R

DATE DUE

JE 4 05			
JE 7 06			

COUNSELING THE DEAF SUBSTANCE ABUSER

by

Fra

DEMCO 38-296

ISBN: 0-9663753-0-0
Library of Congress
Catalog Card Number: 98-66640

ADAMS PRESS
CHICAGO, IL
Distributed by:
Midas Management Company
P.O. Box 27740
Las Vegas, Nevada 89126-1740

COLLEGES, UNIVERSITIES, RECOVERY PROGRAMS, DEAF ORGANIZATIONS, QUANTITY BUYERS
Discounts on this book are available for bulk purchases. Write or e-mail for information on our discount programs.

Author's e-mail address:
Frank_James3rd@hotmail.com

Publisher's Cataloging-in-Publication
(Provided by Quality Books, Inc.)

Lala, Frank James John.
    Counseling the deaf substance abuser / by Frank James
John Lala. -- 1st ed.
    p. cm.
    Includes bibliographical references.
    LCCN: 98-66640
    ISBN: 0-9663753-0-0

    1. Deaf--Substance abuse. 2. Deaf--Counseling of.
3. Twelve-step programs.   I. Title.

HV4999.D43L35 1998   362.29'0872
                                      QBI98-1262

ABOUT THE ARTISTS

THOMAS CARTER HAWKINS, Artist & Illustrator

Special thanks are given to Thomas Carter Hawkins, artist and illustrator, for his outstanding work on the front cover of my book. His artwork is exceptional and unequalled. (P.O. Box 1004, Cypress, CA 90630; TomSoCal29@aol.com).

RUSSELL A. BYE, Computer Graphic Artist

Heartfelt appreciation also for the *color* work on the front cover by computer graphic artist, Russell A. Bye– (El Segundo, CA 310/322-4839 TTY; or 310/322-6173 FAX; RSBye@aol.com).

CATHRINE MYERS, Designer & Artist

And to designer and artist, Cathrine Myers who drew the fingerspelling letters on the cover. A business owner involved in selling deaf products at DEAF EXPO, as well as owner of Fingers Mart– MYCATS@webtv.net).

ACKNOWLEDGMENTS

A great many people have facilitated my progress on this work: I should like to thank everyone. I am deeply grateful and indebted to my two faculty advisors/mentors, Dr. Harlan Lane and Dr. Betty G. Miller for their encouragement, guidance and evaluation of my doctoral dissertation. The quality of scholarly research would not have been possible without their expertise in their respective fields. I am equally impressed with their knowledge and professional backgrounds. To them I owe the confidence to proceed with this work, with their expertise backing me. Dr. Lane definitely qualifies as having a "deaf mind," in that he embodies Deaf culture, thinking in terms of deaf values and perspective, consistently. I, being deaf and growing up in a deaf culture, using ASL and being educated in schools for the deaf, thought I knew much about the subject of deafness, yet Dr. Lane has taught me much. Dr. Miller, the first deaf woman from Gallaudet University to receive a doctorate, and a pioneer in the field of substance abuse, has provided invaluable advise and feedback for me. I consider myself fortunate to have two such capable and prominent mentors!

I am equally indebted to UCLA librarian, Linda Banner, of the Metropolitan Cooperative Library System at the Deaf Resources Office. She provided countless materials including books, computer printouts, photocopied articles and letters for my use in this dissertation. I am equally grateful to Carol Wentzel who unselfishly gave me the use of her immense research materials in the field of substance abuse among the Deaf. She saved me many research hours and considerable expense.

I would also like to thank Jill Marisa Conway, UCLA instructor, for my internship experience in acquiring my

UCLA Certificate in Alcohol and Drug Abuse Counseling, and UCLA instructors and professors, Dr. Terry Davis, Jim Conway, Lou Sanman, Michael Topp, Dr. JoAnne Barge and Leslie Bragg Damski.

I am indebted to Larry Gentile, Chief Executive Director of Behavioral Health Services of the South Bay for my UCLA Practicum-Internship.

I wish to thank the Greater Los Angeles Council on Deafness, Inc., for referring their clients to me at Behavioral Health Services during my Practicum-Internship.

Steve Merkin deserves many thanks for giving me the opportunity to be one of the four founders of the Awakenings Program in Downey and Whittier, California, in 1988. That opportunity gave me the much needed experience to develop skills in working with deaf substance abusers as a counselor, and provided both individual and group settings for counseling and facilitated many subsequent insights and empathy, without which this dissertation might have been a dry and impersonal research paper. It may be impossible to estimate how much I have benefited from working with and listening to my peers in the substance abuse counseling program.

I owe special thanks to my deaf clients of the Awakenings Program for having confidence enough in me to trust me with their most personal thoughts and problems. I have benefited, also, from sharing their lives, and have the pleasure of knowing them, not only as clients, but also as friends.

To the faculty and staff of the California School for the Deaf in Riverside, especially to the late Dr. Richard G. Brill, our first superintendent, and to the late Mr. William E. May and the late Mrs. Esther McGarry, who inspired me to seek education achievement, I am eternally indebted.

I would also like to express my appreciation to the Fourth Alumni Reunion Committee members and to the President Mark R. Sultan for awarding me the first CSDR Outstanding Community Achievement Alumnus Award, in recognition of my efforts and commitment to the Deaf community in the field of substance abuse. I shall always treasure the honor bestowed upon me in this prestigious award.

To UFAF Black Belt instructor, Ron Pohnel, for conveying his conviction and belief in my potential, I offer my sincere thanks and so much more. He instilled incalculable courage and self-esteem in me during my years of karate training under his tutelage. In my quest for the coveted Black Belt (in the Chuck Norris Karate System) Ron taught me the virtues of concentration, commitment, control, courage, dedication, determination, discipline, humility, adaptability, flexibility, patience, perseverance, visualization, toughness, kindness and wholeness. As an *aspiring* Black Belt, I learned from Ron what really counts during training is what an individual achieves spiritually, mentally, emotionally and physically during the process from White Belt to Black Belt. The consciousness aspect of martial arts is the crowning glory of martial arts training. I am thrilled to be a martial artist and a Black Belt in Karate. Ron is a true master and friend without whose coaching, I would not have been recently featured in *Black Belt* in a laudatory magazine article. Ron made it possible for me to acquire the recognition and nomination in receiving the distinctive award, "Karate Athlete of the Year" for 1993.

To Sensei Richard Pietrelli, of Granada Hills Ju-Jitsu Kai, who first taught me the principles of Kodenkan Danzan Ryu Ju-Jitsu, I also offer special thanks. He encouraged me to participate in the tournament which helped augment my self-assurance. I have continued in this path to Black Belt rank. Richard's instruction stresses perfection of character and development of mind and body– in unison.

To Dee Hardison, Mayor of Torrance, and to the City Council of the City of Torrance for presenting me with a congratulatory plaque inscribed, *"In celebration of your birthday and service to the community educating the hearing-impaired and others about alcohol and drug abuse."*

To Assemblywoman Debra Bowen and the California Legislature Assembly for presenting me with a framed Certificate of Appreciation in honor of *"Outstanding Service and Commitment to the South Bay Deaf Community."*

I am humbly appreciative of the awards presented to me and the honors bestowed upon me. This recognition fuels the fire within my soul. The deaf community is very generous in featuring me in their periodicals recognizing my accomplishments. My Alma Mater, Western Maryland College, presented to me their highest award–*"Trustee Alumni Award"*–in acknowledgement of my commitment and efforts extended to the deaf community in the field of substance abuse. These acknowledgements and commendations always encourage me forward in fulfilling my personal aspirations and career goals. Many of these tributes and honors would not have been possible without the scholarships from UCLA and CPU; I am most indebted for the opportunities they provided.

I would like to take this occasion to express my gratitude to the following individuals and organizations:

- To Dr. Robert H. Chambers, President of WMC and Trustee Alumni members for the *"Trustee Alumni Award."*
- To Kentucky Governor, Brereton C. Jones, for *"Kentucky Colonel Commissioned."*
- To John J. Bellizzi, Director of the International Narcotic Enforcement Officers Association for the *"DEA Special Award of Honor,"* which reads: "In Recognition of Outstanding Accomplishment in the Field of Narcotic Law Enforcement."
- To the American Police Hall of Fame for their *"Honor Award"* . . . "Distinguished Achievement in Public Service."
- To the National Rehabilitation Association for their *"Bell Greve Memorial Award."*

Special thanks are given to Thomas Carter Hawkins, artist and illustrator, for his outstanding work on the front cover of my book. His artwork is exceptional and unequalled. [P.O. Box 1004, Cypress, CA 90630; TomSoCal29@aol.com]. Heartfelt appreciation also for the *color* work on the front cover by computer graphic artist, Russell A. Bye–[El Segundo, CA 310/322-4839 TTY; or 310/322-6173 FAX; RSBye@aol.com}; and to designer and artist, Cathrine Myers who drew the fingerspelling letters on the cover. A business owner involved in selling deaf products at DEAF EXPO, as well as owner of Fingers Mart–MYCATS@webtv.net].

In closing, I wish to thank and acknowledge Shara Lee Campbell's contribution, particularly for her patience, understanding and encouragement during the completion of my doctoral dissertation, in spite of her sarcastic teasing about the library being my second home.

PREFACE

This book has come about due to the strong internal commitment of the author to aid the Deaf community and the larger society with the work of his life. Frank Lala has shown the dedication and love for his fellow man which are rewarded with the esteem and respect of his community.

Dr. Lala's life may shed some insight on his high degree of commitment, so a few details about his life seem worth sharing. Frank Lala lost his hearing when he was five years old, and is the son of a mother who lost her hearing when she was twenty-eight years old. She did not learn sign language and was unfamiliar with Deaf culture. Frank grew up in a dysfunctional home afflicted with alcoholism and substance abuse. His mother died of alcoholism and drug abuse.

From such a background, Frank determined to help rid the deaf community of alcoholism and substance abuse. His zeal led him to become one of the founders of a recovery program for deaf people who have abused substances. Dr. Lala has been a counselor of deaf substance abusers for many years and has formed, from his experience, a number of helpful insights. When he leads group recovery meetings, he often explains to the other participants how he is an adult child of alcoholics, and how that has had an impact on his life. Dr. Lala is currently writing a book especially for adult children of alcoholics, as he feels special empathy for that group of people. The work will encompass material to adult children of alcoholics, generally, and specifically for deaf adult children of both deaf and hearing alcoholic or substance abusing parents and to hearing children of deaf substance abusing parents.

The present book is intended to focus attention on the problem of substance abuse in the Deaf community, in order to remediate people's lives affected by addiction, and to provide preventive information and incentives to preclude the development of alcoholism and substance abuse in the next generation.

If you want to contact Dr. Frank Lala for speaking engagements on Deaf Substance Abuse, contact the Midas Management Company for further information.

To order additional copies of <u>Counseling the Deaf Substance Abuser</u>, send $28.95 plus $5.00 postage and handling to:

Midas Management Co.,
P.O. Box 27740, Las Vegas, NV 89126

COLLEGES, UNIVERSITIES, QUANTITY BUYERS
Discounts on this book are available for bulk purchases. Write or call for information on our discount programs.

DEDICATION . . . . .

To the Rev. Lawrence Elliott Cordero

This book of scholarly research is humbly dedicated to Rev. Cordero in recognition for the sacrifices he has made in education, for his noble teachings and for his self-sacrificing devotion to the deaf ministry and the Deaf community in Riverside.

Dr. Cordero is well loved by the Riverside community, deaf and hearing alike. He has inspired and enriched us with his boundless love, unceasing courage and incredible perseverance. He is held in high esteem, for he is responsible for converting more "Deaf Reverends," directly or indirectly, than anyone else we know. He is admired for his immaculate steadfast faith in the face of life's hardships. He unselfishly gave his time and effort in rebuilding the Riverside's Calvary Silent Temple after it was engulfed in flames. The Temple stands as a testimony and monument to his Deaf ministry work. He has received standing ovations and his name is enshrined in a special niche in hearts of the Riverside community. We will always treasure his teachings, which have not gone unheeded by his listeners. We honor him for his God-given gift of pedagogy with homage akin to conferring an honorary doctorate degree. The honor which has immortalized his name for perpetuity stands in the annals of recorded doctoral dissertations at the University of Microfilms International. This revered reward is our way of expressing our gratitude and appreciation for everything he stood for in brotherly love.

In Memory . . . . .

Robert Wayne Bedford • Lynn Eddie Struble
Richard Stafford Stumbo

ix

TABLE OF CONTENTS

xi

LIST OF TABLES

ABSTRACT

The National Institute on Deafness and other Communicative Disorders has estimated that up to twenty-eight million people in the U.S. suffer from hearing impairment of some degree. This includes people born deaf, people who become deaf prelingually, people deafened by accidents or disease, people who lose hearing gradually throughout life and people who throughout their lives are hard-of-hearing to a consistent degree. Researchers estimate that up to 35% of people with significant hearing impairment have abused substances, including alcohol; which is almost double the estimated rate of comparable abuse among people who do not suffer impaired hearing. Vulnerability to addiction and substance abuse may ultimately be seen as an additional risk for people with hearing disabilities. Various populations of deaf people have specific, often different, needs in terms of prevention and treatment of substance abuse. Elderly hard-of-hearing people, for example, have different communication needs from those of deaf children of deaf parents, and these various needs noted may influence vulnerability to substance abuse and addictive behaviors. Social services often have not adequately met the needs of deaf people with substance abuse problems. The author suggests various interacting factors to account for this and makes recommendations for effective prevention and recovery efforts. He critiques a number of existing resources and facilities, and discusses intervention points and methods surveyed discussed.

CHAPTER I

INTRODUCTION

In 1988, some 21 million Americans were identified as having some hearing impairment. These impairments ranged from minimal to severe and were cited as potentially contributing to a variety of psychological, educational, social and vocational disabilities.[1] Perhaps 10% of this group of Americans with hearing loss are severely or profoundly deaf. It is estimated that about 15% of these largely-deaf individuals also suffer from some form of substance abuse.

Comparatively little attention was paid to these multi-disadvantaged Americans until recently. The first published reference to the interaction of hearing disabilities and alcoholism appeared in the Alcoholics Anonymous newsletter *Grapevine* in 1968.[2] The first treatment program designed specifically for deaf alcoholics dates from a decade ago in the San Francisco area.[3] Programs were developed independently in Minnesota, Michigan, and elsewhere in California, but did not proliferate in the country as a whole.

Deaf alcohol abusers have received little meaningful assistance. Additionally, their quest for sobriety was not studied in a timely manner, so that identification of any special needs of this group had been quite tardy. The

---

[1] Judith Randel and William Hines, "New Power for a Divided Minority," Washington Post Health, Mar. 29, 1988, p. 15.

[2] J.B., "AA and the Deaf Mute", The Grapevine. Dec., 1968. pp. 32-33.

[3] Jack Gorey, Rational Alcoholism Services for Hearing Impaired People," J. Rehab & Deaf, Dec. 1979. pp. 6-8.

earliest studies date from 1978 which deal with the incidence of substance abuse among the deaf.[4] These studies found that the incidence of substance abuse among the deaf was about the same as for the population as a whole; in the absence of detailed demographic studies, this conclusion has remained unchallenged.

While solid, large-scale research remains scanty, ample evidence has accumulated that the network of services developed to help substance abusers works poorly for the deaf. Communication between helpers and clients has been and remains a major problem. Even when steps are taken to solve this problem by providing an interpreter, the deaf client typically: a) needs extra time to absorb the materials, due to the probability that they are difficult to comprehend, b) experiences fatigue sooner than do other clients, c) misses many of the nuances of group interaction, and d) may not even be able to see the interpreter clearly, because of poor lighting. After-treatment and community support services for deaf clients are also often minimal.[5]

Even with these daunting considerations, progress has undoubtedly been made in helping deaf substance abusers. Effective programs are increasingly available, scattered throughout the country. Many small-scale studies using a variety of assessment methods and populations have accumulated in the literature. Still lacking is some kind of synthesis, or even a comprehensive survey.

---

[4] S. Johnson & K. Locke, "Student Drug Use in a School for the Deaf", Paper presented at the annual meeting of the National Conference on Drugs; Seattle, WA. 1978.

[5] Alexander Boros, "Alcoholism Intervention for the Deaf", Alcohol Health and Research World: Special Issue: The Multi-Disabled; 5 (2)1981. pp. 26-30.

Background of the Study

The background of the study includes a basic statement regarding types of hearing impairment, the consequences of this disability, and the complicating factor of substance abuse.

Etiology of Hearing Loss

The major causes of deafness are: heredity, illness, accident, aging, and some forms of substance abuse. Heredity is the principal cause, with about half of all deafness in infants the result of genetic factors. Down's syndrome and RH factor incompatibility of the parents' blood are two of the many genetic factors implicated.[6]

Many illnesses can cause deafness. Rubella (German measles) damages the auditory nerves of embryos when contracted by the mother in the early stages of pregnancy.[7] Other prenatal diseases can have the same effect, as can premature-birth, Meningitis, mumps, measles, and other diseases of childhood. High fever, infections, and even some medications all can affect hearing.

Experiential and environmental factors are also involved. I. King Jordan, the new president of Gallaudet University, lost his hearing as a result of injuries in an automobile accident. H. Latham Breunig, a former member of the presidential commission on deafness, was born hard-of-hearing, then he lost more hearing after scarlet fever at

---

[6] Larry G. Stewart, "Hearing-Impaired/Developmentally Disabled Persons in the United States: Definitions, Causes, Effects, and Prevalence Estimates," A.A.D.,(4) 1978. p.491.

[7] Randel & Hines, Ibid. p. 17.

the age of five, and became deaf at age seven as the result of a skull fracture.[8]

Loud noises, either sudden or prolonged, e.g. explosions or rock concerts, respectively, can also damage hearing severely. Hearing tends to deteriorate with age, additionally, and finally, excessive use of alcohol and drugs can also adversely affect hearing.[9]

Types of Hearing Loss

Four major types of hearing loss are recognized. A central hearing loss results from impairment to the nerves or nuclei of the central nervous system. Conductive hearing losses are the results of disease or obstructions in the outer or middle ear. In conductive hearing loss, typically, all frequencies are evenly affected, and remedial intervention often can be taken. Sensorineural hearing loss comes from damage to the sensory hair cells of the inner ear or the connecting nerves; Hearing loss from this cause can range from mild to profound, and remediation is usually impossible. External hearing aids ameliorate the situation, but not the loss itself. Mixed hearing losses involve both the middle and inner ear. Additionally, some writers have identified psychological or *"hysterical"* deafness, where the loss of hearing is psychogenic; when

---

8

[9] Dale C. Wheeler, et al, "Audiometric Configuration in Patients Being Treated for Alcoholism," Drug and Alcohol Depend., 5, 1980 pp. 63-68; S. Polpathapee, et al., "Sensorineural Hearing Loss in a Heroin Addict, "Journal of the Medical Association of Thailand, Vol. 1, 1967. pp. 57-60.

relieved of psychological stresses, persons suffering such cases of deafness can hear again normally.[10]

The extent of hearing loss is an important variable. Approximately two million persons in the United States have a complete, and usually irreversible, loss of hearing.[11] Hearing loss encompasses a wide-range continuum, with many intervals of gradation.

Also crucial is the age at which hearing loss takes place. The most physically disabling condition, albeit not the most emotionally isolating one, occurs when hearing loss precedes the normal development of oral language and speech. In the pre-lingually deaf, oral language development is adversely affected, thus the ensuing emotional and intellectual development of each stage of growth is delayed. Other individuals become deaf at some point after normal language and speech have developed. While these post-lingually deaf have fewer communication difficulties and intellectual disadvantages, loss of hearing at any age can be a traumatic experience requiring medical and psychiatric intervention. Moreover, people who lose their hearing as adults may have to master alternative means of communication at a time when they do not have the advantages of flexibility and mental agility of youth.[12]

The Consequences of Hearing Loss

As with most disabilities, the consequences of deafness can be greatly mitigated, and deafness does not preclude

---

[10] Anthony R. T. Cornforth & Marie M. Woods, "Why Loss of Hearing?" Nurs Times, Jan. 27, 1972. p. 102.

[11] Gallaudet College/National Information Center on Deafness, Deafness: A Fact Sheet; Washington D.C.; Gallaudet Univ. Press. 1984. p. 1.

[12] Cornforth and Woods. p. 102

greatness. Many famous men and women were deaf at some point in their lives, perhaps the most remarkable being Ludwig van Beethoven, who composed his greatest music when he could no longer hear.[13] Countless other deaf people achieve great things, despite their handicap.

Today, hearing loss no longer represents the same degree of impediment to success, in most professions, that it formerly did. As Stepp said, "Two generations ago, young deaf people were treated as if they were retarded, shunted off to state residential schools, and prepared for blue-collar jobs such as printing and sewing."[14] The next generation began climbing the professional ladder, rung by rung, and today's generation has fully arrived. Today, deaf people have entered most of the professions. Starting salaries for Gallaudet graduates have increased markedly in recent years to be commensurate with salaries of hearing people in the same profession.[15]

Nevertheless, hearing loss is a major impediment that can be overcome only with struggle. Congenitally deaf children cannot learn speech as normal children do, through hearing, repeating, and having their speaking behavior reinforced.[16] To complicate things further, parents of deaf infants may not even realize their child's

---

[13] B.M. Schowe, Identity Crisis in Deafness: A Humanistic Perspective. Tempe, AZ: *The Scholar's Press*. 1979. p. 109.

[14] Laura Sessions Stepp, Deaf Generation Leaps" Wall'; Hearing World Breached by New Work Force," The Washington Post, Mar. 21, 1988; pp. 1, 19 at p. 1.

[15] Ibid, p. 19. In 1985, 23.2% of Gallaudet graduates earned $15,000-$19,000 a year on their first job; in 1986, the percentage jumped to 47.6.

[16] Alan O. Ross, Psychological Disorders of Children: A Behavioral Approach to Theory, Research & Therapy, 2nd ed. New York: McGraw-Hill, 1980. p. 205.

deafness, and when hearing loss is finally suspected, the family may have difficulty obtaining a definitive diagnosis.[17] Delays, mixed signals from the professional community, and similar problems may result in developmental impediments which may or may not be overcome at a later date. (The literature dealing with this aspect of the problem will be reported in detail in a later chapter.)

In a perceptive review of the literature on linguistic deficiency and thinking, Furth concluded that pre-lingually deaf children normally suffer developmental lags similar to those of culturally-deprived or culturally-different children. Early linguistic and cognitive deficiencies normally are overcome with appropriate interventions.[18]

Unfortunately, however, agreement is not universal on what constitutes appropriate intervention. The deaf, and those who work with them, remain divided on such matters as *"mainstreaming"* versus special education and the best way to teach communication skills. Hearing parents with a deaf child may not know which way to turn in the face of conflicting advice.

Numerous studies, up to and including the early 1980's found that deaf people experience a high incidence of psychological problems related to deficiencies in conventional communications skills. Lack of empathy, inadequate insight into the impact of their own behavior, inadequately developed impulse-control mechanisms, relatively mild depression, and an array of personality

---

[17] Frank Bowe, "Crises of the Deaf Child and His Family" in Readings on Deafness, Ed. Douglas Watson, New York: New York Univ. School of Educ., Deafness Research & Training Center, 1973. pp. 38-44.

[18] Hans G. Furth, Linguistic Deficiency and Thinking", Psychological Bulletin, 76 (1)1971. pp. 58-72.

disturbances are reported in the literature on the deaf.[19] Some of the same writers who cite these findings also note, however, the absence of definition and measurement of both hearing impairment and of mental illness and emotional disturbance. It is also acknowledged that serious mental illness, as measured by the number of hospital admissions, is no greater among the deaf than among the hearing.[20]

More recent studies are less prone to such generalization. Nevertheless, growing up with a hearing handicap and seeking to cope with a hearing world throughout a lifetime does put a strain on an individual who is deaf, just as being in a minority inherently decreases the probability of one's being experientially understood by the majority.

Until recently, deaf people tended to be economically disadvantaged. Although educated non-hearing individuals found employment at about the same rate as their hearing counterparts, the former tended to have lower-paying jobs.[21] Non-hearing people with little education had much higher levels of unemployment than their hearing counterparts. For example, the 1988 unemployment rate for deaf New England young adults was 17%, while for the hearing young adults of the area, the rate was 11.2%. As acknowledged earlier in this chapter, opportunities for deaf persons graduating from colleges and universities today are

---

[19] Hilde S. Schlesinger and Kathryn P. Meadow, "A Conceptual Model for a Program of Community Psychiatry for a Deaf Population," Community Mental Health Journal, 6 (1)1972. pp. 47-59.

[20] Ibid, p. 49.

[21] Edward C. Carney, "Deaf People in the World of Work," in Readings on Deafness. Ed Douglas Watson, New York: N.Y. Univ. School of Educ., Deafness Research & Training Center; 1973. pp. 134-136.

greater than at any time in the recent past.[22] But earning deficits remain for the mass of relatively uneducated deaf people now in the marketplace.

One study of the employment problem concluded:

> Deficient education and underemployment have been clearly documented . . . Obviously, a deaf person victimized by poor education and under-employment and unemployment will suffer in his social, psychological, family, and spiritual achievements and satisfactions . . .[23]

While this characterization is obviously not relevant to everyone, a significant number of deaf people still feel themselves to be caught in the circularly reinforcing undesirable circumstances. We can understand that these people might turn to alcohol and/or other substances in their search for solace and satisfaction. Of course, the majority of deaf people do not succumb to substance abuse.

The Deaf and Substance Abuse

Studies of small populations indicate that the incidence of substance abuse among the deaf is about the same as that for the general population of the United States. Several authors, extrapolating from these studies, have estimated that in 1980 there were about 73,000 deaf alcoholics; 8,500 deaf heroin users; 14,700 deaf cocaine users; and 110,000 deaf people who use marijuana on a

---

[22] Stepp, pp. 1, 19.

[23] McCay Vernon, "Potential Achievement and Rehabilitation in the Deaf Population", in Readings on Deafness, Ed. Douglas Watson; New York: N.Y. Univ. School of Educ., Deafness Research & Training Center, 1973. p. 96.

regular basis.[24] There are no reliable national statistics based on direct counting. Extrapolated statistics can probably serve, however, to suggest the general magnitude of the problem.

The principal difference between deaf and hearing substance abusers is that the former often cannot find services readily available to the latter. According to Scanlon:

> Where is there an Alanon group for deaf parents of a substance abusing child, and the Alateen, Alatot? These services are provided for the hearing community and they should be available for deaf people. I think we're really seeing the need for assertiveness training for many deaf people, especially for deaf women. Where can you set those up?[25]

Nature of the Study

The study is an exhaustive review of the literature dealing with substance abuse among the deaf population of the United States. Considerable background information

---

[24] J.D. Miler and I.H. Cisin, Highlights from the National Survey on Drug Abuse, (Rockville, MD: NIDA, 1980); n. Zinberg, "Report on the Liason Task Panel on Psychoactive Drug Use/Misuse," in The Yearbook of Substance Use and Abuse, ed L. Brill and C. Winick, Vol. II. New York: Human Sciences Press, 1980.

[25] John Scanlon, "Is there a Need for Mental Health and Substance Abuse Services to Deaf People?" in Mental Health, Substance Abuse, and Deafness, Ed. Douglas Watson, Karen Steitler, Penelope Peterson, and William K. Fulton; Silver Springs, MD. Amer Deafness & Rehab Assoc., 1983, pp. 7-9 at p.9.

on deafness, alcoholism, and drug abuse is reviewed and summarized in order to arrive at precepts, methods, and techniques useful in helping deaf substance abusers overcome their self-destructive habits. Exemplary programs have been identified; their literature studied and described.

Purpose of the Study

This study is intended to help those who work with deaf substance abusers by providing them with relevant background information, descriptive material on successful programs, and valid generalizations based on the literature and sound practice. It is given with the hope that it will be useful in itself, and also might later serve as the basis for published reference regarding the best ways to treat deaf substance abusers. Such published materials can then be disseminated to all who are in the helping professions related to deaf substance abusers. This study, and any published materials which might derive from it, might also be useful to policy makers responsible for programs and budgets.

Need for and Significance of the Study

Becoming a victim of alcohol or drugs is a terrible fate for the individual and a loss for society.[26] The losses are compounded when the victim is already handicapped, and when remediation is difficult to find.[27]

---

[26] Abraham J. Twerski, MD, Self Discovery in Recovery, (Pittsburg, PA; Hazelden Press, 1984). p.7.

[27] Patrick Kenneth Best, "Psychological Differentiation in the Deaf" Doctoral dissertation, Wayne State University, Ann Arbor Michigan, (1974), p.137.

There now exist significant impediments for the deaf in using existing social services. Difficulty of communication can be a major barrier, prohibiting access.[28] If the social service agency does not have staff who sign or interpreters for deaf clients, deaf clients are unlikely to receive much benefit from treatment. Virtually all modes of counseling involve *"talking things out"*; if counselor and client cannot *"talk"* to one another freely, successful treatment is unlikely.[29]

Moreover, even the use of interpreters can pose problems. The deaf client, who typically views his addiction as a *"fall from grace"* may find an interpreter a threat to confidentiality, and thus refrain from disclosing to the counselor in the presence of an interpreter. Client and interpreter, moreover, may have differing communication modes, e.g. American Sign Language vs. Pidgin Sign English.[30]

Trust between counselor and client is essential, but may be difficult to develop between a hearing therapist and a deaf client. Many deaf people have received short shrift from institutions and authority figures in the past, and therefore they tend to be mistrustful and skeptical. According to Chough, when deaf people are in need of professional help, "they feel diminished as individuals, as a

---

[28] Michael A. Harvey, <u>Psychotherapy with Deaf and Hard-of-Hearing Persons: a Systemic Model</u>, Hillsdale, New Jersey; (1989) p.142-147.

[29] Douglas Watson, "Substance Abuse Services for Deaf Clients: A Question of Accessibility" in <u>Mental Health, Substance Abuse, and Deafness</u>, Ed. D. Watson et al., Silver Spring, MD: American Deafness & Rehabilitation Assoc., 1983. pp. 13-16, at p.14.

[30] Ibid, p.21, and <u>Deafness: A Fact Sheet</u>, p 2.

result of paternalistic attitudes on the part of professionals.[31]

Because the deaf community tends to be closely knit, failure to treat one deaf person effectively and with respect can lead to a virtual boycott by the community. Loyalty to those perceived as "like them" and more than a hint of suspicion towards "do-gooders who don't understand" are not uncommon.[32]

Finally, the trust that develops over time in a bi-lateral healing relationship can be difficult to establish when three people (the two plus an interpreter) are linked together, merely because of group and personality dynamics. Alcoholics Anonymous reaches out to all alcoholics, but deaf people have been more likely than other people to lack information regarding the organization and its mission. If deaf people do turn to AA for help, they may find an insuperable language barrier. They may not have the reading skills necessary to comprehend AA literature.[33]

Because deaf substance abusers have such a difficult time finding and receiving the help they require, there is a need for an exhaustive and careful study summarizing facts, experience, and theory scattered in hundreds of

---

[31] Steven K. Chough, "The Trust-Mistrust Phenomenon Among Deaf Persons," in <u>Mental Health, Substance Abuse, and Deafness</u>, Ed. D. Watson, et al, Silver Springs, MD: Amer. Deafness & Rehab. Assoc., 1983. pp.17-19 at p.18.

[32] Barbara Kannapell, "The Trust-Mistrust Syndrome," in <u>Mental Health, Substance Abuse, and Deafness</u>, Ed. D. Watson, et al., Silver Springs, MD: Amer. Deafness & Rehab. Assoc., 1983. pp.20-22.

[33] Edna P. Adler, "Vocational Rehabilitation as an Intervenor in Substance Abuse Services to Deaf People," in Ibid., pp.10-12, at p.11.

published articles. The significance of this study is that it is an honest attempt to meet this very real need.

Definition of Terms

A number of specialized terms have been used in this chapter, and many more will be found in the body of the study. Most of these terms can be defined in context, or they become self-evident if viewed in context. Those which are not self-defining or which are particularly crucial are defined below.

Alcohol abuse: ". . . any use of alcoholic beverages that causes damage to the individual or society or both."[34] "Abuse" implies a lack of control to a point where the individual can no longer function effectively in his/her society.

Communication: The act of transmitting information, thought, or feeling so that it is satisfactorily received and understood by others. Communication is broader than the use of words, including art, signs, and body language.

The deaf may communicate by speaking, speech reading, writing, and manual communication. Manual communication includes: 1) American Sign Language (ASL), which has its own vocabulary, idioms, grammar, and syntax, distinct from those of English; 2) Fingerspelling, which is spelling with the fingers in the air, usually used in combination with ASL or with spoken English (Rochester method); 3) Manual English or Pidgin English (PSE), involving the vocabulary of ASL and fingerspelled words presented in English word order; and 4) Cued Speech, a system of communication in which eight hand shapes in

---

[34] E. M. Jellinek, The Disease Concept of Alcoholism, (New Haven, CN: Hillhouse Press, 1968), p.35.

14

four possible positions supplement the information visible on the lips of the speaker. Total communication is a method combining all possible methods of communication to help deaf children acquire language and all deaf persons to understand. Historically, there have been major disagreements between the proponents of the various schools of communication.[35]

Deafness; Refers to the inability to hear and understand speech. Hearing impairment comprises the entire range of auditory disorders from less than normal hearing to total deafness.

Drug Abuse: Any use of drugs, licit or illicit, in inappropriate ways or amounts, as determined by adverse effects upon the user and/or his society.

Substance Abuse; Any use of alcohol or drugs which interfere with the optimum functioning of the individual or society, or both.

Treatment: The method or technique used to help substance abusers overcome their problem.

Assumptions

Since this is not an experimental or statistical study, only general assumptions have been made. In the broadest sense, it has been assumed that people who are deaf or are hard of hearing may view their hearing loss as a handicap, but that the loss need not be disabling. It is further assumed that the nurturing and development of the rich creative gifts of individual people in what ever physical condition they are, is worthwhile to society, and that time, effort, energy and resources spent enabling people to function at their highest level are worthwhile investments.

---

[35] Deafness: A Fact Sheet; Gallaudet Univ. Press; pp.2-3.

Limitations and Delimitations

The principal perceived limitation of the study is one that is typical of any review of literature: since this is not an experimental study, and the writer's own experience in dealing with deaf substance abusers will enter only obliquely into the treatment of the subject matter, the study can be only as strong as the literature itself. The study will only be as insightful as the literature is insightful; it will only be as complete as the literature is complete, etc. The writer believes that the literature is vast, varied and often useful, and that this limitation is therefore relatively minor.

In addition, certain delimitations have been imposed on the study by the researcher. Only English-language materials have been used, but these include research from outside the United States. Materials in other languages might have been useful had they been available in English-language translation.

The materials researched were limited to alcoholism, substance abuse, and deafness. Occasionally, the writer found it necessary to search through psychological and social work research for answers to specific questions, but this literature was not covered in any systematic way.

Organization of the Study

The study is organized into seven chapters. This first chapter has covered introductory materials, including the introduction, the background, the nature of the study, the purpose of the study, the need for and significance of the study, the definition of terms, the assumptions, and the limitations and delimitations.

Chapter II, Relevant Characteristics of the Deaf Population, describes those characteristics of the deaf population that are related to substance abuse and its successful treatment.

Chapter III covers the literature on alcoholism as it relates to the deaf.

Chapter IV covers the literature on drug abuse and the deaf.

Chapter V covers those programs for deaf substance abusers that have been described in the literature or described for the writer, at his request, for this study.

Chapter VI, Discussion, ties together all the various threads into one coherent whole, and discusses implications of certain viewpoints which have been developed in answer to several pre-eminent and salient questions about deafness, the ramifications of present trends toward prevention and treatment of substance abuse among the deaf, and proposed and/or projected developments in the field.

Chapter VII contains the summary, conclusions and recommendations for future research and practice to help prevent substance abuse among deaf people and to help deaf substance abusers overcome their disabilities and lead normal, productive lives.

CHAPTER II

RELEVANT CHARACTERISTICS OF THE POPULATION

Introduction

The purpose of the study is to help those who work with deaf substance abusers by providing them with relevant background information, descriptive material on programs, and valid generalizations, based on the literature and practice. This chapter shall cover the literature which describes those characteristics of the deaf population that might be relevant to substance abuse and treatment.

This chapter originally was meant to be a comprehensive review of relevant literature using accepted research methodology and dealing with problems of deafness. Unfortunately, some research of this type was found to be misleading and occasionally outlandish. Common problems include the use of atypical populations, such as psychiatric patients, to develop generalizations meant to apply to the deaf population as a whole, extremely small populations, and a lack of understanding of the typical deaf experience. Viewed in its entirety, that literature which purports to be scientific, while falling below the minimum threshold of acceptability, cannot be considered a reliable guide for those who work with deaf substance abusers. Most of such studies, therefore, are not covered in this chapter.

By contrast, some material considered valuable in this researcher's opinion, is *experiential* or in anecdotal form. "Experiential" means written out of experience, rather than in accordance with such research principles as control groups and statistical procedures. As might be expected, much of this is the work of deaf scholars.

Aspects of Population

The latest available figures on the deaf were cited in Chapter I of this study and need not be repeated. It should be noted, however, that all of the figures cited in the literature represent estimates or educated guesses. A recent book on the deaf experience in the United States states flatly: "There are no reliable figures on the number of Deaf people in the United States and Canada."[36] Official statistics generally attempt to estimate or count the number of deaf individuals in the country. It is not possible to develop from these numbers, for example, how many of these people cannot hear at all and how many use some variety of sign language.

Moreover, the experience of more than a century and a half of attempting to estimate or count the deaf population indicates that there are not likely to be any easy solutions. Between 1830 and 1930, the United States Bureau of the Census attempted to enumerate the deaf population without success.[37]

Beginning with the 1970s, the Census Bureau adopted a sampling method; in 1975, interviews were conducted in approximately 44,000 households containing about 134,000

---

[36] Carol Padden & Tom Humphries, Deaf in America: Voices from a Culture, (Cambridge, MA; Harvard University Press, 1988) p.4.

[37] Hearing Impairments in the United States, Statistical Bulletin of the Metropolitan Life Insurance Company, Feb. 1976 (57) pp.7-9 at p.9.

people. Even the authors acknowledged that sampling errors might have tainted the results.[38]

In 1978, Stewart attempted to remedy some of the gaps in the official estimates. According to his figures, about 3.2% of the population (some 6.5 million Americans) had significant hearing loss in both ears. Slightly less than 1% of these were severely deaf, unable to hear or understand speech. Still, this enumeration involved nearly two million people.

The pre-vocational deaf (deaf before the age of 19), constituted 2.3% of the population; the prelingual deaf (deaf before the age of 3) represented almost 1% of the population. In addition, Stewart estimated the numbers of individuals with impaired hearing who were also developmentally disabled. These figures included the deaf who were also autistic, cerebral palsied, epileptic, and mentally retarded.[39]

A significant recent study of the demographics of deafness by Karchmer was based on the 1982-3 Annual Survey of Hearing-Impaired Children and Youth, and the 1983 national norming of deaf students on the Stanford Achievement Text. He noted that the number of students reported to the United States Department of Education by the states did not include deaf-blind students, students with hearing loss included under "multi-handicapped," or

---

[38] Peter W. Ries, "Hearing Ability of Persons by Sociodemographic and Health Characteristics," Vital Health Statistics, Aug. 1982 (140) pp.1-60, at p.2.

[39] Larry G. Stewart, "Hearing-Impaired/Developmentally Disabled Persons in the United States: Definitions, Causes, Effects, and Prevalence Estimates," A.A.D., Jun. 1978 (123) pp.489-98.

students not being served by the states.[40] It may appear, therefore, that students with severe hearing problems are routinely undercounted.

Vernon discussed a number of present, and probable future, trends that will affect the prevalence of hearing impairments. More liberal sexual practices in the larger society have resulted in the transmission of viral pathogens, herpes simplex, and cyromegalovirus, all of which can infect the fetus and cause deafness, cerebral palsy, mental retardation, and other handicaps. The huge bulge of youth deafened by the 1963-65 rubella epidemic will continue to require post-secondary education, training, and other forms of assistance. Moreover, rubella will continue to pose a threat because: a) about 20% of women of child-bearing age have not been immunized, b) the duration of the immunity conferred by existing vaccines is not clear, and c) the prevalence of rubella as a cause of deafness since the presently used vaccine was licensed in 1969 remains about 12-13%.[41]

Psychological Characteristics

Research includes scores of studies dealing with purported psychological problems of the deaf. Many are from foreign countries; some concern themselves with atypical populations, e.g. patients in mental institutions; and all tend to reach conclusions without taking all the variables into account. For example, a British study, after finding that deaf people were over-represented in mental

---

[40] Michael A. Karchmer, "Demographics and Deaf Adolescents," Gallaudet Univ. Press; n.d., pp.29-31.

[41] McCay Vernon, "The Decade of the Eighties: Significant Trends and Developments for Hearing Impaired Individuals," Rehabilitation Literature, Jan-Feb, 1981 (42) pp.2-7.

institutions, admitted that the reason might be *mislabeling*, particularly since there was little communication between patient and staff.[42]

Psychological Health of the Deaf

In a 1969 paper, Vernon surveyed the literature dealing with the psychological factors associated with hearing loss. Some 50 independently-conducted studies indicated that the deaf or hard-of-hearing population has essentially the same distribution of intelligence as the general population. These statistics would seem to indicate that the potential for abstract thought is as prevalent among deaf people as among the hearing. However, educational attainments of the deaf are generally lower than for their hearing counterparts, partly due to neglect or inadequate teaching. As a result, deaf people have been more likely to end up in menial jobs offering little future and financial return, contributing to less than optimum psychological states.[43]

Vernon concluded that the level of schizophrenia was no higher among the deaf than among the general population. However paranoid schizophrenia may be more prevalent among those who became hard-of-hearing later in life than among the prelingually deaf. Less is known about the prevalence of neuroses, character disorders, and other mental problems not considered psychoses. Such kinds of disorders are not easy to diagnose in the deaf population. Vernon offered the following "tenuous" conclusions from his review of the literature: 1) Impulse control problems and

---

[42] John C. Denmark, "Mental Illness and Early Profound Deafness," Brit J of Med Psych, Jun, 1966 (39) pp. 117-124.

[43] McCay Vernon, "Sociological and Psychological Factors Associated with Hearing Loss," JSHR, SEPT, 1969 (12) PP. 541-550.

their related syndromes are more common among the deaf. 2) There is frequent lack of insight, with externalization of blame for psychosocial difficulties. And 3) there is therefore less conscious anxiety or motivation to seek treatment.[44]

Altshuler reported his conclusions based on sixteen years of study of the deaf in New York State psychiatric hospitals. He reasoned that deaf people are precluded from certain accoutrements of sound, in particular the emotionality aroused or transmitted by sound, and therefore often are hampered in the timely development of language. Often oral language usage in people who have not experienced the reinforcing aid of sound is permanently stunted. Awareness of this lack lays an additional burden of stress on the deaf individual trying to communicate orally.

Among deaf schizophrenics, auditory hallucinations occur in about the same proportion as in the hearing population. This is reasonable since hallucinations are presumed to be psychogenic rather than organic in nature.[45]

Altshuler also noted the prevalence of impulsive behavior among the deaf population in New York State mental institutions. He hypothesized that auditory potential was necessary in order for a person to internalize rage. The absence of a given perceptual mode might, he thought, preclude certain adaptive options, while its presence might enable (but not guarantee) the choice. For

---

[44] Ibid. pp. 555-556.
[45] Kenneth Z. Altshuler, "Studies of the Deaf: Relevance to Psychiatric Theory," American Journal of Psychiatry, May 1971 (127) pp. 1521-1526, at p. 1525.

example, the development of insights which encourage control of one's impulses becomes highly unlikely.[46]

Altshuler collaborated with Rainer in another study of deaf in-patients in New York State mental hospitals. In the area of personality and character disorders, the authors noted:

> . . . a lack of empathy, a diminished understanding and regard for the feelings of other people, a lessened awareness of the impact of one's behavior on other people, and the tendency toward impulsive behavior, with limited control and restraint. One corollary of the latter is that rage lies close to the surface without becoming internalized, and indeed little or no retarded, depressive symptomatology was noted.[47]

Paranoid symptoms and projective mechanisms were observed, but were no more prevalent than among the hearing population. However, the writers admitted that they could not tell whether these character traits and symptom patterns were related to absence of verbal language or to deficiencies of parent-child communication in the formative years. The authors state that many observers have noted similarities between some deaf children and culturally-deprived children. They labeled some of their deaf patients *primitive personalities*, referencing a social and cognitive immaturity found among

---

[46] Ibid. p. 1525.

[47] John D. Rainer and Kenneth Z. Altshuler, "A Psychiatric Program for the Deaf: Experiences and Implications," Amer J of Psychiatry, May, 1971 (127) pp. 1527-32, at p. 1528.

those who were brought up with minimal communication at home.[48]

Elements of the family backgrounds of some New York State mental hospital deaf patients would seem to have predisposed them to schizophrenia. These factors included disturbances in parent-child relationships, covert maternal wishes of rejection, and denial of the needs and limitations of the child. Nevertheless, there was no increase in the schizophrenic rate among the deaf population there as compared with the hearing patients of that hospital.[49]

In a later article, Altshuler attempted to trace significant developmental differences between deaf and hearing children. The absence of auditory potential in a newborn child limits its ability to its surroundings, and may inhibit its development, he reasoned. Sound soothes a troubled baby during the early, symbiotic period of development. Later, when the child is more clearly learning to individuate and develop a sense of self, hearing its mother in the next room often boosts confidence enough that the toddler is encouraged in exploring the world. Without hearing, spontaneous mimicry and learning derived from that are impossible, Altshuler states. The deaf child has the capacity and readiness for language development, but he/she needs help which may not be readily available.[50] As stated before, without verbal communication between parent and child, the internalization of control by the child is extremely difficult. (Altshuler apparently assumes the deaf child is born into a

---

48 Ibid, p. 1528.

49 Ibid, p. 1529.

50 Kenneth Z. Altshuler, "The Social and Psychological Development of Deaf children: Problems, Their Treatment and Prevention," Social and Psychol Development, Aug., 1974 (119) pp. 365-76, at p. 368.

hearing family; if the parents are able to communicate with the child in nonverbal ways, the consequences sketched by Altshuler would not necessarily follow.)

From the standpoint of hearing parents, deafness in their child is usually an invisible handicap for at least the first few months of life. Parents may note that something is wrong, but may have difficulty finding a doctor who is able to make an accurate diagnosis and provide useful advice. Parental reactive depression may result in confused, ambivalent treatment, then, of the child. Unfortunately, such crises tend to develop at the stage of development when the child is trying to pass from symbiosis to individuation. Once the deaf child enters the world outside the family, there ensues a struggle to teach communication and content. A tendency may develop for the youngster to remain dependent instead of exploring, and to learn largely by rote instead of insight.[51]

"In view of the foregoing," Altshuler writes, "It is nothing short of miraculous that the majority of deaf children develop to be normal neurotics like the rest of us."[52] With the minor exceptions previously noted, major forms of psychotic illness are no more frequent among the deaf than among the hearing.

However, deaf children are by no means a homogeneous group. Some are born with multiple handicaps, complicating their prognosis for normal development still further. About 10% of all deaf children are born to deaf parents. In this case, most of the factors that militate against development of the deaf child do not apply. The parents know what to expect and how to cope. Deaf parents' communication with their deaf child is more facile

---

[51] Ibid. pp. 369-70.
[52] Ibid., p. 370.

than that of hearing parents with a deaf child. Deaf children of deaf parents are often described as better adjusted, they have higher achievement test scores, and receive higher teacher ratings on items relating to maturity, responsibility, sociability, initiative and appropriate sex-role behavior than do deaf children born to hearing parents.[53]

In 1978, Altshuler wrote an important paper on the question of whether there really was a "psychology of deafness." A number of researchers have reported important differences between hearing and deaf subjects, with the latter being characterized as socially immature, emotionally labile, volatile and brittle, with ego rigidity, having difficulty with abstractions, etc. However, Altshuler points out, the research on which these, and other such, generalizations are based may be tainted by the use of tests on which the deaf might be expected to do less well than hearing people. Almost any study using a standard psychological test interprets results in accordance with data standardized on hearing populations. Moreover, even if the results are taken at face value, there remains the question of whether the outcome is a stereotype or a composite. Not every deaf person will be aberrant in all, or any, of the characteristics measured by particular research instruments; nevertheless, some people view the research as describing a "typical" deaf person. In addition, those who work closely with deaf persons emerge with "clinical impressions," which may be reported, but do not constitute clinical facts.[54]

---

[53] Ibid., p. 370.
[54] Kenneth Z. Altshuler, "Toward a Psychology of Deafness?" J. Communication Disorders, Apr., 1978 (11) pp. 159-69, at pp. 159-60.

In order to differentiate between ephemeral and intrinsic factors, the author participated in a cross-cultural study with New York State and Yugoslav colleagues. The study compared psychological test results of normal deaf and hearing adolescents in New York State and Yugoslavia. The two environments were considered so different that the effects of deafness itself, rather than cultural influences might be expected to emerge. The results of the study indicated that the deaf in both countries scored higher for impulsivity than the hearing adolescents in both countries. There was a striking absence of overlap between deaf and hearing sub-groups in both countries. Moreover, a related but separate investigation of deaf patients in Yugoslavian mental hospitals showed that those patients demonstrated impulsive, aggressive, and bizarre symptoms similar to those noted of deaf patients in New York. The results suggest either that the tests are meaningless (deemed unlikely by the author), or that they tapped different aspects of what is considered impulsive behavior. The author suggests that these studies should be expanded to adolescents whose parents were themselves deaf, or of hearing parents who diagnosed the problem early and communicated with their deaf children in sign language. Pending such studies, the author does not believe it possible to interpret what role sound alone plays in development. It would therefore be erroneous to conclude that "a psychology of deafness" is justified from these studies alone.[55]

A study of the type and prevalence of psychiatric illness among deaf people was published by Lebuffe and Lebuffe. Because hearing is the sense best adapted for the continuous scanning of the environment, it has often been

---

[55] Ibid., pp. 160-168.

postulated that deafness might dispose the individual toward paranoia. In fact, most of the relevant studies indicate that this outcome is only likely when a hearing person loses the sense of hearing, usually late in life. There is no indication that the pre-lingually deaf are likely to show paranoid traits. Because deafness in an infant might result in major emotional upheavals in the parents, and also might result in faulty mother-child communication, schizophrenia has been thought to be likely to afflict the deaf. However the extreme of psychosis is not verified by empirical evidence, which shows that the pre-lingually deaf are not predisposed to schizophrenia. Severe depression requiring hospitalization is extremely rare among the deaf, as is the classic obsessive-compulsive neurosis. On the other hand, deaf people are not immune to mild and moderate feelings of depression or discouragement.

Here again, there is a difference between the pre-lingually deaf and those who lose their hearing relatively late in life, with the latter being much more prone to severe depression. Deafness is a severely handicapping condition, and yet deaf people do not, as a group, rank significantly at the pathological extreme on the continuum of mental health.

Impulsivity is an often-noted characteristic of the pre-lingually deaf, but it does not normally assume significant proportions (e.g. criminal behavior), and it may well reflect developmental delays rather than any permanent character traits. There is no evidence of increased psychosocial problems among the deaf; their divorce rate, for example, mirrors that of the general population. Despite continuing language problems in some cases, the evidence suggests that deafness delays, but does not limit, the development of intelligence.[56]

Evans and Elliott attempted to develop screening criteria for the diagnosis of schizophrenia in deaf patients. They pointed out that misdiagnosis is all too common; mental health professionals have been known to diagnose individuals with unrecognized deafness as schizophrenic, and to maintain the erroneous classification for 25 years. When confronted with gesticulating, excited patients who cannot be understood, schizophrenia is often used as a "wastebasket" classification. The authors suggest using Schneider's criteria scales because they do not include symptoms that might be indistinguishable from deafness. Even using these scales, great care is essential, and the patient should, optimally, be interviewed in sign language.[57]

Critchley and his colleagues agreed that communications problems, even when sign language is used, make psychiatric diagnosis of deaf people extremely difficult. Psychiatrists traditionally have noted the presence of thought disorder in the diagnosis of schizophrenia, but the language barrier makes this difficult to access in deaf people. Schneider's criteria, which depend on the analysis of hallucinations, have generally been accepted as the best way to diagnose schizophrenia in deaf populations. An experiment with deaf patients conducted by the authors found that 10 of 12 deaf patients tentatively

---

[56] Francis P. Lebuffe and Leon A. Lebuffe, "Psychiatric Aspects of Deafness," Primary Care, June, 1979 (6) pp. 295-310.

[57] J. William Evans and Holly Elliott, "Screening Criteria for the Diagnosis of Schizophrenia in Deaf Patients," Arch Gen Psychiat, Jul, 1981 (38) pp. 787-90, and Debbie Cole "Sign Language and the Health Care Professional" Robert E., Krieger Publ. Co.; Malabar, FL. 1990 p.ix.

classified as schizophrenic had experiences which, in hearing patients, would be described as auditory hallucinations, a sign of schizophrenia. Many of the patients used the sign for talk or talking to describe the experience. One patient described hearing a "voice like a bell." The authors found this aspect of the experiment difficult to understand. In addition, 10 of the 12 subjects described visual hallucinations. The writers concluded that great caution was necessary in classification because "the nature of communication, where thinking ends and vocalization begins, is imperfectly understood."[58]

In a recent interview, Harlan Lane attacked the credibility of much of the psychological research on the deaf, specifically in the area of methodology. Going back to the 1920s, he found that various researchers, usually on the basis of inappropriate tests, had labeled deaf people's behavioral patterns as: aggressive, androgynous, conscientious, hedonistic, immature, impulsive, lacking in initiative, limited in interests, showing slow motor development, presenting undeveloped personality, possessive, rigid, stubborn, suspicious, and lacking in confidence. The emotional nature of deaf people, if one were to believe every report ever written, would include the following often contradictory and mutually exclusive characteristics: displaying no anxiety, depressive, easily emotionally disturbed, lacking in empathy with other people, explosive, easily frustrated, irritable, moody, showing neurotic behaviors, having a predisposition toward paranoid states, passionate, displaying psychotic reactions, serious, temperamental, and insensitive to others' needs.

---

[58] E.M. Critchley, John C. Denmark, Frank Warren, and Kathleen Wilson, "Hallucinatory Experiences of Prelingually Profound Deaf Schizophrenics," Brit J of Psychiatry, Jan, 1981 (136) pp. 30-2.

Clearly these can not all be generic characterizations of deaf people. Extrapolating from one person's observed personality characteristics to assert that they should also apply to other persons, merely on the basis of shared dysfunction of the ears has not shown any validity.

One of Lane's conclusions is that, in order for deaf people to benefit to any significant degree from the aid offered them, they must have control of the systems and agencies directed at them. In particular, deaf professional workers should be involved in the process of designing and administering psychometrics and other measures upon which research is to be based, implying that experience is the only path to understanding.[59]

Lane suggests that deaf people are more inherently qualified to be sensitive to the needs of other deaf people. A problem with implementing this admittedly solipsistic view arises because there have been few, if any, deaf individuals qualified to address the psychological and psychiatric problems of the deaf. The situation is certainly improving, although there are not yet enough deaf mental health professionals to treat all the deaf clients presenting themselves for treatment. In terms of research, deaf psychologists and psychiatrists, with insights borne of their own experience, might have avoided making some of the more gregious generalizations which can be found in literature regarding deaf people.

Much of the stricter research of the recent past seems to agree with Lane. Study after study lists stereotypes of psychological profiles of the deaf offered by very early studies, and concludes that there is no evidence for acceptance of these descriptions. Researchers such as

---

[59] Lisa Allphin, "Harlan Lane: Psychology of the Deaf: Dangerous Stereotypes?" <u>DCARA News</u>, May 1988, pp. 1-2.

Altshuler concluded that there was no such thing as a "psychology of the deaf," but at most, only the psychology of a particular form of socio-cultural deprivation. This deprivation does not stem from the lack of hearing, but from the lack of help from parents, significant others, and helping professionals. The controlling mechanism of possible future pathology is not the auditory deficit, per se, but the quality of interpersonal relationships which develop as a result of that deficit.

To know, merely, that a given individual is deaf is to know nothing significant about that specific person's psychological make-up; group psychological studies are similar to insure statistics in that they contain information about probability, incidence percentage, etc., rather than precise predictions that composite conclusions will apply to any one individual. Pre-lingually deaf people are as varied as are others of the human race. The literature on deaf people is full of clinical observations, case studies, and self-report evidence offering accumulative evidence of personality trends and vulnerability in certain areas. Research makes that point on the basis of reason, evidence, and scientific method rather than on the basis of emotion and undocumented assertion. Moreover, psychological literature on deaf people stresses the importance of early diagnosis and treatment of deafness, to minimize its effects in the lives of deaf people. Current literature reveals graphic examples of the tragic waste of human potential that ensues when deaf children and adults are misclassified and relegated to the back wards of institutions, rather than receiving appropriate and adequate treatment.

The Psychological Consequences of Hearing Loss

Research summarized in the previous section dealt mainly with pre-lingually deaf people. Considerable attention has also been paid to the psychological problems associated with late-onset deafness, particularly deafness among geriatric populations. However, since the problems of the post-lingually deaf are of a different order and are less central to the focus of this work, they will be covered in less detail.

According to Rousey, the loss of hearing, either sudden or gradual, constitutes a threat to psychological integrity of an individual. Loss of hearing results in mourning for something precious that has been lost; the world suddenly (or gradually) has become dead where it was alive before. There is fear of being cut off from one's normal society, even when hearing aids can be used. There is often a loss of self-esteem involved. The loss of hearing often meets with projection and denial. These and related factors greatly complicate the treatment of hearing loss.[60]

Cornforth and Woods generally agree with Rousey. They declare that "the impact of sudden severe deafness is one of the most psychotraumatic that an individual can experience."[61] The most common result is a severe reactive depression, sometimes leading to suicide attempts.

Mahapatra investigated links between hearing loss and mental health. In one experiment, he found a significantly higher incidence of psychiatric illness among post-lingually

---

[60] Clyde L. Rousey, "Psychological Reactions to Hearing Loss," J. Speech and Hearing Disorders, Aug, 1971 (36) pp. 82-9.

[61] Anthony Cornforth & Marie M. Woods, "Progressive or Sudden Hearing Loss," Nursing Times, 17 Feb, 1972 (68) pp. 205-7, at p. 201.

deaf people than among the general population.[62] The same author in another study used the Cornell Index to show that the post-lingually deaf revealed a greater propensity than did the controls to psychiatric and psychosomatic disturbances.[63]

An article in the British journal, *Lancet*, summarized what is known about the consequences of deafness that strikes late in life. Depressive reactions are among the most common emotional reactions, and the whole family can be affected. Of the functional psychoses, paranoid psychosis seems to be the most likely outcome of depressive reaction. The writer points out that "prelingual deafness constitutes a sensory deficit, acquired deafness a sensory deprivation."[64] While the pre-lingually deaf usually acquire manual language, the elderly deafened cannot be expected to do so. Communication with these individuals is very difficult, adding to the expected negative prognosis of treatment.

One of the few dissenting voices regarding deafness was that of Rosen, who concluded, on the basis of an exhaustive review of the literature, that "the hearing impaired as a group have not been established to differ from the general population on psychiatric or psychological variables."[65] Her reasons were: 1) Clinical decisions are often made on the

---

[62] S. B. Mahapatra, "Psychiatric and Psychosomatic Illness in the Deaf," Brit J. of Psychiatry, Nov, 1974 (125) pp. 450-1.

[63] S.B. Mahapatra, "Deafness and Mental Health: Psychiatric and Psychosomatic Illness in the Deaf," Acta Psychiatrica Scandinavia, June, 1974 (50) pp. 596-611.

[64] "Deafness and Mental Illness," The Lancet, 16 Oct, 1976 (7990), p. 837.

[65] Jeanette K. Rosen, "Psychological & Social Aspects of the Evaluation of Acquired Hearing Impairment," Audiology, May-June, 1979 (18) pp. 238-52, at p. 249.

basis of answers to informal questions. 2) Hearing disability questionnaires vary widely and have not been validated. 3) Attitude surveys of the general population have found little sympathy for, or understanding of, problems of people with impaired hearing. 4) Hearing handicaps vary in nature and seriousness depending on the situation and the interlocutors. And 5) Accordingly, self-report scales which are not verified by acoustical testing may be misleading. It may be argued that her stated reasons do not observably prove her assertion; they only point to the lack of proof of common contrary assumptions.

Rosen's conclusions were disputed by Luey, who wrote from the perspective of a social worker. Communication problems almost always cost the deaf person some friends, she noted, because people are often over-extended, and when they believe they can't handle everything well, the first areas to be neglected are "extras" like sensitivity to people whose needs seem to be different than their own. When a newly-deafened person feels that a friend has let him down, a sense of alienation from society creeps into the disappointment, connecting the hearing loss with the social problem. Newly deafened persons frequently experience an identity crisis as a result of major changes in their lives. At some point in the adjustment process, the deafened individual passes through a crisis similar to that experienced by most people going through catastrophic change. The adjustment process consists of the usual phases of denial, anger, bargaining, and guilt, before a constructive adaptation can take place.[66]

---

[66] Helen S. Luey, "Between Worlds: The Problems of Deafened Adults," Social Work in Health Care, Spring, 1980 (5) pp. 253-65.

Psychological Treatment

Deafness clearly complicates the psychological or psychiatric treatment that may be required for any psychological illness or condition. Relatively few articles have addressed this problem: some of these are summarized in the following pages. Before presenting these reports, it should be noted that the field of treatment for psychological disabilities is highly fragmented among theoretical lines. e.g., Peterson lists six major approaches to counseling and psychotherapy: 1) Cognitive, with major proponents Ellis, Beck, and Raimy; 2) Learning Theory, propounded by Dollard & Miller, Wolpe, Kanfer, and Phillips, Rotter & Meichenbaum; 3) Psychoanalytic, led by Freud, and amended by Horney, Alexander and Jung; 4) Perceptual-Phenomenological, represented by Kelly, Berne, Perls, Lewin, and Rogers; 5) Existential, as represented by May, Frankl, Buber, and Kirkegaurd; and 6) Eclectic, most clearly propounded by Harte and Thorne.[67] These broad, general classifications may undercount, e.g., the range of different schools of psychoanalytic theory and practice (Adler, Jung, and Sullivan). Each school of thought interprets psychological problems in the light of its own theoretical perspective and prescribes its own treatment modalities.

Moreover, although the practitioners of particular schools of thought believe that their theories and treatment methods work better than others, empirical evidence has not consistently revealed this. One major evaluation concluded that "Empirical studies do not produce any clear-cut winners when psychotherapies are compared with each

---

[67] C.H. Patterson, Theories of Counseling and Psychotherapy, Fourth Ed., New York; Harper & Row, 1986.

other."[68] This does not mean that some are not more effective than others, but that there is no conclusive evidence to show which is consistently best in terms of patient outcomes.

On the other hand, all of the respectable therapies do seem to benefit most patients most of the time. All seem to have in common the idea of a helper, or therapist, who attempts to establish a helping relationship with a patient. Why the relationship is helpful has not been answered conclusively by research, but it is thought that providing a person a milieu of unconditional acceptance and offering the unwavering presumption that the client can affect his circumstances, contribute to the development of self-confidence in the client. When the client is given a chance to ventilate thoughts, without fear of being criticized, and to receive insights via gentle interactions, progress in psychological health is often perceived.[69]

In addition, chemotherapeutic interventions have become common and are effective for the treatment of many psychological illnesses. According to one authority, "Effective and relatively safe medical treatments are now available for most of the major psychiatric illnesses."[70] Some forms of psychosis, neurosis, and character disorder do not respond well to drugs, however. And, in all cases, a patient under medication needs close medical supervision.

---

[68] R.J. Spitzer & D.F. Klein, (Eds.) Evaluation of Psychological Therapies, Baltimore, MD: The Johns Hopkins University Press, 1976. p. 16-17.

[69] Ibid.

[70] Ross J. Baldessarini, "Chemotherapy," in The Harvard Guide to Modern Psychiatry, Ed. Armand M. Nicholi, Jr., Cambridge, MA: The Belknap Press of Harvard Univ. Press; 19078, pp. 387-432, at p. 430.

Most researchers have stressed the need to have helping personnel able to converse with patients in their own language. Denmark and Eldridge declared that the most pressing need in dealing with deaf psychiatric patients was for personnel to be trained in sign language. They noted that "communication between doctor and patient is more important in psychiatry than in any other branch of medicine, for it is the psychiatrist who relies most completely on his patient's powers of verbal expression and his own ability to understand the patient to effect change.[71] While this research is comparatively old, it remains true that, in psychiatry, language is the diagnostic and healing medium.

The same point was made by Altshuler and Rainer. "For effective psychiatric work with most deaf patients, a knowledge of manual language is a sine qua non."[72] In New York State mental hospitals, the most widely applicable approach was individual therapy, supportive in nature and designed to achieve insight. Group therapy restricted to members of one sex was ineffective, but results improved when groups were mixed. Self-government in group therapy was not effective because it was soon converted into a dictatorship; firm but flexible leadership by the staff proved the best access to therapy.

In another article, Denmark repeated his belief that many deaf patients can derive a great deal of help from specialized psychiatric services, provided helping personnel are aware of the unique problems of the deaf, and have sign

---

[71] John C. Denmark and Raymond W. Eldridge, "Psychiatric Services for the Deaf," The Lancet, 2 Aug, 1969 (614) pp. 259-262, at p. 259.

[72] Kenneth Z. Altshuler and John D. Rainer, "Observations on Psychiatric Services for the Deaf," Mental Hygiene, 17 Sep. 1971 (133) pp. 28-31.

language skills. He cited a report of the International Research Seminar on the Rehabilitation of Deaf Persons which recommended that all personnel dealing with deaf people should be "adequately trained in all methods of communicating with the deaf."[73] The author felt there was an urgent need in the United States for the development of such facilities.

Deafness is more than a medical fact; it can include social, emotional, linguistic, and mental facets. Thus, according to Schlesinger and Meadow, the deaf individual may require services from a number of organizations and disciplines, including medicine, audiology, speech therapy, special education, vocational counseling, welfare departments, courts and probate assistance. Even when all these agencies and services are providing parallel, and not contradictory information, the results can be overwhelmingly confusing. An effective program of community psychiatry ideally involves co-ordinating efforts of all the people involved. In addition, the community psychiatrist is in an ideal position to act as an agent for social change in the area of deaf education.[74]

Robinson reported on a special program for the deaf at St. Elizabeth's Hospital in the District of Columbia in 1963. At that time, group therapy sessions using sign language were started, and they soon proved useful. In 1970, the program was expanded into a 30-bed facility with a full-time staff. Sign language and finger spelling are now the principal methods of communication, although other means

---

[73] John C. Denmark, "Psychiatry and the Deaf," Current Psychiatric Therapies, 1971 (11) pp. 68-72.

[74] Hilde S. Schlesinger & Kathryn P. Meadow, "A Conceptual Model for a Program of Community Psychiatry for a Deaf Population," Commun Mental Health J., Feb, 1972, (8) p. 47-59.

are not discouraged. The goals of the group therapy sessions are: to allay anxiety, improve self-esteem, improve interpersonal relations, and to expand social interaction. Group therapy may be supplemented with family therapy, and often leads to individual therapy. The advantage of the latter system is that patients will often reveal important sensitive materials in private that they would not in a group. Activity therapies, such as dance, drama and mime, psychodrama, drawing, painting and sculpting have also been found to be useful. Hospital personnel for these services were trained at Gallaudet College.[75]

Shapiro and Harris reported the use of family therapy in treatment of the deaf with psychological problems. The authors believe that problems of deaf individuals are largely related to family problems, and that family therapy, therefore, serves as the best vehicle for treatment. Studies reported elsewhere in this work assert that deaf parents generally cope much more effectively with the psychological needs of a deaf child than do hearing parents, but all families would desire enhanced functioning.[76]

An article by Robinson on the St. Elizabeth's psychotherapy program provided these prescriptions for effective treatment: Therapists should not assume that any one method of communication is best for use with the deaf. The method should be negotiated between therapist and patient. Because some deaf people have limited vocabularies, the therapist must personalize the level of sophistication of his/her communication. Some therapists may need to use an interpreter, if their signing skills are

---

[75] Luther D. Robinson, "A Program for Deaf Mental Patients," Hospi & Commun Psychiat, Jan, 1973 (24) pp. 40-42.

[76] Rodney J. Shapiro and R. J. Harris, "Family Therapy in Treatment of the Deaf: A Case Report," Family Process, Mar, 1976 (15) pp. 83-96.

inadequate, if the client approves; although questions of confidentiality and rapport discourage this practice. Finally, despite strides made in treating mentally ill deaf persons, demands for service continue to exceed the supply of motivated, qualified therapists.[77]

Hoyt and his colleagues interviewed ten therapists and supervisors with clinical experiences in working with deaf people to determine their views on major issues. These highlights were noted:

    1. Communication. Most forms of therapy involve "talking through" problems. With deaf clients and hearing therapists, communication becomes, at times, nearly impossible. Yet therapists assert that the ability of a person to disclose himself/herself fully and honestly to at least one other person is a prime measure of psychological adjustment.[78] Ideally, deaf clients who sign should be seen by therapists fluent in sign language. The use of an interpreter complicates the usual "one-on-one" relationship which many therapists believe is necessary, in order for healing to occur. With an interpreter present, the normal process of transference may not develop, or the interpreter may become the patient's "authority figure." Moreover, the patient may be unwilling to trust anyone but the therapist with sensitive or painful disclosures. If no signing therapist is available, and an interpreter is used, problems with this less than optimum means of communication should be discussed explicitly with the client. The therapist

---

[77] "Gold Award: Mental Health Services for the Deaf: St. Elizabeth's Hospital, Wash., D.C.," Hospital and Community Psychiatry, Oct, 1978 (29) pp. 674-677.

[78] Sidney M. Jourard. The Transparent Self: Self Disclosure and Well-Being. N.Y., N.Y.; Van Nostrand, 1964. & Abraham H. Maslow. Towards a Psychology of Being, 2nd ed. New York, Van Nostrand, 1968. p. 212.

may state his/her awareness that sharing deeply personal thoughts in the presence of an interpreter may be difficult with the client, to aid the client in realizing that this reluctance is normal.

2. Diagnosis and Evaluation. Difficult under the best of circumstances, problems of diagnosis are greatly exacerbated when communication between client and therapist is unsatisfactory. Diagnostic personnel need to distinguish carefully between lack of oral language skills and pathologies, e.g. Therapists might normally give some weight to disturbed speech patterns, as evidence of disturbed thought or distraught emotions. Because the syntax of American Sign Language is different from that of standard English, what might be natural in one might appear distorted in the other. The evaluating/diagnosing therapist, then should be aware of these cautions. Ideally, he/she should thoroughly understand both languages.

Other family therapists, e.g. Satir, Jackson, and Watzlawick, have concentrated on dysfunctional communication and miscommunication which is often common in over-extended families. They speak of the phenomenon of *double bind*, wherein chronic under-communication and miscommunication work to discourage people to trust their own perceptions. Watzlawick, Beavin and Jackson note: "The paradoxical behavior imposed by double-binding . . . is in turn of a double-binding nature, and this leads to a self-perpetuating pattern of communication. The behavior of the most overtly disturbed communicant, if examined in isolation, satisfies the clinical criteria of schizophrenia."[79] Their thesis is that examining

---

[79] Paul Watzlawick, Janet H. Beavin, and Don D. Jackson, Pragmatics of Human Communication, A Study of Interactional Patterns, Pathologies, and Paradoxes. N.Y.; W.W. Norton & Co.; 1967. p. 215.

an identified patient without due consideration of his milieu–primarily the other people he/she lives with, promotes a false presentation of mental illness symptomatology. When viewed as a whole, family interactions and group dynamics make sense of much that otherwise would be classified as at least bizarre.

3. Special Features of Therapy with the Deaf: Therapists need to explain basics of the treatment mode, including: influences of unconscious dynamics, certain concepts such as the linking of past influences to the present, and insight that feelings influence actions but are not, themselves, behavior. Clients require understanding that talking about feelings is therapeutic–even if the feelings the client can articulate at that time consist only of hostility or disdain for the therapist. Therapists need additional cautions against being directive within the therapy session. They need to frequently ascertain that the client understands and is actively participating in the choices of therapy.[80] (Much of this advice seems predicated on the existence of proclivity toward misunderstanding. if both therapist and client use the same language, such problems may be minimized.)

Socially Related Emotional Characteristics

This section covers literature review of research articles dealing with sociological and socially matrixed emotional problems of the deaf. These articles are reported in chronological order.

---

[80] Michael F. Hoyt, Ellen Y. Siegelman, and Hiolde S. Schlesinger, "Special Issues Regarding Psychotherapy with the Deaf," Amer. J. Psychiatry, Jun, 1981 (138) pp. 807-811.

In an article on the quality of life for handicapped people, Jackson and Engstrom report on the success of theatre for deaf people.[81] In 1967, actress Ann Bancroft and director Arthur Penn conceived the idea of a deaf repertory theatre while attending a performance of *Othello*, given by deaf players at Gallaudet College. They visualized the company as an aesthetic enterprise and as a way of expanding employment opportunities for deaf persons. After deaf people compensate for difficulties in communicating, almost from birth, they tend to excel in non-verbal expression–including body language, and therefore are naturally emotive. The National Theatre of the Deaf has been a success commercially, artistically, and as a means of fostering understanding between deaf and hearing communities. Moreover, it served as the spark for the creation of other dramatic groups for deaf people, notably the Chicago Experimental Theatre for the Deaf.

In an experimental British study, Bowyer and Gillies investigated the hypothesis that partially-deaf children have more social-emotional problems than do severely deaf children, and that the former, therefore, should not be mainstreamed. The two groups were studied in four different schools using a combination of written tests and teachers' ratings. Bowyer and Gillies found that neither group was maladjusted. The writers attributed this happy conclusion to the better medical care and early treatment of all these children had received, including, the receipt of hearing aids, when they were deemed necessary.[82]

---

[81] Dorothy G. Jackson and George A. Engstrom, "The Quality of Life," J of Rehabilitation, Jan-Feb, 1971 (37) pp. 10-12.

[82] L.R. Bowyer and J. Gillies, "The Social and Emotional Adjustment of Deaf and Partially-Deaf Children," Briti J. Educ. Psych, Nov, 1972 (42) pp. 305-308.

In 1973 a team of New York University researchers surveyed methods of dealing with emotionally disturbed children with identified behavior problems. Among deaf children, 1-3 out of 10 were believed to have emotional and behavioral disorders, and children suspected of having these disorders were being kept out of the classroom. Therefore, educators could not avoid addressing the problem. A model program was developed, using principles which had been shown effective with hearing children. Children were introduced to sign language, and their parents were encouraged to learn sign language also. An atmosphere of genuine concern and acceptance was fostered in the classroom.[83] (Although the researchers did not differentiate between the various program changes which were revealed in overall improved student outcomes on academic measures, it seems likely to this researcher that improving communication between parents and children, and between teachers and children, at least partially contributed to the program's success.)

Jacobs attempted to survey the adult community of the Deaf, describing the group as being closely knit, seeking their own kind for mutual pleasure and benefits, including ease of communication. Because the Deaf comprise such a small portion of the population, Deaf adults usually form only small communities, except perhaps in larger metropolitan areas. They experience the advantages and disadvantages of life in small towns/villages everywhere–stemming primarily from the premise that everyone knows everyone else. Gradually the Deaf community has evolved a network of organizations, ranging from local to national

---

[83] Doris Naiman, Jerome D. Schein, and Larry Steward, "New Vistas for Emotionally Disturbed Deaf Children," American Annals of the Deaf, Aug, 1973 (118) pp. 480-487.

levels. While these organizations serve a social function, their primary aim is to be of service to deaf people. These organizations include the National Association of the Deaf, the International Association of Parents of the Deaf, the Gallaudet College Alumni Association, the American Athletic Association of the Deaf, several national /international religious groups, and many others.[84]

McLaughlin and Andrews investigated the reading habits of deaf adults. Their subjects were 36 members of a church organization and were mainly unskilled workers in manual jobs. virtually all of the subjects said they read a local newspaper for an average of 37 minutes a day. In addition, most of the group said they read one or more magazines on a regular basis, with *TV Guide* the most popular. Relatively few read books, but the Bible was the main choice of those who did. Deaf people over age 50 listed themselves as the most avid readers. Those who had used sign language in school were more interested in reading than were those who had used oral communication. The researchers concluded, from their 36 subjects, that reading habits of deaf adults, as designated by a self-report measure, were not significantly different from those of hearing adults of comparable educational background and occupational category.[85]

Schiff and Ventry reported the results of an investigation into the communication problem of hearing children with deaf parents. The quality of parents' speech to their children traditionally has been considered to have significant implications for the child's speech and language

---

[84] Leo Jacobs, "The Community of the Adult Deaf," American Annals of the Deaf, Feb, 1974 (119) pp. 41-46.

[85] Joseph McLaughlin and Jean Andrews, "The Reading Habits of Deaf Adults in Baltimore," American Annals of the Deaf, Oct, 1975 (120) pp. 497-501.

development. About half of the 52 children were considered to be developing speech and language normally; most of these had mothers who used sign language with them. However, since 14 of the 52 children were discovered to have severely limiting disabilities, not much can be deduced from the study.[86]

Andrews and Conley developed classroom activities to provide deaf teenagers with information and skills to correct misconceptions they might have had about crime and the law. Deaf students are hardly immune to the temptations prevalent in their society, and temptation comes in a variety of guises, from drugs to shop-lifting. Additionally, deaf children may have obtained a distorted idea of crime because they may have comprehended only a portion of the message portrayed by radio and TV. Glamorized detective shows or programs which offer scant plot to cover the primary offering of high-speed car chases or other stereotypical violence of the genre may, indeed, contribute additionally to deaf teenagers' misconceptions about the law. The researchers' proposed activities included reading "wanted posters," filling out job applications which normally seek information on felony records, compiling a scrapbook of crime stories from the press and magazines, receiving a classroom visit from a police officer, touring the local jail, and role-playing relevant situations. In addition to providing students with a better grasp of concepts of crime and the law, their

---

[86] Naomi B. Schiff and Ira M. Ventry, "Communication Problems in Hearing Children of Deaf Parents," The Journal of Speech and Hearing Disorders, Aug, 1976 (41) pp. 348-358.

activities were positively correlated with motivating students to improve their reading and writing skills.[87]

Becker interviewed 200 people in the San Francisco Bay area who were born deaf or who had become deaf in the first few years of life, to determine how they perceived and dealt with stigma. Researcher and subjects communicated in sign language, and accumulatively, results indicated that for most of the subjects, the experience of stigma began at an early age. They were born of hearing parents with whom they were never able to communicate perfectly. Their parents faced the difficult choice of whether to have their children attend a local school to learn speech and lip reading or to go away to school to learn American Sign Language. At the time the subjects were growing up, users of sign language were generally stigmatized. Some parents reinforced this feeling by making clear their distaste for signing. For this reason, and as a result of unpleasant experiences with the hearing world, many of the subjects reported negative experiences of contacts with society in general. The deaf people in the study group tended to form a separate and distinct society as a result of a process Becker calls "normalization." The San Francisco area deaf group gave their primary loyalty to their own group, and conformed completely to its norms. As part of the normalization process, they dissociated themselves from others who suffered a different social stigma, such as ethnic and racial minorities, the socially deviant, and those with other disabilities.[88]

---

[87] Jean Andrews and Janet Conley, "Beer, Pot, and Shoplifting: Teenage Abuses," American Annals of the Deaf, Dec, 1977 (122) pp. 557-562.

[88] Gaylene Becker, "Coping With Stigma: Lifelong Adaption of Deaf People," Social Science and Medicine, Jan, 1981 (158) pp. 21-24.

The National Technical Institute for the Deaf offers a course called "The Psycho-Social Aspects of Deafness" to small groups of college-bound deaf students. According to Skyer, the rationale for the course is that students with hearing impairments may lag behind their hearing counterparts in the diversity and richness of prior experiences and in their reservoir of factual information regarding social and personal issues. The major goal of the course is to provide students with opportunities to understand the dynamics of hearing-deaf social and familial interactions, and to comprehend the impact of their deafness on their educational, social and emotional growth. The course outline includes: 1) an overview of education of the deaf from Grecian times to the present; 2) different forms of communication; 3) impact of deafness on language and educational development; 4) mechanisms of adjustment and family development; 5) attitudes of society toward deafness and the deaf individual's attitudes toward his own deafness and other deaf people, as well as appropriate coping mechanisms; and 6) roles of deaf adults. The course operates as a seminar in which students are encouraged to participate in discussions and share their feelings. Students enrolled in the course have opportunities to interact with hearing people on campus.[89]

Lisowski investigated the process of living as a deaf person communicating via ASL with 12 pre-lingually deaf persons living in a housing development near a medical center. In all 12 subjects, the socialization process took place at a residential school, wherein the students developed an ad-hoc family life, rather than developing a

---

[89] Solange C. Skyer, "Psycho-Social Aspects of Deafness Course as a Counseling Tool for the Hearing Impaired," American Annals of the Deaf, June, 1982 (127) pp. 349-355.

biological family life. All of the 12 overcame any deprivation of "outside" society which this may have implied. All but one of these people used sign language predominantly and wrote their messages for hearing people. Whether by choice or necessity, all of the subjects limited their social ties to immediate family or to other deaf individuals. None of the subjects felt deprived; since they had never heard, they did not miss what they had never known. On the whole, they revealed somewhat negative attitudes toward hearing people, perhaps because of their perception that the hearing world discriminated against them, or because of a lack of intimate familiarity with the hearing world. All were considered conservative in social orientation.[90] Although, admittedly, this study was quite small, and used only self-report measures, it may be representative.

Andersson studied sociological variables of deafness in a cross-cultural investigation in Sweden and in the United States. Sweden was at that time a comparatively homogeneous country. Deafness there was considered a serious handicap, and deaf people were mostly segregated, having their own school, clubs, and supportive services, all sponsored and financed by the government. The result, according to Andersson, is that deaf people in Sweden comprise a separate and well-defined group, with little contact the larger society. In the United States, deafness is regarded as being less severely handicapping than it is in

---

[90] Kathleen Anne Lisowski, "A Naturalistic Study of the Experience of Living as a Deaf Person," (Ph.D. dissertation, Humanistic Psychology Institute, 1980) pp. 288-311; see also Gaylene Becker, "Lifelong Socialization and Adaptive Behavior of Deaf People" Understanding Deafness Socially ed. Paul Higgins & Jeffrey Nash; Charles C. Thomas, Publ.; Springfield, Ill. n.d. pp. 59-63.

Sweden, he notes, and accordingly, in the U.S., the demographics of the deaf population are more diverse. Andersson states that the National Association of the Deaf encourages deaf persons to remain in the larger society, rather than encouraging small group development at state and local levels. In the U.S., some deaf children go to residential schools, while others are mainstreamed within public schools. At the university level, students may attend any school for which they are qualified, providing interpreting services are available. The American ideal is assimilation, but, in fact, deaf people in the U.S. often form separate social groups for a number of reasons. Facile communication is one decided advantage.[91]

Most of the studies surveyed for this section describe the sociology of a particular deaf group, and it would, of course, be erroneous to attribute the same characteristics to other deaf groups or individuals. Extension via accumulative detail is risky. As a welcome alternative, it is instructive to study biographies of deaf persons who have achieved greatness in the larger society. A few examples will suffice to illustrate the contrast. Erastus "Deaf" Smith lost his hearing at the age of one, but became the greatest scout and legendary fighter of the conflict between Texas and Mexico. Smith coped with his hearing loss by training a dog not to bark but to alert him to intruders by tugging at his pants. John Carlin was born deaf in 1813. Without any formal schooling, he became a major American artist and writer, and he exerted a major influence in the decision to found Gallaudet College. Mabel Hubbard Bell, wife of the inventor of the telephone, developed total deafness at the

---

[91] Yerker J. O. Anderson, "A Cross-Cultural Comparative Study: Deafness," (Ph.D. dissertation, University of Maryland, 1981, pp. 115-123).

age of five, but lived an active social life, preventing her husband, a natural recluse, from going into semi-hibernation.

Numerous other examples could be cited; there is hardly a field of endeavor in which profoundly deaf individuals have not flourished, often with neglected or inadequate schooling or other immense hardships to overcome.[92] If it was possible for these individuals to thrive–even excel–then deafness, per se, cannot preclude people from experiencing rich, full lives in their various circumstances.

Cinema and television play important roles in American social and emotional life. Both have been shown to reflect popular opinion and to mold attitudes. Schuchman's book on deafness and the film entertainment industry examines the way deaf people have been portrayed through analysis of more than 200 films and television episodes. The author has much sensitivity to Deaf culture, stemming from the fact that both his parents were profoundly and pre-lingually deaf.[93] Schuchman's thesis is:

> . . . the film and television industries have dealt with deafness in a manner similar to their stereotyped treatment of ethnic and racial minorities. Thus, entertainment has been a substantial contributor to the public's general misunderstanding of deafness and to the perpetuation of attitudes that permit discrimination against deaf citizens.[94]

---

[92] Robert Panara & John Panara, Great Deaf Americans, Silver Spring, MD., T.J. Publishers, n.d.) passim.

[93] John S. Schuchman, Hollywood Speaks: Deafness and the Film Entertainment Industry, Urbana, IL: University of Illinois Press, 1988.

[94] Ibid., pp. ix-x.

Schuchman acknowledges that the film industry did not create these stereotypes, which even prevail in scholarly literature, created by professional people who should have observed more precisely. The film industry, however, did unthinkingly reinforce these stereotypes.

In the early days of film, the medium was regarded as a great boon by the deaf community. Silent films could be enjoyed by deaf and hearing people alike, on equal terms. Silent films posed no impediment to the use of deaf screen actors, so deaf actors were frequently employed. Since sign language was under massive attack in the United States and abroad, deaf educators used film technology to teach and enrich deaf students. However, even during this "golden age," deaf actors usually did not portray deaf characters on the screen; they had little opportunity to influence the popular image of deafness. Increasingly, the stereotype of deaf people as "dummies" evolved. "Hearing aids, ear trumpets, and sign language itself were transformed into visual gimmicks designed to elicit laughter, and it became common for characters to feign deafness in order to catch or trick a villain."[95]

Film makers' unable to resist the quick prat-fall may have contributed to further stereotyping deaf people, but at least deaf people enjoyed employment on the silent screen. However, the equal access enjoyed by the deaf as performer and audience came to an end in 1927-28, when the silent era ended and talking pictures emerged.

The advent of talking pictures caused consternation in the deaf community. The inexorable march towards sound deprived deaf people of the ability to participate in what was becoming an important part of American socio-cultural life. A number of distinguished film careers by deaf

---

[95] Ibid., pp. 28-29.

performers ended abruptly. During the period from 1928 to 1948, the image of deaf characters in film media steadily worsened.[96] Silence was often portrayed as stupidity, as in the film "The Dummy;" catering to public stereotypes, and erroneous public expectations encouraged further short-cuts by film makers, which distorted reality. Profoundly deaf characters were depicted as perfect speakers, as in the case of Loretta Young playing the deaf wife of Alexander Graham Bell in "The Story of Alexander Graham Bell." Characters described as pre-lingually deaf were portrayed as expert lip-readers; and deaf characters were frequently portrayed as steeped in misery because of their affliction. In a revealing twist, film makers produced more convoluted plots by having villains or heroes at times to mask their identities by faking deafness.[97]

Throughout the first two decades of "talking" pictures, the deaf community complained bitterly about the emerging Hollywood stereotype of deaf people. In particular: "It is the word *dumb* that we despise, detest and loathe, for there is among the hearing public, a wide misconception of the use of the term *dumb* in reference to the deaf.[98]

Hollywood attempted to correct the demeaning stereotype with the filming of "Johnny Belinda," with Jane Wyman, the story of a deaf girl treated like a dummy, who blossoms when taught signs, numbers, and the alphabet. A dozen films, including two musicals, dealing with deafness in some fashion were produced in the 1950s. "Flesh and Fury," with Tony Curtis, is the story of a deaf boxer who regains his hearing following an operation and then loses it again during a championship fight. According to

---

96 Ibid., p. 50.
97 Ibid., pp. 44-50.
98 Ibid., p. 53

Schuchman, "the film is more sensitive to deafness than any prior motion picture, particularly in its depiction of Callan's/Curtis' confusion when his hearing is restored by the operation."[99]

Two films, "Crash of Silence" and "The Story of Esther Costello," dealt fairly realistically with the way deaf children are taught to communicate. Films during the 1950s represented a modest step forward, in that some form of sign language was used, permitting more rounded and believable deaf characters. But most of the films contained outlandish sequences and continuing slights to deaf people.[100]

One of the most successful films of the 1960s from the perspective of Deaf culture, was "The Miracle Worker," starring Ann Bancroft and Patty Duke, and based on materials from the autobiography of Helen Keller. Although it is emotionally moving and was crafted to gain sympathy for the deaf-blind heroine, it nonetheless equates success with speech.[101]

"Children of a Lesser God," was the first film in 60 years to employ deaf actors and actresses in all the deaf parts. Based on a successful Broadway play which received several Tony Awards, the film version was also very well received by the general public. Nevertheless, the film version de-emphasized "deaf politics" in order to accentuate the love story. Moreover, the camera routinely cut off the signs or obscured their visibility, so as to be largely incomprehensible to deaf audiences. Additionally, there were few captioned versions of the film, so there were

---

99 Ibid., p. 57.
100 Ibid., p. 64.
101 Ibid. p. 65.

relatively few opportunities for deaf audiences to view the film.[102]

Schuchman finds television marginally better than film. Closed-caption technology makes the medium more accessible to deaf people than is film. As a regulated industry, also it is somewhat more responsive to public pressure than is cinema. Following a protest campaign in 1978-1979, the television industry began to hire more deaf actors to play appropriate roles; from 1980 to 1986, there were 24 identifiable deaf roles in TV dramas, of which 18 were portrayed by deaf actors. On the whole, concludes Schuchman, "television has not met all of the expectations of deaf people, but it certainly has come a long way since its initial popularity in the 1950s, and it certainly is more accessible than motion pictures."[103]

Padden and Humphries, members of the deaf community, and scholars who study their community's language and society, attempted to "collect,organize, and interpret examples of the cultural life of Deaf people."[104] The result is a rich mosaic of deaf life and a necessary corrective to the literature which studies deaf people as subjects in experiments, but which is inadequate in revealing their inner lives.

Although their book may be difficult to summarize, a few important insights are visible. Scholarly writings about deaf people traditionally have focused on disability and pathology. Classifications have stressed the facts and degrees of hearing impairment as if these were the most

---

[102] Ibid., pp. 82-86.

[103] Ibid., p. 97.

[104] Carol Padden and Tom Humphries, Deaf in America: Voices From a Culture, (Cambridge, MA; Harvard University Press, 1988) p.v.

important facts about the people being studied. "Other facts about them, notably those about their social and cultural lives, are then interpreted as consequences of these classifications."[105] However deaf people have much outside the fact that they do not hear that is salient in describing and understanding them. For instance, they have a rich language of their own, one that is capable of "insight, invention, and irony."[106] The larger society could benefit from understanding how deaf people perceive their world.

Children without hearing at birth, or those who lose hearing early in life, do not know they are deaf or different. If they are born into a deaf family, they fall naturally into the patterns of sign language; if children are born into a hearing family, they notice that some people move their lips, but they do not know why. Increasingly, it becomes the outside world which defines them. Sometimes they may be sent away from their families to residential schools. If deaf children were to be raised among deaf people, secure in their sign language and the shared knowledge of the group, they would not need to fall "into darkness, nonexistence, and despair," as some do, suggest Padden and Humphries. Deaf people may experience the larger society dictating to them, without signs of empathy or sensitivity. The most flagrant example of this has been the effort, at various times and places, to ban the use of signs in favor of *oralism*. Padden and Humphries descry this, saying, "If signed language is snatched away from deaf people, they can only fall into despair . . ."[107] Padden and Humphries point out that many terms used in sociological research on the deaf

---

105 Ibid., p. 10.
106 Ibid., p. 11.
107 Ibid. p. 36, and Dolnick, E. "Deafness as Culture;" The Atlantic; v. 292, #3; Sep. '93; p. 39.

convey the message that deaf people have lessened status. e.g. The distinction is made in the literature between pre-lingual and post-lingual deaf, referring to those who lost their hearing before they acquired spoken English and those who became deaf after learning English, respectively.

The distinction ignores those who have learned sign language as a first language, and hence are native users of a human language, like those who are "post-lingually deaf." The terms, as would be expected within an official frame with HEARING as its center, emphasize the role of onset of hearing loss and the presence of English, rather than the age at which any human language, including ASL, is acquired.[108]

In the vocabulary of ASL, "deaf" represents normality, and "hearing" the highest degree of deviation from the norm; it is all a question of perspective.

Human children are born with innate abilities for learning language, but they are dependent on other language users to instruct them. Hearing children will babble naturally, gradually forming words and grammatical constructions, with positive reinforcement for increasingly discernible approximations to words their elders use. Similarly, deaf preschool children emulate signing adults. If they are isolated from mature sign users, they will develop their own sign language, intelligible to themselves and their playmates, but not to others.

But in an environment which actively seeks to suppress signing, such children may have their development arrested or distorted. Moreover, they will be deprived of what other

---

[108] Ibid., p. 48.

children take for granted, a language that is potentially as much an art as it is a means of communication.[109]

Harlan Lane discusses some of these same themes in his introduction to a compilation of some of the classics of deaf language and education (de Fontenay, Desloges, de L'Epee, etc.). He points out that "the relations between a minority using one language and the enveloping society using another are often the subject of heated dispute."[110] The examples are legion–minorities in the United States who demand bilingual education, Basques in Spain, Kurds in Iraq, and people from Syria, Turkey and France in Canada. Such a conflict exists between deaf people who wish to educate their children in ASL and the surrounding communities which espouse English. Indeed, the "history of the deaf in the United States is the history of a struggle, in which, by a bitter irony, the community of signers is pitted against their would-be benefactors, those English-speakers charged by the nation with improving the plight of the deaf.[111]

According to Lane, the conflict stems from the hearing establishment's refusal to view signing as other than pathological. ASL was viewed as a poor substitute for "real" language; the "enlightened" solution was to rehabilitate signers with special educators and speech pathologists. Perhaps the objective (to integrate deaf people into the greater American society) was benign, but it was based on ignorance and had deplorable results. Decades of Oralism

---

[109] Ibid., pp. 56-121.

[110] Harlan Lane, ed. The Deaf Experience: Classics in Language and Education, (Cambridge, MA: Harvard University Press, 1984), p. 1.

[111] Ibid.

failed to produce individuals who could speak well enough to make their way in the hearing world.[112]

Intelligence

It is not immediately apparent why an individual's hearing should affect the brain between malfunctioning ears. Nevertheless, a number of studies, primarily based on posited links between language and thought, have tried to investigate deafness in relationship to intelligence. Some scholars assert that the absence of auditory stimulation and the lack of systematic reinforcement of learning through speech interferes with developing intelligence.[113] In passing, we note that arguments still swirl over the nature of "intelligence," and whether it exists as one unitary trait or as a collection of variables.[114]

Furth wrote a major article incorporating literature review and research on the thinking of deaf children. He pointed out that pre-lingually deaf children not taught sign language at an early age may grow up without any systematized conventional language. However, these children nevertheless "construct their own symbols as they are needed for the development of thinking."[115] The thinking processes of deaf children are presumed to be

---

112 Ibid., pp. 2-13.
113 Walter A. Luszki, "Hearing Loss and Intelligence Among Retardates," American Journal of Mental Deficiency, July, 1965 (70) pp. 93-101.
114 Adrienne Harrie, "Are Brains Genetic? The Intelligence Controversy," The New York Times book Review May 31, 1981; pp. 11, 22.
115 Hans G. Furth, "Linguistic Deficiency and Thinking: Research with Deaf Subjects, 1964-1969." Psychological Bulletin, July, 1971 (76) pp. 58-72.

similar to those of hearing children, and therefore, development of thought processes must be explained without recourse to verbal processes. The author quotes approvingly Jean Piaget's view that language is not a constituent element of logical thinking. Evidence provided by a number of researchers with deaf children offers confirmation of Piaget's view.

Youniss investigated implications of deafness on intelligence. He acknowledged having once assumed that the growth of intelligence depended on mastery of a language. He cited surveys of deaf adults in New York State and in Frederick County, Maryland, which did not validate such a link. Deaf children deprived through chance or social policy from acquiring a formal language nevertheless showed no deficiencies in intelligence. (Of course, some of these children might have had a signed language.) Youniss also explained this phenomenon in terms of Piaget's theories. Crudely put, symbols did not drive intelligence forward, but were created and used by intelligence. Youniss also pleaded with other researchers to be very careful in testing deaf children with conventional measures of intelligence.[116]

Kusche and her associates assessed the differences in intelligence and achievement of deaf adolescents from three different family constellations. These were: 1) 19 deaf children with deaf parents; 2) 19 controls with hearing parents and hearing siblings; and 3) 20 deaf children with deaf siblings and hearing parents, together with their 20 controls. The tests covered performance scale I.Q., vocabulary, reading comprehension, and language

---

[116] James Youniss, "Intelligence: Implication of and for Deafness," Advanced Experimental Medicine and Biology, 1972 (30) pp. 151-159.

achievement. The deaf students with deaf parents learned to sign earlier, and had higher I.Q.s and achievement scores than did any of the other groups. All the deaf children scored higher than their control groups. The authors speculated that, in families where deafness is hereditary, deaf parents with superior nonverbal intelligence would be the ones most likely to become successful, marry, and have children–passing their traits on to their children.[117]

Education

Bonvillian and his colleagues reviewed the educational and psycho-linguistic implications of deafness. They concluded that deaf people are not deficient in intellectual competence, inferring that weaker skills in English and lower educational achievement require other explanations beyond the fact of deafness. Essentially, the deaf use another language entirely, and should not be compared to hearing students using oral language. Sign language is an organized and structured symbolic system whose acquisition mirrors the acquisition of spoken language. The authors believe the case for allowing deaf children to acquire sign-language is very strong. Teaching written English is also important in the education of deaf children in the United States, as written language is the sole means of communication between deaf and hearing worlds. ASL should be used, in the U.S., as the medium to teach English and other disciplines. The wider use of captioned television programs (using ASL) would have educational benefits and

---

[117] Carol A. Kusche, Mark T. Greenberg, and Tracy S. Garfield, "Nonverbal Intelligence and Verbal Achievement in Deaf Adolescents: An Examination of Heredity and Environment." American Annals of the Deaf, August, 1983 (128) pp. 458-466.

serve to reduce the isolation deaf people experience from the dominant hearing community.[118]

According to Hook, back in 1958, 42% of children with hearing loss in a national sample had some learning disability in addition to the loss of hearing. This survey was conducted by the Office of Demographic Studies of Gallaudet College. Since then, medical advances have made it more likely that high-risk infants will survive in greater numbers, so that the incidence of children with multiple handicaps will also have increased. These learning disabilities include: perceptual handicaps, brain injuries, minimal brain dysfunction, dyslexia, and developmental aphasia. Diagnosing and treating these conditions in children with hearing impairments are made more difficult because measurement is virtually impossible. Often, children classified as learning impaired make rapid progress when taught sign language and finger spelling.[119]

Sims and his colleagues offered a statistical study examining the consequences of different methods of instruction on academic achievement and the ability to speak. The subjects were 108 students at the National Technical Institute for the Deaf. Background to the study included conflicting recommendations from different "experts" on how best to educate the pre-lingually deaf. Oral communication proponents advised parents to have the deaf child live and grow in an atmosphere were orality is stressed from the beginning. The opposing view holds that profoundly deaf children will not learn to speak

[118] John D. Bonvillian, Veda R. Charrow, and Keith E. Nelson, "Psycholinguistic and Education Implications of Deafness," Human Development, 1973 (16), 321-345.

[119] Pamela E. Hook, "Learning Disabilities in the Hearing-Impaired," Ear, Nose, and Throat Journal, July, 1958 (58) pp. 303-309.

intelligibly anyway, and only ASL can help them become more skillful in key academic areas. the subjects were divided into two groups, those with relatively good speech and those with poor speech. Both groups were tested for competence in abstract reasoning, reading comprehension, written language, mathematics, and noted regarding overall college grade-point average. There were no statistical differences between the two groups of college students in their academic attainments. According to the authors, 28% of the students who attended schools where oralism was stressed developed functional speaking ability.[120] (The writers do not clarify what they mean by "functional.")

Bodner-Johnson pointed out that teachers of deaf children are often called upon to educate the parents as well. How well are they trained to perform this function? A survey indicated that there was considerable interest in the idea, but that little was being done. The answer to this discrepancy between interest and action, the author suggested, might lie in the general need for most universities to cut costs, an underlying conservatism, and in the changing nature of the American family (divorce and working mothers). Moreover, there appeared to be a trend to concentrate academic resources on preschool parent-infant relations and to ignore the relationship of the older deaf child and his/her parents. The author recommends establishing study groups to chart ways of meeting the need in the area of instructing parents of deaf children.[121]

---

[120] Donald G. Sims, Linda Gottermeier, and Gerald G. Walter, "Factors Contributing to the Development of Intelligible Speech among Prelingually Deaf Persons," American Annals of the Deaf, May, 1980, (125), pp. 374-381.

[121] Barbara Bodner-Johnson, "Professional Preparation of Parent Educators: A Survey and Recommendations," American Annals of the Deaf, October, 1980 (125), pp. 931-936.

Another study by Bonvillian examined 40 deaf and 20 hearing students' free recall of visually presented words varied systematically with respect to signability and visual imagery. By "signability" was meant words that could be represented by a single sign. Half of the deaf students had deaf parents, the other half had hearing parents. For deaf students, recall was better for words that had sign-language equivalents and high-imagery values. Hearing students remembered words best that had high imagery values. The hearing students recalled significantly more words. In immediate recall, deaf students with deaf parents reported using a sign language coded strategy more frequently and recalled more words correctly than did the deaf students with hearing parents. These results underlined the importance of sign language in the memory and recall of deaf persons.[122]

Williams surveyed 56 administrators of residential school for the deaf representing the 50 states, the District of Columbia and territories, to determine their admissions policies. The schools enrolled 90% of all the deaf students in residential schools. Student referrals are based primarily on the severity of hearing loss, acceptance depended on the school's ability to provide an appropriate program within staffing and programming limitations. Local school districts are the major sources of referrals for students admitted to state-operated residential schools for the deaf. Seventy percent of the schools surveyed retained a high degree of autonomy in admission decisions to prospective students. In particular, children with multiple handicaps in addition to deafness are likely to be denied

---

[122] John D. Bonvillian, "Effects of Signability and Imagery on Word Recall of Deaf and Hearing Students," Perceptual and Motor Skills, June, 1983 (56), pp. 775-791.

admission on the grounds that the schools do not have the capability to adequately serve them. The author questions whether this power is justified, given declining financial resources at the state and local levels and the provisions of Public Law 94-142.[123]

Wolk and Schildroth studied the strategies used by deaf students when taking a reading comprehension test. They found that deaf students favored answers based on association cues unrelated to the overall meanings of the previous paragraph or stimulus sentence. For example, in the type of test where a number of choices follow a paragraph, the deaf students are more likely to focus on the choices and choose one, rather than to focus on the paragraph to be interpreted. Such a choice-dependent strategy will often lead to lower test scores, since comprehension is being tested. The average deaf student comes to a reading comprehension test with relatively stronger word recognition and association skills than his (relatively weaker) linguistic skills of syntactical analysis and interpretation. Therefore, these children tend to focus on what they know best, the words. The authors believe that children with hearing loss need to be taught in ways that will emphasize meaning rather than word acquisition. They question whether multiple choice tests are useful for deaf children. In addition, they believe that providing an experiential basis for reading is even more important for the deaf than for the hearing child. [124]

---

[123] Peyton Williams, Jr., "Admission Policies and Practices of State-Operated Residential Schools for the Deaf," Exceptional Children, April, 1984 (50), pp. 550-551.

[124] Steve Wolk and Arthur Schildroth, "A Longitudinal Study of Deaf Students' Use of an Associational Strategy on a Reading Comprehension Test," Journal of Research in Reading, August, 1985 (2), pp. 82-93.

The most important issue in education for the deaf involves the oral-signing controversy. This controversy seethes more among hearing specialists than among the deaf, themselves, who not only prefer, but love their sign language. Lane repeated approvingly the words of Charles-Michel de l'Epee (1712-1789):

> Every deaf-mute already has a language . . . He is thoroughly in the habit of using it, and understands others who do. With it, he expresses his needs, desires, doubts, pains, and so on, and makes no mistakes when others express themselves likewise. We want to instruct him and therefore teach him French. What is the shortest and easiest method? Isn't it to express ourselves in his language.[125]

By the middle of the 19th century, growing numbers of deaf children in the United States and Europe studied in sign language. Nearly half of the teachers of the deaf were themselves deaf; "today, they are a rarity."[126] Three decades later, the tide turned against sign language. Alexander Graham Bell used his wealth and prestige to promote oralism. The 1880 Congress of Milan, unattended by the Deaf themselves, espoused oralism with the slogan: "Long live speech!"[127]

At the end of the Civil War in the United States, there were 26 schools for the deaf, all of them using ASL; by 1907, there were 139 schools, and in all of them, ASL was

---

[125] Lane, The Deaf Experience, pp. 6-7.
[126] Ibid., p. 11.
[127] Ibid., p. 12.

forbidden.[128] In the 1960s and 70s, recognition grew that ASL was indeed a language, unlike English, but with its own rules and richness of expression. Coupled with the patent failure of oral rehabilitation to work, the pendulum has begun to shift once again. Moreover, this time, deaf people are themselves active in causing the change.

Vocational

There has been considerable research on the vocational needs and status of deaf children and adults. The literature includes both teaching strategies and various aspects of the working world of deaf people.

Rowland described the strengths and weaknesses of deaf workers, as evaluated by their employers and supervisors. From questionnaires sent to 80 businesses in the Los Angeles area, she compiled information. Employers and supervisors most often used oral and written communication with deaf workers, but a significant minority was able to use ASL. Deaf workers were rated generally about the same as hearing employees. In particular, they were rated as safety-conscious as their hearing counterparts; they were not judged to be safety hazards. Principal strengths of these deaf workers were: dependability, ambition, pride in craftsmanship, willingness to learn, acceptance of supervision, valuing their jobs, tenacity on the job, and positive attitudes. Areas of weakness were: immaturity, lack of self-confidence, susceptibility to criticism, inability to read and write effectively, lack of interaction with fellow employees, higher absentee rate, lack of patience, lack of acquired lore commonly called "common sense," and weakness in

---

[128] Ibid., p. 3.

following abstract directions. Employers thought that the emphasis in vocational counseling and training should be on developing good work attitudes, rather than on specific skills and knowledge.[129]

Dodd studied occupational stereotypes related to sex and deafness. The subjects were entering freshmen at the National technical Institute for the Deaf, and the instrument was the *Job Lists Test*. Males tended to stereotype jobs by gender more than females did. Older deaf students tended to stereotype more jobs as inappropriate for deaf people. Students who rated occupations as strongly stereotyped by sex also rated them as strongly appropriate for hearing workers. The author concludes that educators and counselors should liberate young students from such limiting views of their own potential by revealing the fallacies of stereotypes.[130]

Wright studied graduates from the California School for the Deaf at Riverside between 1972 and 1976; there were 123 respondents to a questionnaire. More than 80% of the respondents took some form of postgraduate education. Some 67% were employed; 30% had never found employment. Nearly half of the respondents indicated that their employment was not related to their academic studies. English, reading and mathematics were rated the most useful academic courses and business education and homemaking were ranked as the most valuable vocational courses. Two-thirds of the graduates felt that the

---

[129] Carolyn Raye Rowland, "Strengths and Weaknesses of Deaf Workers as Evaluated by Employers and Supervisors," (Master of Arts Thesis, California State University, Long Beach, CA, 1978.)

[130] Judy Egelston Dodd, "Overcoming Occupational Stereotypes Related to Sex and Deafness," <u>American Annals of the Deaf,</u> October, 1977 (122), pp. 489-491.

California School for the Deaf had prepared them for college but not for the job market, a complaint they share with hearing students of their schools. Two findings of the study indicated the need for more careful preparation of deaf students for the job market: 1) 30% had been unable to find work; and 2) half of the respondents had an annual salary under $5,000 a year.[131] Considerations such as the comparative merits of vocational training and more abstract educational endeavors, in a long range view, were not addressed in this study.

Farrugia attempted to determine the vocational interests and attitudes of deaf persons aged 16-19, and to see how they differed from hearing persons of the same age. In general, he found that deaf students tended to prefer manual over academic and cultural activities. The deaf students seemed to have lower aspirations than did their hearing counterparts. The students' self-report measures indicated that the deaf students' scores resembled most the hearing students of ages 12-15. The author suggests that those responsible for vocational training for deaf people might wish to emphasize areas such as art and numbers, where low scores were not linked to hearing loss.

Banowsky attempted to ascertain whether or not certain personality factors relevant to long-term employment differed between pre-lingually deaf adults and the general population. differences in sources of job satisfaction were also considered. The findings of these self-report measures indicated that personality factors associated with long-term employment were different between the two populations. The deaf subjects assessed themselves as being tough-

---

131 Charles L. Wright, "Follow-Up Study of the Graduates from California School for the Deaf at Riverside, 1972-1976." (Master of Arts Thesis, California State University, Long Beach, 1979.)

minded (self-reliant, unsentimental, acting on practical, logical evidence). There were no differences between the two populations in their views of areas of work, pay, promotions and supervision. The deaf workers had a significantly less positive opinion of their co-workers than did hearing workers. The author concluded that deaf workers may need to come to terms with working in situations where their "down to earth" approach will not necessarily coincide with the more intuitive approach of their co-workers. However, given the unreliability of assessing personality with self-report measures, the author warns that this study's findings should be regarded only as tentative.[133]

The Black Deaf

Minorities in the United States historically have had a difficult time gaining respect for their individuality and achieving their rights. The deaf are a case in point, but deaf members of other minorities have had to struggle all the harder. There is a sparse literature on black deaf people, but little regarding the deaf of other minority groups, including people of Hispanic culture.

Moores and Oden (1977) discussed the, then current, educational situation of black children. They pointed out that census figures indicating a lower incidence of deafness among black people are probably misleading, since there is no medical reason to believe that incidence of deafness varies by race. Possibly white researchers undercounted the black deaf population because they worked primarily

---

[133] Alfred Wm. Bannowsky, Personality Factors, Job Satisfaction, and Long-Term Employment of Prelingually Profoundly Deaf Adults (Ph.D. Dissertation, California Institute of Integral Studies, 1983.)

with white deaf groups from which black people may have been excluded. Black people, they stated, were also under-represented in school programs designed for deaf students, perhaps as a consequence of late diagnosis of deafness among black people of lower socio-economic means, and thus less access to these programs. Even when the diagnosis of deafness is made in a timely fashion, black parents may not be as well informed as white parents regarding services available to them. On occasion, they noted, a deaf black child is summarily classified as mentally retarded, and is enrolled in a wildly inappropriate program. This type of error may be responsible for the disproportionately large number of black children reported to be mentally retarded. It is possible that other deaf minority children may still be subject to similar neglect and misclassification.[134]

Luetke-Stahlman noted the small number of minority teachers involved in special education, compared to regular education. She suggested a need for teachers who share cultural characteristics with their students, "so that these teachers' perceptions do not result in self-fulfilling prophecies about a child's limited ability."[135] A 1981 study indicated that the number of black deaf students had increased to 17% in the U.S.; yet the number of black teachers was only 3.3 percent. The study shed no light on why black educators have shunned special education.

Taft queried a sample of 67 black deaf residents of the District of Columbia in 1983. Black deaf people in that

---

[134] Donald F. Moores and Chester W. Oden, Jr., "Educational Needs of Black Children," American Annals of the Deaf, June, 1977 (122), pp. 313-318.

[135] B. Luetke-Stahlman, "Recruiting Black Teacher-Trainees into Programs for the Hearing-Impaired," American Annals of the Deaf, October, 1983 (128), pp. 851-2, at p. 851.

sample had a higher job success rate than did clients with other disabilities. More black females found work than did black males, possibly because the available jobs subsisted largely of clerical and domestic work. Almost all the members of the sample had previous work experience; about half had received vocational training; and about two-thirds obtained jobs in areas related to their work experience or training. The study, accumulatively, indicated that properly trained, deaf, black individuals can find employment of some kind.[136]

A major contribution to the literature of deaf Americans of minority extraction was a book written by Hairston and Smith. *Black and Deaf in America* cites major problems of black, deaf Americans such as: under-education, underemployment, poor communication skills and unfavorable self image. Individual differences do exist, however, and stereotyping is not helpful in understanding individual people. black deaf people are subject to the same racism experienced by other black people, and they may suffer a double stigma in being deaf. There is little socialization of black deaf people with deaf caucasians, although such associations might aid in overcoming misperception. All the problems deaf white children encounter are compounded for deaf black children, and the frequent inability of black parents to cope with the usual bureaucracies of helping professions can be a further burden, further diminishing the probability that the family unit can adequately fulfill the needs of the black deaf.[137]

---

[136] Brenda Taft, "Employability of Black Deaf Persons in Washington, DC: National Implications," <u>American Annals of the Deaf,</u> August, 1983 (128), pp. 453-457.

[137] Ernest Hairston and Linwood Smith, <u>Black and Deaf in America,</u> Silver Spring, MD: T.J. Publishers, 1983.)

Summary

After surveying the mass of studies which purport to document and/or explain the unique needs of the deaf, it is apparent that more knowledge in all these areas surveyed would aid us in formulating helpful guidelines and techniques to empower deaf people to live "whole" lives, rather than lives sharply circumscribed by arbitrary limitations of society's willingness and ability to accommodate their non-hearing status. It would also be quite useful for research pertaining primarily to one particular aspect of hearing impairment, e.g. gradual deafness in the elderly, to be clearly labeled as such, since relevant/salient characteristics vary vastly, discouraging generalization. Such areas as susceptibility to depression among deaf persons, e.g., seem clearly to be linked with age, economic means, availability of another person in whom to confide and other such factors, more than with the factor of deafness. Additionally, it would be optimum if investigators would increasingly consider research designs which offer adequate standards of reliability and validity.

Hearing loss has been the focus of research about deaf people for many years, with its assumption of direct correlation to other factors being considered. Although this is sometimes relevant, it clearly is not the entire picture. We need to examine our assumptions about "normality" which underlie research hypotheses in studies of the Deaf.

CHAPTER III

DEAFNESS AND ALCOHOL ABUSE

This chapter will present a broad overview on alcoholism as it relates to deafness. There is a plethora of research literature on alcoholism, its development, its causes, its effects, its involvement in other maladies, and its treatment. This chapter reviews research studies within several topic areas. The following aspects are investigated in the first section of this chapter: 1) basic definitory, delimiting matter about alcoholism; 2) a review of both short and long term physical, mental, emotional and social effects of alcohol abuse; 3) current thought regarding the etiology and epidemiology of alcoholism, including predisposing influences, such as genetic propensity of some people toward alcoholism; 4) a view of socio-cultural and psychological circularly interweaving factors which contribute to and/or maintain alcohol abuse; and 5) a listing of some variables which may influence an individual's willingness to seek treatment for alcohol addiction.

In the second section of this chapter, each of these considerations, singly, or in clusters, when appropriate, is reviewed, in the light of the literature, with special emphasis regarding to its/their possible impact(s) on deaf people. Some parallels are drawn between the two groups of people, and then, further division into specific populations of deaf people are referenced in regard to alcoholism.

Alcohol and Alcoholism:

Alcohol is a poison. Alcohol is addictive for many people. These two simple truths and their combined impact have been declaimed, researched, proven many times and expressed in many ways more complex and convoluted than this.[138] Not every person who uses alcohol becomes alcoholic, of course.[139] Nevertheless, alcoholism thrives and continues to trap people into lives of reduced potency, dissatisfaction, and loss of the sense of self-determination.[140]

Alcoholism afflicts deaf people just as relentlessly and severely as it does hearing people. The combined effects of alcoholism and deafness pose a significant threat, not only to the Deaf community, but to the larger hearing community as well, because of the potential contributions to society these people might otherwise offer.

For medical and legal purposes, the presence of 0.15% alcohol in the blood is regarded by many authorities as the level of onset of intoxication.[141] All forms of alcohol are transformed by the body's chemistry into ethanol, and are thus interchangeable in their alcohol component. Short term effects of alcohol abuse include both intoxication, or drunkenness, and acute alcoholism. Obvious short term effects of alcohol intoxication are often the subject of gross parody and slap-stick humor. The "drunk" is recognized by his decreased inhibitions, such as acting the buffoon; blurring of the senses, e.g. seeing double; diminished

---

[138] Jean Kinney, M.S.W. & Gwen Leaton, Loosening the Grip, 2nd ed.; St. Louis, MO; C.V. Mosby Co. 1983 p. 28.

[139] Ibid. p. 11 & p. 71, and Mary M. "Choices," Center City, MN., Hazelden, 1984 p. 5.

[140] Vernon E. Johnson I'll Quit Tomorrow: A Practical Guide to Alcoholism Treatment; San Francisco, CA; Harper & Row; 1980 pp. 1-7.

[141] Harvey Schlossberg, The Autokinetic Phenomenon: Alcohol and Auditory Modification; Doctoral dissertation; Yeshiva Univ.; N.Y. 1971. p, 108.

physical control, e.g. the inability to walk a straight line or to place a finger on the nose,[142] and impaired judgment, e.g. racing a train across a track.[143] The dangerous proclivity of alcohol to combine synergistically with other drugs as a CNS depressant is also a considerable factor affecting people's lives; e.g. surviving loved ones deplore the unnecessary deaths of those who took barbiturates after imbibing.[144] Alcohol's potential to trigger or exacerbate feelings of self-denigration, remorse and helplessness, both during intoxication and afterward, is also well documented, embedding despair.[145]

More rare than either acute intoxication or chronic alcoholism, but still potentially lethal, is acute alcoholism, differentiated by the DSM-III from acute alcohol intoxication.[146] Throughout DSM-III, diagnostic criteria for disorders related to the abuse of alcohol are listed in groups of symptoms, not in terms of a single presenting symptom, so the diagnosis of acute alcoholism is not as clear-cut as that of chronic alcoholism.[147]

Acute alcoholism is only occasionally seen in hospital emergency admissions, and the person afflicted with it cannot tolerate alcohol even in small amounts. In layman's

---

[142] Kinney & Leaton, p. 13.

[143] Celia Dulfano, Families, Alcoholism & Recovery: 10 Stories, Center City, MN; Hazelden, 1982 p. 12.

[144] Stanley E. Gitlow, M.D. "The Clinical Pharmacology and Drug Interactions of Ethanol" in Encyclopedic Handbook of Alcoholism, E. Mansell Pattison, M.D. & Edward Kaufman, M.D. editors, N.Y.; Gardner Press; 1982 pp. 354-356.

[145] Abraham J. Twerski, M.D. Self Discovery in Recovery; Center City, MN; Hazelden, 1984 pp. 3-5, 107.

[146] A.P.A., Diagnostic and Statistical Manual of Mental Disorders; 3rd ed. Wash., D.C., 1980.

[147] ibid.

terms, this comparatively rare disorder is known as "allergy to alcohol."

Most people, however, do not develop acute alcoholism. After an introductory period of acclimation to alcohol, most people develop a fairly high level of tolerance for alcohol for a long period of time, allowing the person to believe he/she is only a social drinker, not an alcoholic. In fact a *sudden* drop in the person's normally high tolerance level for alcohol is one of the more visible symptoms of alcoholism's physiologically advanced stages.[148]

Chronic alcoholism, of course, occurs much more commonly and represents a tragic waste of life.[149] *Alcoholics Anonymous* defines an alcoholic as "a person who has lost the power to control drinking," and considers alcoholism to be both a physical and spiritual disease.[150] Many measuring instruments have been developed to try to make the diagnosis of alcoholism more precise; the Iowa Alcoholic Stages Index is one of the more commonly used, but even it relies on self-report assessment, which is subjective. The DSM-III offers the following criteria for diagnoses of third stage alcohol dependence: 1) a pattern of pathological alcohol use, 2) impairment in social or occupational functioning due to alcohol use, 3) duration of disturbance of at least one month, and 4) change in either toleration or withdrawal manifestations. (See Table I)

---

[148] Harold A. Mulford, "The Epidemiology of Alcoholism and its Implications," in Encyclopedic Handbook on Alcoholism, Pattison & Kaufman (eds.) N.Y.: Gardner Press, 1982 pp. 451-452.

[149] Alcoholics Anonymous, 3rd ed.; Alcoholics Anonymous World Services, Inc., N.Y. 1976.

[150] Yale H., The Beginners' Meetings, Center City, MN., Hazelden, 1984 p. 1.

Table I

The following material is the profile given by DSM-IV as Criteria for the Diagnosis of Alcohol Abuse/Dependence, relating to the third stage of alcoholism.

I: Pattern of Pathological Alcohol Use

*   Need for daily use for adequate functioning
*   Inability to cut-down or stop
*   Repeated efforts to control by going on wagon or restricting drinking to certain times of day.
*   Binges (at least 2 days)
*   Drinks more than one fifth per day
*   Blackouts
*   Drinking exacerbates serious physical disorder
*   Drinks non-beverage alcohol

II: Impairment in Social or Occupational Functioning

*   Violence while intoxicated
*   Absence from work
*   Loss of job
*   Arrest for intoxicated behavior
*   Arguments or difficulties with family or friends

III: Tolerance to Alcohol or Withdrawal Symptoms

* Tolerance change
* Need for increased amounts to achieve desired effect, or diminished effect with same amount
* Withdrawal symptoms
* Morning shakes and malaise after cessation or reduction relieved by drinking

IV: Medical Complications of Dependence

* Hepatitis, cirrhosis
* Peripheral neuropathy
* Gastritis
* Alcohol withdrawal delirium/DTs
* Dementia associated with alcoholism
* Other, including neurological damage, withdrawal seizures, CBS, etc.

Pattison and Kaufman, among other researchers, point out that alcoholism is medically construed as a syndrome, and note that the syndrome is multivariate–that is, multiple variations of the syndrome may present themselves both among different people and within the same individual at different stages of the disease.[151]

The compilers of the third edition of the handbook, *Alcoholics Anonymous,* estimated that, in 1976, the incidence of alcoholism in the United States was thought to be as high as one person in ten, using the broadest definition of alcoholism. Public health services data, at that time, and admission statistics of detoxification units totaled over ten million people in the US, although the recidivism rate is acknowledgedly high, and some of these may have been re-admissions. Alcoholics Anonymous, in 1984, reported over 2,000 groups meeting in various Los Angeles neighborhoods, alone. Over 100 countries have A.A. chapters. Related support groups such as Al-Anon and Al-a-Teen continue to thrive,[152] and public and private treatment programs dealing with unhealthy addictions have increased significantly within the last ten years.

Physical Effects of Alcoholism:

The effects of chronic alcoholism appear gradually, insidiously, and increase steadily, but they interweave among the various parts of a person's life, consistently

---

[151] E. Mansell Pattison, M.D. and Edward Kaufman, M.D., eds. "Prologue: Purpose, Concept, and Plan," in Encyclopedic Handbook of Alcoholism, N.Y.; Gardner Press, 1982. p. xxix.

[152] Alcoholics Anonymous, 3rd ed.; A.A. World Services, Inc.; N.Y., 1976, p. xxii & 121, and Leslie Ward "After 50 years, AA is still going strong." The L.A. Herald Exam. Nov. 17, 1985. p. A10.

deteriorating the quality of life.[153] Undermined personal relationships and minimized perceived options are two of the earlier visible results of alcoholism, but a sizable number of both physical and non-physical ills remain hidden in the early stages of alcoholism. Loss of ability to hold a job and strict legal sanctions are cited as two of the more powerful constraints occurring in the middle stages of alcoholism.[154]

Regarding the physical and physiological effects of chronic alcoholism, research citing the following is included: Chronic alcoholism: 1) destroys brain cells & CNS synapses, which do not regenerate; these brain lesions are often in the area of memory and involve diminished learning capacity. 2) weakens the functioning capacity of liver, pancreas, and other organs, 3) can produce convulsions/seizures and other system-overload symptoms. 4) undermines cardiovascular fitness, and 5) interferes with the normal function of assorted other parts of the human body. Specifically, alcohol rots the brain; several sciences offer at least partial explanation and details of the process. In terms of the biochemistry of alcohol and the process of alcohol metabolism, Tewari and Carson conclude:

> Ethanol significantly affects brain protein and RNA metabolism following long-term ingestion. Since these macro-molecules have wide and diverse structural as well as functional significance in the brain, it would not be too surprising that ethanol-induced changes in behavior might partly be ascribed to changes in brain protein and RNA metabolism. For example, impaired learning,

---

153 Ibid. pp. 30-34.
154 Ibid. p.p. 35, 43.

observed in animal behavior experiments, as well as psychological evaluation of FAS children, may be related to altered RNA and protein metabolism, since, in addition to their function as cellular constituents in cellular regulations, RNA and proteins have been implicated in learning and in many other neural processes.[155]

These researchers report that not only do severe neuropathies, resulting in memory dysfunction and altered brain protein metabolism, ensue from chronic alcoholism, but that there is growing evidence that alcoholism increases the potential of a person to develop cancer of the mouth, pharynx, larynx, esophagus, liver and lungs. Additionally, abnormally decreased endocrine secretion has been shown to be caused by alcoholism adversely affecting the luteinizing of testicular and ovarian hormones.[156]

Blum details significant neurophysiological effects of alcohol, particularly the deleterious effects on neuro-transmitter functions, and unequivocally concludes that prolonged abuse of alcohol results in significant brain damage, particularly learning impairment and memory loss. He further notes:

It appears that alcohol is not simply a local anesthetic agent; nor is it a simple protein denaturant; nor is it only a toxic pathogen, nor is it a false neurotransmitter . . . , nor is it an opiate receptor against or an antagonist; nor is it a releasor

---

155 Sujata Tewari and Virginia G. Carson, "Biochemistry of Alcohol and Alcohol Metabolism," in Encyclopedic Handbook of Alcoholism, Pattison & Kaufman, eds.; p. 99.
156 Ibid., p. 101.

of biogenic amines and other neuropeptides like the enkephalins or endorphins; nor is it an intoxicant; nor is it an addictive agent leading to total devastation of the individual and his/her family. It is all of the above; and that is why society is compelled to continue to understand its biological activity.[157]

Medical aspects of alcoholism are both multiple and devastating. alcoholism is a progressively degenerative disease, which, if not treated, ultimately results in death. Editors Pattison & Kaufman commissioned various medical specialists to survey the direct effects of alcohol on the brain, including chronic neuropsychiatric disorders associated with alcoholism, personality alterations in chronic alcoholics, and effects on the brain of malnutrition associated with chronic alcoholism. Acute effects of neurological injury, nutritional deficiency, hepatic decompensation and withdrawal from alcohol might take weeks or even months, but only after that detoxification phase could an assessment of persistent brain injury be made, it was concluded.[158]

Contrary to the myths which surround alcoholism, only a small degree of its degenerative processes occur during the later, visible stages. The bulk of ills which collectively interweave to render most alcoholics helpless, develop invisibly over a long period of time.

Alcohol is recognized to be detrimental to health in such diverse areas as the skeletal system, skin diseases, sleep

---

[157] Kenneth Blum, "Neurophysiological Effects of Alcohol," in Encyclopedic Handbook on Alcoholism, Pattison & Kaufman, eds.; p. 127.

[158] Pattison & Kaufman, eds. ibid, Joseph P. McEvoy, "The Chronic Neuropsychiatric Disorders,"

disorders, impaired reproductive function, the gastrointestinal tract, impairments especially associated with alcoholism such as withdrawal and delirium tremens, cirrhosis of the liver and pancreas disease, severe impairment of both respiratory and cardiovascular systems.[159]

Of particular interest from the standpoint of this work is the research of Wheeler, DeWolpe and Rausch. They wanted to examine hearing acuity in relationship to alcohol consumption. Not much research has been done on the relationship between alcohol and hearing loss, so these researchers observed 52 alcoholic subjects, and showed, via audiograms, consistent patterns revealing a bilateral high-frequency drop in hearing acuity. This loss was seen to be related to drinking time, but independent of the variable of age. Wheeler et al. suggest a definite relationship between length of time of heavy drinking and hearing loss.[160]

Schlossberg (1971) investigated the autokinetic phenomenon, specifically testing whether the presence of alcohol modified auditory response. He found that alcohol does affect the perceptions, but that sound did not influence the amount of movement perceived. There were sufficient indications, however, to suggest that sound had the effect of *inducing* the autokinetic phenomenon, and seemed to be involved in controlling the speed of perceived movement.[161]

---

[159] Pattison & Kaufman, eds. Encyclopedic Handbook of Alcoholism, Gardner Press, N.Y.; 1982, & David H. Knott & James D. Beard; "Effects of Alcohol Ingestion on the Cardiovascular System," pp. 332-343.

[160] Dale C. Wheeler, Alan S. DeWolpe, & Marie A. Rausch, "Audiometric Configuration in Patients Being Treated for Alcoholism," in Drug and Alcohol Dependence, 5, (1980) pp. 63-68.

[161] Harvey Schlossberg, p. 110.

Luterman (1982) sought to determine whether alcohol intoxication affected brainstem auditory evoked responses (BAER). He believed that BAER information would be valuable for estimating hearing thresholds of difficult-to-test subjects, and would also aid in determining the site of lesion within the brainstem. He found that alcohol did effect BAER in a diffuse manner, not limited to localization, but the amount was not statistically significant; however, this research may have important implications for deaf people.[162]

Another study (Jeter, 1975) compared the reflex and voluntary contraction of middle ear muscles in normal people and in alcoholics, and reached these conclusions:

1. There are clear differences between middle ear impedance changes produced by Eustachian tube activity and by middle ear muscle activity.
2. The middle ear muscles can be voluntarily contracted by some individuals.
3. There are differences between middle ear impedance changes produced by the acoustic reflex and by orbicularis oculi contraction or voluntary contraction of the middle ear muscles.[163]

The effects of alcohol upon sensory evoked and upon spontaneous cerebral potentials have also been

---

[162] Barry F. Luterman, Human Brainstem Auditory Evoked Responses During Alcohol Intoxication and Recovery; Doctoral dissertation, University of MO; 1982; pp. 64-66.

[163] Irma K. Jeter. Reflex and Voluntary Contraction of the Middle Ear Muscles in Normals and Alcoholics. Doctoral dissertation; University of Maryland, 1975. p. 117.

investigated. (Salamy, 1972). The relationships proved to be quite convoluted, leaving the researcher to conclude that there was a definite effect, but that the processes were not clear-cut. He stated, "Whether the effect of alcohol is to actually decrease excitatory activity or to increase inhibitory drive or both, cannot be said."[164] Implications of such finding could be helpful, preventively.

Weingartner and colleagues noted the reduction of verbal retention in alcoholics,[165] and Van de Vusse found that long term abuse of alcohol produces deficits in verbal learning ability, directly correlated to age.[166]

Accumulatively the weight of years of major research underscores the fact that alcoholism is a fatal disease affecting all bodily symptoms. The abuse of alcohol may produce many adverse consequences, and not all of these are strictly seen as physical alcoholism pathology, but all are public health problems interrelated with alcoholism.

Predisposing Factors of Alcoholism:

Is there a genetic propensity toward Alcoholism? A number of family studies of incidence of alcoholism have

---

[164] Albert Salamy. The Effects of Alcohol Upon Sensory Evoked And Spontaneous Cerebral Potentials; Doctoral dissertation; The Univ. of OK; 1972. p. 172, and Benj. Kissin, "The role of physical dependence and brain damage in the protracted alcohol abstinence syndrome." Advances in Alcoholism, 2 (11) 1981.

[165] H. Weingartner, L.A. Faillace, & H.G. Markley; "Verbal retention in alcoholics" in Quarterly Journal of Studies on Alcohol, 1971, (32) 293-303.

[166] David Van de Vusse, Verbal Learning in Alcoholics: Semantic vs. Acoustic Encoding Processes. Doctoral dissertation; Wayne State Univ.; 1978. p. 79.

been done. Some longitudinal studies survey parents and children over a period of years; some researchers study the incidence of alcoholism in twins, both monozygotic and dizgotic, especially twins not raised in the same home (to compensate for the blurring effects of environment). And a few studies of adopted children of alcoholics have been done, following the children's transitions into adulthood to see if they developed alcoholism even out of the environment of an alcoholic home. Murray and Stabenau discussed possible genetic factors in alcoholism predisposition, after reviewing many studies, including longitudinal and adoption case studies, and concluded that there is a modest but significant genetic influence predisposing given individuals toward alcoholism or some similar outlet for psychological distress. Specifically they note:

One of the reasons why researchers have been slow to elucidate the exact nature of the genetic predisposition is that they have been looking for simple answers. The present evidence is incompatible with simple Mendelian inheritance through a single dominant gene, and sex-linked inheritance has also been excluded. Any successful etiologic model must obviously take into account environmental factors such as price and availability of alcohol, plus the effects of occupation and family attitudes to alcohol. It is furthermore, unwise to assume that the same genetic factors contribute to an individual's likelihood of becoming dependent on alcohol as influence, for example, the same individual's chances of committing a crime while drunk. For these reasons, polygenic models have been suggested in which multiple genetic factors

interact with powerful environmental influences at
several different levels.[167]

Psychological/Emotional Predisposing Factors in
Alcoholism:

What makes one person, more than another, become
dependent on alcohol? In addition to the hypothesized
genetic linkage, considerable speculation regarding
emotional aspects of vulnerability to alcoholism has been
done, both by scientific researchers and curious laymen.
Alcoholic courage is a hackneyed phrase referring to the
myth alcoholics have allowed themselves to accept, without
examining it closely, which builds the habit of taking a
drink when facing a task thought to be difficult unpleasant,
or otherwise calling for more resources than they believe
are available to them without alcohol. The prevalence of
this term implies that people afflicted with alcoholism feel
inadequate and fearful that they cannot handle
circumstances of their life without alcohol.

Woititz posits that adult children of alcoholics are at
risk and especially vulnerable to addictions, themselves. In
noting how adult children of alcoholics receive inadequate
role-modeling from parents, and thus develop immaturely,
he delineated a number of emotional problems observed in
alcoholics, with the implication that a causative circular
correlation might be found therein. Among the
characteristics listed as frequently seen were: excessive

---

[167] Robin M. Murray and James R. Stabenau, "Genetic Factors in
Alcoholism Predisposition," in Encyclopedic Handbook on
Alcoholism, Pattison & Kaufman, eds. 1982. p. 142, and M.
Eckart, et. al., "Health Hazards associated with alcohol
consumption." Journal of the American Medical Assn., 246 (6)
1981, pp. 648-666.

dependency, inability to appropriately express emotions, low frustration tolerance, emotional immaturity, high levels of anxiety in interpersonal relationships, low self-esteem, grandiosity, feelings of isolation, perfectionism, ambivalence toward authority, guilt, denial, obsessions, continual worry, confusion, false hope, disappointment, euphoria, sex problems, and inability to appropriately handle anger.[168]

Twerski documents alcoholism as one of the more easily accessible retreats for persons of low-self esteem. He says:

> . . . there are numerous ways people try to cope with life based on their misconceptions of themselves, and unfortunately, many of these reinforce the negative self image rather than overcome it. Whenever the factors that render a person vulnerable to alcoholism exist, the complicated syndrome of alcoholism emerges including the characteristic self-disapproval and self-deprecation. And it becomes even more difficult to overcome a negative self-image.[169]

Kinney and Leaton (1983) note several emotional factors which may motivate alcohol abuse. Anxiety and the desire for a sense of control over one's environment are two

---

[168] Janet G. Woititz, Ed.D. <u>Adult Children of Alcoholics,</u> 10th printing; (Hollywood, FL; Health Communications, Inc.; 1983) p. 105.

[169] Twerski, <u>Self Discovery in Recovery,</u> (Center City, MN.: Hazelden; 1984). p. 26.

motivations they discuss, but, of course, these are present in everyone, and not everyone becomes alcoholic.[170]

Psychological Consequences of Alcohol Abuse:

The transformation of personality which occurs in the alcoholic has been noted and lamented by multitudes of people affected by it, including the alcoholic himself/herself in rare moments of insight. In a work intended to serve as a guide to the treatment of alcoholism, Vernon Johnson says:

Very different sorts of people become alcoholic, but all alcoholics are ultimately alike. The disease itself swallows up all differences and creates a universal alcoholic profile. The personality changes that go with the illness are predictable and inevitable, with some individual adaptation, of course. When we describe the behavior of a victim of this disease, there is always instant recognition by members of the family. The classic description fits almost any individual alcoholic to a startling degree.[171]

Some of the personality characteristics which typify alcoholics include: extreme mood swings, diminished awareness of their tacit "messages," increasing irritability, increasing delusional material in thought processes, (e.g.

---

[170] Jean Kinney and Gwen Leaton, Loosening the Grip: a handbook of alcohol information; 2nd ed.; (St. Louis, MO.: The C.V. Mosby Col; 1983) p. 11-14.

[171] Vernon E. Johnson, I'll Quit Tomorrow: A Practical Guide to Alcoholism Treatment, (San Francisco, CA; Harper & Row, 1980) p. 5.

outlandish rationalization of drinking behavior), minimal self-insight, steady erosion of the ability to handle unforeseen circumstances, and circularly reinforcing stress resulting from even partial insight.[172]

Woititz (1983) speaks compellingly about heart-rending effects of two of the commonly perceived traits of alcoholics: low frustration tolerance and immaturity.[173] These are such classic traits, almost anyone who knows an alcoholic can cite examples of them, and even if the alcoholic has no insight regarding these, he or she still suffers from the interaction of these traits and their consequences.

Some of the very characteristics which may have led a person to the abuse of alcohol, unfortunately, are ones which are reinforced by alcoholism. Thus an exit-less circle is created, trapping the alcoholic. A cluster of related personality constellations assume cohesiveness, analogous to the powerful root system of crab-grass, eroding the alcoholic's sense of efficacy and increasingly altering the alcoholic's personality. The inability to handle anger, difficulty in delaying gratification, willingness to ignore reality and evade the truth about one's degree of addiction, passive-aggressive behavior, excessive guilt, and narcissism are traits which can be seen both as pre-disposing and as results of alcoholism.[174]

Speaking of emotional losses charged to alcoholism, Wegscheider (1981), paints a discouraging picture:

---

[172] Ibid. p. 4.

[173] Janet G. Woititz, p. 7.

[174] Abraham J. Twerski, Self Discovery in Recovery; (Center City, MN.; Hazelden, 1984) pp. 34-46 & 50.

When he first began to use alcohol socially, we can assume that even though he may have been immature, he was nevertheless a fairly whole person . . . From that initial state of relative wholeness, his personal potentials began to erode. The loss became visible earlier in some areas than others, and we shall inventory the various potentials . . . in the order in which healthy functioning appears to be lost. But I want to add a word of caution: any system of ordering these changes can be misleading, because the loss is actually taking place in many parts of the alcoholic's being simultaneously. With the physical potential, for instance, it is hard to say whether personal appearance or sexual satisfaction deteriorates first. A sloppy appearance certainly is not going to enhance one's opportunity for sexual satisfaction; on the other hand, decreased sexual desire can reduce one's motivation to look appealing to a sexual partner.

The erosion of personal potentials seems to begin with the feelings. Anger . . . , fear . . . , shame . . . , guilt . . . , feelings of worthlessness and remorse, and depression ensue. When the burden of painful emotion reaches a point he can no longer tolerate, he begins to repress them—to turn them off. Gradually he is not so aware of the fear and guilt. But blocking out the bad does not bring back the good. Instead, he is left with no feelings at all—numb, "turned off," no longer able to relate to other people or events as a human, feeling being. Then, in the late stages of his addiction, he loses even the ability to repress, and the realization of his true situation descends on him in a flood of desperation and despair.[175]

As a counselor of teen-aged alcoholics and substance abusers, Krupski (1982) has written very sympathetically regarding the emotional debris alcoholism leaves. She notes that under ordinary circumstances, adolescence is a vulnerable developmental period. Under ordinary circumstances an adolescent may experience frequent mood-swings, violent oscillations of self esteem, a heightened sense of self-absorption, be extremely touchy, and exhibit more than a little ambivalence about relying on or repudiating parental support. She notes that once an adolescent becomes addicted to alcohol, "no circumstances remain ordinary. The distress of adolescence is accentuated and distorted in a whirlwind of alcohol-induced confusion."[176]

Effects of Alcoholism on People Around the Alcoholic:

In addition to the effects of alcohol on the psyche of the alcoholic, there are tremendous psychological effects wreaked on individuals in the wake of the individual alcoholic. Spouses, children, parents, friends, neighbors and colleagues of alcoholics are all affected adversely. Battered wives and children, living with alcoholics who may exhibit no frustration tolerance, certainly develop coping mechanisms; but these aids, which were intended to help them function, may not enhance their psychological health,

---

[175] Sharon Wegscheider, Another Chance; (Palo Alto, CA.; Science and Behavior Books, Inc. 1981) pp. 70.

[176] A.M. Krupski, Inside the Adolescent Alcoholic, (Center City, MN.; Hazelden; 1982) p. viii.

and may render these "support" people needing remedial attention themselves. Stresses of accumulated compensating and/or *covering* for a loved one who is not functioning do take an observable toll on the health of the individuals striving to "cover" for the alcoholic. Dulfane writes:

> Alcoholism is a chronic disease which typically takes ten to fifteen years to develop. By the time an alcoholic comes to therapy, therefore,his friends, family and associates have been dealing with the impact of progressive alcoholism for years. The children may never have known adequate parenting. The spouse is by definition either over-burdened, or, perhaps, defeated . . . The chaos in the family, its instability, the lack of an adequate role model, etc., are not the stuff of a healthy childhood.[177]

Nearly all the studies surveyed included poignant, even heartbreaking anecdotes and pronouncements, such as the following:

> Of all illnesses which affect family life, none is more devastating than that of alcoholism. The steady sense of security, love and warmth necessary for adequate development of children are so unpredictably present in such a home that a child has difficulty developing the trust and confidence in himself and others which he will need for successful living. Neither the alcoholic father nor the alcoholic mother can play adequately the role of parent, so

---

[177] Celia Dulfano, <u>Families, Alcoholism and Recovery: 10 Stories</u>, (Center City, MN., Hazelden, 1982) p. 8.

that there are gross failures of identification in the growing child–a condition which can warp all his further relationships. Treatment must be directed toward overcoming the alcoholism in the parent, as well as helping the child to adjust to the difficult family situation.[178]

The current popularity of the term *dysfunctional family* is, in part, due to the aspect of many disorders, such as alcoholism, of involving many people and of involving non-specific objects of abuse. i.e. Today's alcoholic may be tomorrow's drug addict. The emotional fall-out of one person's alcoholism can involve all of the people within the influence of that alcoholic. For this reason, family-systems therapies focus not merely on the identified patient, but on the under-girding, psychological functioning of the entire family. Interlocking and mutually re-enforcing sets of rationales of afflicted people, circumstances, and agendas of the various personalities involved all influence the particular course the disease of alcoholism takes as it follows the path of least resistance.[179]

Regarding dysfunctional families, Virginia Satir (1973) wrote of her observations:

It is a sad experience for me to be with these families. I see the hopelessness, the helplessness,

---

[178] R. Fox, "The Effect of Alcoholism in Children," Paper distributed by the National council on Alcoholism. New York, 1976.

[179] Milton H. Erickson, M.D., in the Foreward to <u>Change Principles of Problem Formation and Problem Resolution</u>, by Paul Watzlawick, John Weakland & Richard Fisch. (N.Y.; W.W. Norton & Co.; 1974) p.x.

the loneliness. I see the bravery of people trying to cover up–a bravery that can eventually kill them. There are those who are still clinging to a little hope, who can still bellow or nag or whine at each other. Others no longer care. These people go on year after year, enduring misery themselves, or, in their desperation, inflicting it on others.[180]

The psychological profile of the family of an alcoholic is attempted by Wegscheider (1981). She pin-points seven identifiable areas in which the family interacts in the pathology of the alcoholic. 1) A pattern of denial and delusion regarding the extent alcohol plays in the problem; 2) Acutely painful feelings are put out of awareness; 3) Emotional defenses are so highly developed that the people are rigid and compulsive. i.e. Repressed feelings have become locked in as attitudes, anger has gone underground and become resentment, fear has become withdrawal, and guilt has become avoidance behavior, and thus hurting people hurt people themselves; 4) The self-esteem of individuals in the family is exceedingly low; 5) Behavior appears rigidly fixed, compulsive, and obsessive; 6) Communication is blocked, due to denial and delusion, and 7) Insight and education alone are ineffective in ameliorating the situation.[181]

Another formidable symptom seen in dysfunctional families is the prevalence and persistence of mixed messages. Mixed messages influence emotionally-dependent people to disregard their own perceptions and to fear to take any initiative stemming from their own

---

[180] Virginia Satir, Peoplemaking, (Palo Alto, CA.; Science and Behavior Books, 1973) pp. 10-12.

[181] Wegscheider, (Ibid). pp. 55-56.

impulses. Mixed messages alcoholics send to their loved ones create *double binds,* wherein the person is construed as *wrong* no matter which choice he makes, thus stress is never reduced. Such confusion and emotionally draining practices are thought to be conducive to the development of schizophrenic reactions.[182]

The prevalence of support groups such as Al-Anon and Ala-Teen also give evidence that a huge number of people associated with alcoholics feel violated and in need of emotional healing. The number of people identifying themselves and seeking treatment as adult children of alcoholics (ACOA) has increased steadily in the last decade.

Sociological Considerations of Alcoholism:

As alcoholism increases its addictive hold and makes inroads upon a person's psychological reserves, it also increasingly interferes in the person's ability to function normally. Alcoholism has been cited as contributing to many personnel problems, including diminishing work productivity and the ability to work well with others, thus threatening socio-economic security and physical safety. When one has blackouts, delirium tremens, or other severe after-effects of bouts of alcohol abuse, the ability to retain employment decreases dramatically. Indeed, it is often the overt threat of losing one's job which brings an alcoholic to a point of insight sufficient to seek treatment. Unless one is financially wealthy, alcohol soon erodes one's economic status. *Skid row* is not merely a cliché; it is a reality. Thousands of people victimized by alcoholism know that reality first-hand.

---

[182] Watzlawick, et al. Pragmatics of Human Communication, (N.Y.; W.W. Norton & Co.; 1967. pp. 91-96.

In addition to economic reverses, alcoholism also contributes to loss of social standing. This is another of the circularly reinforcing factors which traps people already suffering from other aspects of alcoholism. A person becomes known as a *boozer* or *lush*, and is passed over on various occasions by people who formerly were friends. The incipient alcoholic often has enough awareness to recognize the snub, and is so sensitive that the resulting depression is enough of an excuse to plunge the person back into another bout of uncontrolled drinking, which further compounds his/her situation. The sequence can start anywhere in the circle; the difficult part is to create an exit. Outside intervention is nearly always required, since the alcoholic is increasingly delusional regarding his/her own problem and also regarding the ability to cope with circumstances.[183]

The loss of driving privileges is usually insufficient to create insight in the alcoholic; it is usually rationalized and the legal restriction is ignored. Thus, the potential of the alcoholic to have additional negative impact on his society increases; fatal automobile and boat accidents, in which alcohol is a factor, influence not only the alcoholic, but also all other victims of the accident. Statistics regarding the number of accidents involving alcohol abuse vary considerably and are imprecise, but police and insurance figures place the loss of life from alcoholism very high on the list of factors causing accidents. Waller (1982) says alcohol is the single most important factor yet identified in serious and fatal motor vehicle crashes. She quotes

---

[183] Vernon E. Johnson, *I'll Quit Tomorrow*; (San Francisco, CA; Harper & Row, 1980) p. 4.

estimates placing alcohol as the culprit in fully half of all fatal crashes.[184]

Epidemiology is the study of the distribution of a disease and concomitant etiologic factors which might influence its distribution. Distribution is described either in terms of prevalence, which is the number of active cases in a specified population in a given time, or in incidence (the number of new cases occurring during a given time period.) Epidemiologists study alcoholism to determine: 1) How many people become alcoholic? 2) Who are they—what characteristics set them apart from people who do not become alcoholic? and 3) Are there certain risk factors or identifiable conditions which make it more likely that a person will become alcoholic? A number of studies have tried to answer these basic questions, but only tentative and as yet unverified answers have been suggested. No studies were found, in the area of epidemiology, which focused specifically on, or were restricted to, deaf people. Since some of the epidemiology studies, however, point up factors which may be present in deaf populations as well as hearing populations, summaries of their findings are included.

Incidence and prevalence of alcohol abuse by women was surveyed by Wilsnack, and it was found, despite many similarities between alcoholic men and alcoholic women, certain differences, possibly attributed to gender and its cultural consequences, were observed in the degree of openness of drinking patterns.[185] Gay/lesbian people were studied by Brandsma and Pattison to see if discernible

---

[184] Patricia A. Waller, Ph.D., "Alcohol and Highway Safety," in Pattison & Kaufman (Ibid); p. 395.

[185] Sharon Wilsnack, "Alcohol Abuse and Alcoholism in Women," in Pattison & Kaufman; Ibid. p. 732.

differences between them and the larger society existed in the incidence of alcoholism. These researchers concluded that homosexuality places a person at a much higher risk of developing alcoholism, because the typical social life of that population is intertwined with the use of alcohol.[186]

The multietiologic factors contributing to alcohol abuse among children were surveyed by Rice, in an effort to stem the increasing incidence of children addicted to alcohol. After studying 5,100 children, she found that by junior high school age, drinking played a very large part in the lives of many of the subjects. School administrations expressed concern about heavy drinking on the premises, but the children themselves showed no insight that their drinking was a problem. This study, and others, show parental drinking in the home to be a contributing factor to the children's development of alcoholism. There seems to be an implied expectation about drinking from one generation to the next. Hypotheses to explain this, such as the possibility that children may use alcohol as a shortcut to an adult role, frequently arise, but they remain only theories.[187]

The geriatric population's abuse of alcohol was surveyed by Maletta, showing that a great diversity of geriatric populations have been studied and a wide range of prevalence of alcohol abuse has been reported. One team of researchers listed the proportion of elderly people seeking alcoholism treatment to vary between 5 and 54% of treatment center admissions. Only a very small percentage of people institutionalized for alcoholism are over age 60, however. This may be construed to mean that elderly

---

186 Jeffrey M. Brandsma and E. Mansell Pattison, "Homosexuality and Alcoholism," in Pattison & Kaufman, Ibid. p. 740.

187 Matilda M. Rice, "Alcohol Use and Abuse in Children," in Pattison & Kaufman, Ibid. p. 759-767.

alcohol abusers do not seek treatment, or that the rate of alcoholism in geriatrics populations is naturally low, or that alcoholism among the elderly may not be the presenting problem, and thus may not be adequately diagnosed, or a number of other suppositions. Since the elderly are not a homogeneous group, further study could focus on various subgroups to investigate for the abuse of alcohol.

There is some clinical evidence to support the theory that late-onset alcoholics have a better prognosis of treatment than do life-long heavy drinkers, but even that tentative hypothesis is subject to the vagaries of variable motivation, degree of autonomy of the person, etc. Altogether, alcohol abuse in the elderly is not seen as a single faceted problem.[188]

Finally, Carroll and Schnoll surveyed people who abused both alcohol and other drugs. They state that the trend of thought now is away from the idea that addiction is substance-specific, and toward the recognition of personality patterns of addiction and abuse of whatever is most convenient. Thus, in many psychiatric hospitals, the often-used doctor's phrase *drug of choice* has hollowly mocked their efforts to free patients from drug dependency. Using, as a base, Eaglevill Hospital, a rehab center which offers treatment for alcohol and drug abuse, Carroll and Schnoll found that prognosis, using combined treatment methods, was often no better than when individual addictions were addressed singly. However, since alcoholics and drug addicts continue to frequently abuse more than one substance, and the presumption of *addictive personalities* seems a likely handle for therapists to use in

---

[188] Gabe J. Maletta, "Alcoholism and the Aged," in Pattison & Kaufman, Ibid. pp. 779-790.

treating afflicted populations, a wider, multi-faceted perspective is encouraged.[189]

Mulford (1982) acknowledges the muddied nature of the etiologic, and particularly epidemiologic, research and of the difficulty of obtaining acceptable definitions, noting problems related to interpreting data which emerges when factors are not constant. He cites one study which identified a factor which could put a person at risk in developing alcoholism–that of being reared in a home where alcohol is served, but notes that even that finding is open to questionable interpretation, due to other varying constraints.[190]

Age at which a person starts drinking has also been studied as a factor putting a person at risk in developing alcoholism, as has urban-rural origin and/or place of residence,[191] but none of these has been proven to be statistically significant, across time for multiple populations as yet. Overall we are left to conclude that epidemiology of alcoholism varies according to time and place, from society to society, can vary for different segments of the same society, and can even vary through time, for a specific population.[192]

---

[189] Jerome F. X. Carroll and Sidney H. Schnoll, "Mixed Drug and Alcohol Populations," in Pattison and Kaufman, Ibid. pp. 742-752.

[190] Harold A. Mulford, "The Epidemiology of Alcoholism and Its Implications," in Pattison & Kaufman, Ibid. p. 445.

[191] "The Iowa Problem Drinker Prevalence Rates, by risk populations and by selected early socioenvironmental factors." from "Stages in the Alcoholic Process" by H. Mulford, in Journal Studies of Alcoholism, (38) 565; 1977.

[192] Mulford, (ibid.) p. 454.

Cultural Factors in Willingness To Seek Treatment:

Although many adults, across cultures, occasionally drink alcohol, in not all cultures do people become alcoholic. In fact the concept of using alcohol to combat stress and/or emotional problems is rare in third world countries. The fact that these cultural variants are learned, rather than innate, implies that they can be unlearned, and therein lies hope.

Regarding the cultural variance in alcohol abuse, Heath notes that drinking problems vary among cultures as direct results of beliefs, behavior, attitudes and values. He says, "The ways in which members of a group view drinking and its consequences obviously influence their willingness to seek various kinds of help for themselves or recommend it for others."[193]

Heath notes examples which may be perhaps especially relevant to deaf people who are trying to "fit" into a hearing world.

Particular kinds of problems are often thought to be unusually prevalent among various populations, as causes rather than results of heavy drinking. One of the most common of these among minority groups is that of "anomie," a term sometimes used to refer to one's loss of traditional norms, and at other times to refer to one's inability to achieve new norms, however enthusiastically they may be embraced. This is sometimes explained as the dilemma of the marginal man, an individual supposedly caught between two worlds and not comfortable with either

---

[193] Dwight b. Heath, "sociocultural Variants in Alcoholism," in Pattison & Kaufman; (ibid.) p. 435.

the dominant or the subordinate society's way of life.[194]

Sociocultural variance is as important as are physiological and psychological influences, when we are trying to understand the myriad interlocking factors involved in alcoholism. Drinking behavior and attitudes are learned within the context of one's family and one's particular culture. Patterns of belief and behavior are modeled by combinations of examples, direct teaching, rewards and punishment, and other formal and informal influences in which norms and mores are transmitted within a culture. In the case of alcoholism, the variety of cultural paths and patterns convey major implications in terms of access and treatment for alcoholism. heath urges caution in relying too much on cultural aspects of alcohol abuse, saying, "On some occasions, unfortunately, a superficial concern for sociocultural variants can be counterproductive. Inappropriate generalizations from one minority population to another can not only be ineffective but insulting and alienating."[195]

Joseph Westermeyor postulates that economic and class factors may masquerade as ethnic and cultural factors in the access to treatment for alcoholism. He notes:

> Groups at a socio-economic disadvantage in a society also come to alcohol treatment at a disadvantage. They possess features inveighing against optimal outcomes, (i.e. more are single, divorced or separated; more are unskilled and

---

[194] Ibid., p. 434.
[195] Ibid., p. 438.

unemployed; they have few material and social resources; there are more arrest records, etc.)[196]

While this, obviously doesn't apply to all poor people, or imply that when disadvantaged people fall prey to alcoholism, their expected prognosis is inherently limited, it does behoove us to note its implications. Attempts at remediation will only be pursued when some hope exists.

Other researchers also have noted that access to treatment for alcoholism may be affected by cultural and socio-economic variables. Westermeyer noted that such things as ease of getting help, including such factors as proximity and anonymity, familiarity with the expected experience, and the person's acceptance of the need for help all affect an individual's willingness to seek treatment for alcoholism.[197]

Zimberg described a prohibitive stigma associated with alcoholism in the Jewish population he studied, concluding that the stigma of being identified as an alcoholic, with its concomitant cultural sense of shame and guilt, was enough to keep many people from seeking treatment of alcoholism.[198] In the Deaf culture, a similar shame and stigma associated with alcoholism have existed for years, and it may be possible to extrapolate from Zimberg's population to see that similar factors, among additional factors of discouragement (e.g. lack of concern from the

---

[196] Joseph Westermeyer, "Alcoholism and Services for Ethnic Populations," in Pattison & Kaufman (ibid), p. 714.

[197] Ibid., p. 713.

[198] S. Zimberg, "Sociopsychiatric perspectives on Jewish alcohol abuse: Implications for the prevention of alcoholism," American Journal of Drug and Alcohol Abuse., 4 (1977) p. 571-579.

hearing world) may operate in the deaf culture to further discourage individuals from seeking treatment for alcoholism.

Heath, et al., also comment that cultural norms and variations have considerable implications for the treatment of alcoholism, and they call for culturally appropriate treatment, and for other specific cautions of implementation in minority populations.[199]

Klein lists four methods of overcoming problems of "difficult to use" excuses for cultural minorities not seeking treatment for alcoholism: 1) Provide easier geographic access–proximity to the community; 2) Include culturally identical people on the staff; 3) Design treatment programs which encompass socio-cultural variables; and 4) Demonstrate sensitivity to ethnic and socio-cultural factors.[200] A subsequent chapter in this work specifically addresses guidelines for addiction treatment centers.

Westermeyer offers a set of clinical guidelines for cross-cultural treatment of chemical dependency, noting several demographic and clinical variations, e.g. Average volumes of alcohol under 250 grams a day were consumed by white alcoholics in the United States and Australia, but the average volume of alcohol consumed among Native Americans ranged from 250 to over 400 grams per day. Certain time-limited and binge drinking bouts also seemed to be culturally linked.[201]

---

[199] Heath, (ibid.) p. 713.

[200] J. A. Klein and A. C. Roberts; "A Residential Alcoholism Treatment Program for American Indians," Quarterly Journal for the Study of Alcohol, 34 (1973) pp. 860-868.

[201] J. Westermeyer (Ibid.) p. 711.

Is there a cultural bias in the treatment of alcoholism? Westermeyer hedges:

> Ethnic bias in treatment for alcoholism is most manifest in regard to access to treatment programs. Economically disadvantages/minorities are admitted to treatment less often than epidemiological findings would warrant. Once engaged in treatment, however, they generally have fully availability of services. They persist in treatment and their outcome is comparable to that of others.[202]

Culture A Factor in Outcome of Treatment?:

Regardless of sociocultural factors which may predispose a person toward alcoholism, the degenerative processes are no respecters of persons, and cut through national, age, gender and racial lines, mandating outside help if recovery is to occur.

A few alcoholism treatment programs have been created for certain minority groups, including deaf people, with varying degrees of success. Westermeyer unequivocally states, regarding ethnically oriented treatment programs, "There are as yet no indications that these programs have outcome results superior to programs without an ethnic emphasis."[203] No longitudinal outcome research is available, since these groups are fairly new. However, many eyes are focused on their progress, so that corrective feedback may be incorporated into future programs.

Underscoring a basic premise of A.A. regarding the importance of motivation and a willingness to accept help

---

[202] Ibid. p. 715.
[203] Ibid., p. 715.

that is available, for favorable prognosis, Smart & Gray conclude, "Outcome is best predicted by what the patient brings to treatment, not what happens to him (or her) there."[204]

Implications of Alcoholism Research for Deaf People

How vulnerable are deaf and hard-of-hearing people to alcohol abuse? Dr. Betty G. Miller, herself a certified, deaf alcoholism counselor, says,

> Alcoholics look for excuses to avoid treatment and we must break through this "denial attitude." In the case of a deaf person, the excuse becomes a glaring reality–deafness. While the basic elements of the disease are the same, the deaf person tends to feel them with a greater intensity. Loneliness, depression, social alienation, a low self-esteem–all these elements are heightened with a deaf person.[205]

Debra Guthmann, of Minnesota's Chemical Dependency Program for Hearing Impaired Youth quotes the Drug Free Schools and Communities Act of 1986 as saying that people are at high risk of developing a drug or alcohol problem if they have "experienced mental-health problems or long-term physical pain due to injury." She notes that the Federal Office of Substance Abuse Prevention has developed a number of categories to identify youth with increased risk of developing an abuse problem. Within this

---

[204] R.G. Smart and G. Gray, "Multiple predictors of dropout from alcoholism treatment"; Archives of General Psychiatry, 35 (1978) pp. 363-367.

[205] Betty G. Miller, Ed.D., CAC; "Empowerment" in The Counselor, May-June (no year) pp. 24-25.

list, along with having a parent who abuses substances, or being economically disadvantaged, or a school drop-out, is having a physical disability.[206]

Ms. Guthmann cites three fairly well known recent studies of substance abuse among specific populations of deaf people, (Isaacs, Buckley and Martin, 1979; Johnson and Locke, 1978; and Boros, 1981) summarizing their conclusions to suggest that the incidence of substance abuse among deaf people is no higher than in the larger society.[207] Using Ms. Guthmann's statistic, we deduce that there are some 73,000 deaf alcoholics in the United States, however some estimates posit over one million people with impaired hearing who have exhibited problems handling alcohol.

Waltzer cites studies by Steitler and by Pelc, agreeing with their independent conclusions that substance abuse among deaf students appears to be higher than among hearing students. She says that up to one out of seven deaf people who use drugs or alcohol becomes addicted, and states that feelings of isolation, communication difficulties, reduced educational and job opportunities, confusion about cultural identity, and mental health problems contribute to this high vulnerability.[208]

The Institute on Alcohol, Drugs and disability offered a review of the literature relative to alcohol, drugs and

---

[206] Debra Guthmann, M.A. "Saying 'No' in college: How to Deal w/Substance Abuse Among Deaf and Hard Of Hearing Students," Paper prepared via the Minnesota Chemical Dependency Program for Hearing Impaired Youth, n.d. pp. 1-14.

[207] Ibid. p. 1.

[208] Deborah R. Waltzer, "A Sobering Tale: Drug and Alcohol Abuse and Recovery in the Deaf Community," in Focus, a paper printed by the Drug Prevention Programs in Higher Education, U.S. Department of Education. n.d.; pp. 17-25.

disability in 1989. They compiled a comprehensive bibliography of literature relative to alcohol, drugs and disability. It is not the purpose of this work to incorporate the details of existing bibliographies, but to note their availability and helpfulness in listing available studies.

We do not wish to stereotype deaf or hard-of-hearing people or to blunt critical examination via overly simplistic insights. While it is obvious that deaf people are individuals and deserve to be met on a one-to-one basis, with no pre-conceptions interfering with complete perception and reception in each encounter, it is equally obvious that a number of concerned researchers have exerted considerable time and effort trying to deduce if there exist discernible points of commonalty, in order to more adequately meet the needs of deaf and hard of hearing people.

Boros (1981) and Isaacs et al. (1979) specified two problems faced by deaf alcoholics. 1) There is a tendency, in the Deaf community, to be closed to outsiders, therefore maintaining cultural mores and not absorbing of the larger culture. 2) The values in the Deaf community place a strong stigma against drunkenness when interacting with those outside the Deaf community. Thus, deaf alcoholics, tend to "hide" their drinking problems with the Deaf community and feel cut-off from help.[209]

Moore (1992) states that many experts believe the incidence of alcoholism among deaf people is at least equal to that of the hearing population. He offers the following

---

[209] Boros, A. "Activating solutions to alcoholism among the hearing impaired: Drug dependence and alcoholism." in Social and Behavioral Issues, Schecter, A.J. ed. (N.Y.; Pleum Press, 1981) and Isaacs, M.; Buckley, G., & Martin, D., "Patterns of drinking among the deaf." American Journal of Drug and Alcohol Abuse, 6 (4) 1979, pp. 463-476.

supplemental reasons, in addition to mentioning several already noted in this work:

Other factors which may contribute to risks for substance abuse by individuals who are deaf range from a lack of understanding of health education information (Kleinig & Mohay, 1989) to differences in information processing patterns among the deaf (Chalifoux, 1989). The inability of existing social systems to respond to the needs of the deaf also contribute a great deal of elevated risks for substance abuse, and this includes a complete lack of awareness about substance abuse services for persons in the deaf community (Whitehouse, Sherman, & Kozlowski, 1991).[210]

Moore and Ford offer evidence that deaf people may be at increased risk in developing addiction, because of factors inherent in their lives, e.g. ready access to psychoactive drugs for pain or balance maintenance, their decreased visibility in society if they maintain separatism, and acceptability of drug use by others in their peer group.[211] And the late Larry Stewart, who was a psychologist and

---

[210] Dennis Moore, Ed.D. "Substance Use Patterns of Persons with Hearing Impairments: a Regional Study"; paper presented at: "The Next Step: A National Conference Focusing on Issues Related to Substance Abuse in the Deaf and hard of Hearing Population"; July 5-8, 1992; Denver, CO. p. 1.

[211] Dennis Moore, Ed.D. & Jo Ann Ford, M.R.C.; "Prevention of Substance Abuse Among Persons With Disabilities: a demonstration model." in Addiction Intervention with the Disabled Bulletin, Fall, 1990, Vol. 12, NO. 1, p. 1.

substance abuse treatment program director, echoed the previously mentioned factors.[212]

Numerous hypotheses abound regarding the physiological way in which deafness impairs people's functioning. Some of these are more plausible than others, however. McCay Vernon (1969) hypothesized that the dismal educational standing of many deaf children, despite their normal distribution of intelligence, particularly citing their difficulty in learning oral languages, might be accounted for by lesions of the central nervous system, which he presumed accompanied the hearing loss.[213] A few people accept the concept of a *deaf psychology*, implying that because deaf people have double-burdens, unique personality structures and dynamics may evolve, but evidence has not supported the idea that there is anything intrinsic in deafness to comprise psychological uniqueness.

Levine (1960) implied that if deaf people constitute a unique psychological profile, their differences from the larger population may be attributed, not to inherent, organic variances—such as deafness, but to socio-cultural factors, such as isolation.[214]

---

[212] Larry G. Stewart, "Hearing Impaired Substance Abusers" paper included in S.T.A.M.P. program materials. n.d. p. 4.

[213] McCay Vernon, "Multiply-Handicapped Deaf Children: Medical, Educational, and Psychological Considerations" (C.E.C. Research Monographs). Washington, D.C.; Council for Exceptional Children. (1969) & M. Vernon, "Multi-Handicapped deaf children: types and causes" in The Multi-Handicapped Hearing Impaired. D. Tweedie & E.H. Shroyer, eds. Washington, D.C.: Gallaudet Univ. Press, 1982. pp. 11-28.

[214] E.S. Levine, The Psychology of Deafness, N.Y.; Columbia Univ. Press, 1960.

Michael A. Harvey (1989) speaks of the common phenomenon of a disability *spreading* to become a handicap, or allowing a handicap to be disabling. This implies extending one's objectively-measurable medical condition to include experiential difficulties of adjusting/functioning in one's environment.[215] He reasons that people experiencing self-doubt in adjusting to hearing loss could greatly benefit from knowing that certain stresses normally accompany the process. Open, frank discussions, rather than denial and evasions, about how these stresses affect the individual, the family and friends could be supportive and therapeutic, in and of themselves.[216]

With these cautions in mind, certain parallels may be at least tentatively drawn, which might illuminate the problem of substance abuse among people with hearing loss. Both the abuse of alcohol and the experience of hearing loss are conducive to the individual's retreat from society.[217]

The sense of belonging to and being accepted by a group is important to successful human development; the feeling of "not belonging," and of the experience of receiving "unequal treatment" are often cited by people in the minority. This experience generally results in either of two forms of responses. It may increase group solidarity among those who feel rejected by the dominant element in the community, or it may generate self-denigration, and result in preservation, in attempts to emulate the dominant group.

---

[215] Michael A. Harvey, <u>Psychotherapy with Deaf and Hard-of-Hearing Persons: A Systemic Model,</u> (Hillsdale, N.J., Lawrence Erlbaum Assoc., Publ.; 1989) p. 97.

[216] Ibid., p. 123.

[217] Larry Stewart (ibid.) p. 5.

The literature reveals examples of both paths taken by deaf and hard-of-hearing people.[218]

Both the experience of hearing loss and substance abuse/alcoholism frequently are characterized by feelings of isolation and "not belonging."[219] Bobbie Beth Scoggins, the deaf creator and director of an enormously successful video which features a cartoon character, says, "Studies show there's about a 35% rate of use or misuse (of drugs), but I would say it's closer to 50% because of isolation, low self-esteem, and lack of employment among the deaf."[220]

Both chronic alcoholism and deafness or hearing loss, to state the obvious, involve physical disability related to receiving sensory input from one's environment, i.e. hearing loss is the physical disability in impaired hearing, which greatly impacts one's communication and may affect ancillary aspects of one's life also. As we have seen from the literature cited earlier in this chapter, studies on alcoholism show multiple disruptions of perception, (e.g. seeing double, balance problems, and hearing loss), among other many physical effects related to chronic alcoholism.

Both deaf or hard-of-hearing people and chronic alcoholics, as shown in the literature, may employ denial and evasion, to avoid facing unpleasant realities. Regarding the tendency to not acknowledge negative aspects of the deaf experience, a great deaf lady, Grace Murphy, noted,

---

218 Harlan Lane, The Mask of Benevolence, Ibid., pp. 64-65, & 103-107.

219 Betty G. Miller, Ed.D., CAC, Ibid. p. 25.

220 Rosalinda Johnson, "Tobey's Tales wins apple, gives deaf children a boost" in Tribune News, April 26, 1991. Local News section.

There would be no purpose in writing this book if I pretended that life is only sweetness and light. It has been the pretence (sic) of the deafened (to this effect) that has made half their difficulties.[221]

Isaacs (1979) documented denial on a fairly large scale among deaf alcoholics. He reported that preliminary efforts to create alcoholism treatment services for people with hearing impairment were met with "massive denial by the organized Deaf community, of the existence of the problem, as well as occasional active hostility to its being raised as a possibility."[222]

Closely related to the phenomenon of denial, perhaps overlapping it, is the concept of *stigma*, alluded to elsewhere in this work. Part of stigma appears to be willingness to accept guilt for something external to oneself, and/or unwillingness to be associated with anything which one believes is somehow shameful. The National Information Center on Deafness reprinted a paper developed by the Virginia Division for the Deaf and Hard of Hearing (1985), which includes the following partial explanation of the cultural stigma deaf people may feel about alcoholism:

---

[221] Grace B. Murphy, Your Deafness Is Not You, (N.Y.; Harper & Bros; 1954). preface.

[222] M. Isaacs (1979) cited by Linda Cherry in "Review of the Literature Relative to Alcohol, Drugs and Disability; Disability in Our Culture: An Overview. Paper developed as part of the California Alcohol, Drug and Disability Study (CALADDS) conducted by the Institute on Alcohol, Drugs and Disability; San Mateo, CA; n.d.

The first barrier deaf persons experience in utilizing existing alcoholism treatment programs is the deaf community's perception of alcoholism. Many deaf persons see alcoholism as a personal weakness and a moral sin. This outdated view of alcoholism if attributed to the isolation deaf persons experience and their limited information on current trends in treatment. The stigma that the deaf community places on alcoholism discourages deaf alcoholics from admitting their drinking problems and from getting treatment.[223]

Also referring to the stigma of alcoholism, Sabin (1988) writes that it still exists in the Deaf community, and Moser says:

A reluctance to enter treatment on the part of the deaf population resulting from the stigma that is attached to the problem, further frustrates the effort to treat. Because the deaf community is tighter and has a strong grapevine, substance abuse carries more of a stigma than in the general population.[224]

---

[223] "Alcoholism and Deafness" a NICD reprint; originally appeared in Reporting for Hearing Impaired Virginians; from the Virginia Division for the Deaf and Hard of Hearing; Winter, 1985.

[224] Nancy Moser of the Center on Deafness at the University of CA, San Francisco, quoted in "Handicapped Persons: Many barriers to be overcome in treating addiction in the deaf," in Reference Guide to Addiction Counseling, n.d., n.a.; p. 4., and Gaylene Becker, "Coping with Stigma: Lifelong Adaptation of Deaf People," in Social Science & Medicine 158 (1) January, 1981, pp. 21-24.

In both alcoholism and deafness studies the propensity toward dysfunctional communication and family life are frequently cited as primary problems deterring treatment. Earlier in this chapter we noted the work of family systems therapists, (Satir, Watzlawick, Jackson, etc.) on dysfunctional families. A number of characteristics of dysfunctional family life can be seen to parallel the experience of a person undergoing hearing loss or feeling isolated and ostracized in a hearing world. These characteristics include: a preponderance of mixed messages, renouncing one's own perceptions in favor of others', creation of *double binds*, in which the individual is perceived as wrong—no matter what, accompanying the fear of being abandoned if one does not abrogate individual rights and embrace unacceptable alternatives. [225]

Gordon Allport noted from his studies of deaf children, that, in order to make a satisfactory life-adjustment, the deaf child "needs to know from an early age that his conditions of security are in some respects unlike those of an average child." [226] This awareness of being isolated, of differing qualitatively from the norm, does not usually contribute to a child's natural, healthy psychological development, but often brings first denial, then anger and bitterness. To the extent that these "negative" emotions

---

[225] P. Watzlawick, J.H. Beavin, & D. Jackson Pragmatics of Human Communication: a study of interactional patterns, pathologies, and paradoxes, (N.Y.; W.W. Norton & Co. Inc., 1967) pp. 87-95 and David Risser, "Program Helps Deaf Students Hone Living Skills," Expressions publ. by the Self-Actualization Institute for the Deaf, Inc.; Vol. 1; originally printed in Los Angeles Times, August 27, 1987. pp. 1-3.

[226] Gordon Allport in K. Lewin, Resolving Social Conflicts, (N.Y.: Harper & Bros. 1948) p. vii.

have no appropriate outlet and are turned inward, the psychological health of the child is adversely affected.

From accumulative literature considering why disabled people sometimes abuse substances, a number of hypotheses have been presented. Four factors were identified most often: 1) People with disabilities have relatively easy access to drugs, e.g. painkillers, and widespread avoidance behavior on the part of parents, educators and others keeps recognition of the problem of over-medication or abuse of drugs at bay. 2) Disabled people, just as do other people, imitate their peers and are prey to peer pressure to behave similarly to group norms in order to be included 3) Disabled people often attempt to assuage frustrations and anxieties with alcohol and other chemicals, as they see people in the larger society model such behavior, and 4) Disabled people often feel that they are an oppressed minority, so a desire for justice creates the phenomenon of *entitlement*, wherein people, over a period of time, come to believe they deserve compensation for their suffering and possibly unjust treatment. Numbness via alcohol/chemicals keeps them from focusing on the reality that they alone cannot alter their treatment by others.

Psychologist Lee Meyerson, himself deaf, constructed a theory regarding the various social adjustments of deaf people. He noted three perceived patterns.

Pattern number one (1) is comprised of the Deaf community who disassociate themselves from the hearing community and "perceive safety in a small but well-ordered world" of their fellow Deaf people. People who share the Deaf culture, are fluent in sign language, and have loved ones in the group may tend toward this category. This category also can apply to people who have become deafened late in life, but who have managed to find havens of acclimation via lip-reading, and/or options, primarily in large urban areas, for sympathetic relationships with other people undergoing similar experiences. There has been no research replicated sufficiently to link specific patterns of emotional difficulties with this group of deaf people who have strong emotional support systems.

Pattern number two (2) is identified as practiced by those who resist awareness of their deafness and strive to interact with hearing people without any special consideration. Allport noted many emotional hazards for people who choose the mainstreaming route; the perils include chronic anxiety, self-doubt and ambivalence toward oneself and one's acquaintances, and internalized, debilitating resentment.

Adjustment pattern number three (3) is chosen by people who can, at least in theory, value the large area of commonalty that exists between those who are deaf and those who hear, seeing that the ability to hear is far from central to the core of humanity. Affirming our essential humanness, similar aspirations, needs and emotions helps people to rise a meta-level in their perspective. Thus the individual manifestations of human variegation are seen as just that, and not as labels, indictments or reasons for dis-affirming either self or others.[227]

The high moral ground is the ideal, Allport says, but tolerance should be shown to everyone in their individual choices. Indeed the divisions between the three identified adjustment patterns is not rigid nor one-way. Just as people experience variance in their moods and emotions, generally, they may also feel like interacting primarily with people who are most likely to understand them at certain

---

[227] Lee Meyerson in B.M. Schowe's Identity Crisis in Deafness: a humanistic perspective, (Tempe, AZ; The Scholars Press; 1979) pp. 49-53.

times. They may feel like asserting their uniqueness or to venture to try to understand someone perceived as *alien* at other times. All this is within the range of normal human variation of mood and confidence level.

Just as the personality profiles of alcoholics in the larger society begin to be less differentiated, and alcoholics assume a common, recognizable profile as their disease encroaches on their lives, deaf people who abuse substances are observed to have characteristics similar to that profile and to each other, and become less individually distinct personalities. Grant, et al., (1982) noted self-doubt, tendency toward paranoia, dependence on external guides rather than internal, low tolerance levels, poor impulse control, poor communication skills, intermittent depression, immaturity and feelings of isolation and inferiority in deaf alcoholics.[228] We do not have conclusive evidence that this personality-cluster was merely the path of least resistance for these people, but we have accumulative research, cited in chapter two, which tags people studied who felt impaired by hearing loss or societal neglect, as vulnerable to these same psychological problems.

Patrick Best, in a dissertation for Wayne State University, found that deaf children manifest a significantly different development pattern of psychological differentiation than do hearing children; he particularly noted abnormally high impulsivity levels in deaf children, as have other researchers such as Altshuler.[229] Does this "high impulsivity" put them at extra risk of becoming alcoholic, since alcoholics also are observed to display high

---

[228] T.N. Grant, C.A. Kramer & K. Nash "Working with Deaf Alcoholics in a Vocational Training Program," Journal of Rehabilitation of the Deaf, 15 (4) 1982, pp. 14-20.

[229] Patrick K. Best, "Psychological Differentiation in the Deaf", Doctoral Dissertation; Wayne State Univ., 1974, p. 163 & 177.

impulsivity? We don't have clear evidence on this; we do have the observation that trying to discover which came first, (the emotional characteristic of poor impulse control or the addictive behavior) may be impossible and non-productive, since they seem to mutually reinforce each other.

It may seem self-evident that such things as feelings of isolation and extreme loneliness are unhealthy psychologically for human beings, but explicit research expresses that thought from a positive standpoint. Maslow studied psychologically healthy individuals and deduced their common characteristics. Among healthy people functioning at a high level of self-actualization, a feeling of benevolence toward and empathy with one's world and specifically one's acquaintances was most salient.[230] Pre-lingually deaf children, playing together, communicating via sign language, and unaware that they may be labeled "impaired" by others, may approach Maslow's outlined ideal of psychological self-actualization as fully as may individuals in any other hypothesized group. They are not mistrustful, bitter, nor inclined to retreat from the world. Until unfortunate experiences with people who do not accept their uniqueness quell the naturally optimistic natures of these deaf children, they are not perceived to be at psychological risk. They are certainly not prime candidates for substance abuse. Therefore, we can deduce that there is not a specific quality inherent in being deaf which predisposes one toward substance abuse.

Sidney Jourard, best known for his work, *The Transparent Self*, states unequivocally that to be fully healthy psychologically, an individual must have at least

---

[230] Abraham H. Maslow, Toward a Psychology of Being, 2nd ed., (N.Y.; Van Nostrand Reinhold Co., 1968), pp. 197-207.

one other human being with whom he/she can be completely honest and can disclose one's innermost feelings. He cites the degenerative effects of feelings of isolation and feeling different from one's peers.[231] It would appear that deaf people who, in reaction to wounds to the psyche from insensitive people, retreat into loneliness and tacit rejection of their uniqueness, are at least further distancing themselves from healthy psychological functioning, and may be seen to be making themselves vulnerable to cul-de-sac retreats such as alcoholism and drug addiction.

Both alcoholism and experiences ensuing from adult-onset hearing loss are perceived to diminish a person's ability to trust his fellow man. Kannapell writes movingly of the *trust-mistrust phenomenon* among deaf people, generally, and notes that one of the classic characteristics of alcoholics, deaf or hearing, is that they increasingly distrust people. She focuses on five possible reasons for mistrust of hearing people by deaf people. In each instance a perceived difference in personal power between the deaf person and the person mistrusted was involved.[232]

Similarly, Chough discussed factors involved in the lack of trust of people exhibited by deaf people. He reviewed Erickson's developmental stages of life and other theories, and closed with recommendations to help the development of trust between deaf and hearing clients and counselors. Chough's pointers are: 1) Hearing counselors should learn, and be fluent in, ASL, and deaf clients should be patient with their counselors. Willingness to learn their language for improved communication may provide evidence of good intentions, at least, and may aid deaf people to trust

---

[231] S. Jourard, (Ibid.) pp. 33-41.
[232] Barbara Kannapell, "The Trust-Mistrust Phenomenon," reprint distributed by NICD, n.d.

hearing people. 2) Both client and counselor should try to communicate their own experience as much as possible. Hearing people need to understand feelings of the deaf, and deaf people need to understand hearing people's constraints. 3) A positive attitude should be maintained. 4) Neither Deaf nor hearing parties should engage in manipulative behavior. Chough says, "If a counselor is to be perceived as wise and trustworthy, he/she should not be a dupe, any more than he/she should be paternalistic.[233]

Among the parallels of the deaf experience and an alcoholic's experience are various physical and/or physiological aspects which are affected by hearing disorders. Certain hearing disabilities are linked to disturbance of the sense of balance, e.g. Meniere's disease, and alcoholism both affect one's sense of balance, and speech centers within the brain have been noted as being affected by both alcoholism and deafness. Even the senses of smell and taste can be affected in both deaf-related circumstances and alcoholism.[234]

These parallel characteristics have been observed by researchers on alcoholism or drug dependency and on deaf people. In certain instances, it may have been assumed by researchers that the variable of deafness was the one observed, however closer scrutiny of the research may offer additional hypotheses to explain the findings. If, however, even some findings are valid, it is imperative that deaf people, who may be at great risk of developing alcoholism or drug addiction, be aware of the potential pitfalls.

---

[233] Steven K. Chough, D.S.W. "The Trust Vs. Mistrust Phenomenon Among Deaf Persons."

[234] National Institute on Deafness and Other Communication Disorders Clearinghouse, paper distributed by the National Institutes of Health, Bethesda, MD. n.d.

Because deaf people do not comprise one homogeneous group, but consist of people born deaf, people who become deaf before they learn oral language, people who gradually become hard-of-hearing, those who become deaf due to accidents and other such circumstantial demarcations, generalizing across the area of hearing-restriction, with respect to emotional characteristics, beliefs and attitudes, vulnerability to addiction, and other variables is neither wise nor helpful.

Harlan Lane (1992) warns of the perils of extrapolating personality characteristics observed in individuals to generalize about deaf people as a whole. (See Chapter II.) He compares various traits accumulatively attributed to the deaf to Burundi's outlandish list of traits attributed to Africans by colonialists.[235] Despite the impossibility of so many mutually contradictory qualities applying to a single person, some agreement by two decades of researchers on observed behavioral traits of certain deaf populations, e.g. deaf adolescents born to hearing parents, in a number of aforementioned studies, comprise composite profiles, which may be instructive.

(Table II is a reproduction of traits most consistently ascribed by researchers cited in this chapter to people with adult-onset deafness, parallel to traits attributed to alcoholics by clinicians.) This particular population of deaf people was chosen to profile primarily because of the great need of early intervention with them regarding vulnerability to addiction.

---

[235] Harlan Lane, The Mask of Benevolence: Disabling the deaf community, (N.Y., Alfred A. Knopf, 1992) p. 35.

Table II

A Comparison of Descriptions of
People Deafened in Adulthood & Alcoholics
(from researchers, clinicians, teachers, therapists,
employers & social workers)

Adult-onset deafness been noted to be conducive to:	Alcoholism has been has noted to contribute to:
* Retreat from society Sense of "not belonging"	* Retreat from society Sense of unacceptability
* Feelings of isolation/ loneliness	* Feelings of loneliness/ being abandoned
* Low self-esteem/poor self-image	* Deteriorating self-esteem
* Intermittent feelings of depression/ moodiness	* Widely varying moods from euphoria to depression
* Denial and/or projection	* Denial and projection
* Stigma & shame leading to "hiding" behaviors	* Stigma & shame & hiding one's drinking
* Motor skills affected by deafness	* Motor skills affected by alcohol
* Dysfunctional communication patterns	* Impaired communication systems

* Over-extended
  family life

* Decreased will to
  overcome/conquer
  ills of life

* Low frustration tolerance

* Diminished ability to
  to trust others

* Resorting to passive-
  aggressive or
  manipulative
  behaviors

* Overall sense of
  helplessness
* Sometimes psychotic
  reactions

* Troubled or defeated
  families

* Circularly reinforcing
  defeatist factors

* Increasingly low
  frustration tolerance

* Increasing paranoid
  feelings

* Manipulating others
  without conscience

* Gradually enveloping
  despair
* Sometimes psychotic
  reactions

A list of characteristics ascribed by observers to deaf children compared to alcoholics might list such commonalties as immaturity and poor impulse control, but such a comparison seems specious to this researcher in that many, if not all, children are by definition immature and most everyone has to learn impulse control. Saying that deaf children lag behind other children in this regard could be regarded as tautological, since their sensory impute, from which these qualities derive is limited. Children mature, however, and learn impulse control, while people ensnared in addiction, unless they receive help, worsen in these variables. Thus, even though we might, in theory, be able to identify a precise moment when the psyches of the two groups seem nearly congruent, the directionality of movement in the two populations is opposite. Presumably the overlap of similarity will diminish if the deaf children do not succumb to alcoholism or drug addiction, so pointing out their similarity to alcoholics is pointless. Intervening at their points of vulnerability to addiction, however, is very much to the point.

Some inconsistency and contradiction in characteristics attributed to deaf people as a whole may be due to the wide range and variability of qualities which all people, deaf or hearing, have the potential of expressing. Some of the inconsistency and contradiction, however, may be due to the general public's sloppy use of terminology, including lumping together all populations of the deaf, and extrapolating conclusively from a few instances. We shall venture a few thoughts, using this insight, and then subdivide the category of deaf people, to examine possible relationships in the various people whose hearing is impaired referenced in terms of vulnerability to alcohol abuse.

<u>Pre-lingually deaf persons & other people who comprise the
Deaf culture:</u>

Among deaf populations, people, such as those known as
pre-lingually deaf, born to deaf parents, who have grown up
within a loving culture of other people like themselves, who
share a common language (e.g. ASL), and have a sense of
commitment to their group may not encounter snubs nor
impatience they might otherwise feel from the larger
society, and thus may not feel isolated or lonely. People
who find their social, intellectual, cultural, physical and
emotional needs met primarily within a closely-knit group
of people may be seen as less vulnerable to the prompting of
loneliness toward addiction, than later-deafened people
might be, who may not have such peer groups.

While alcohol use in residential schools of the deaf has
been cited as a problem in the past, particularly when
signing was discouraged, current awareness of the students'
needs, increasing peer pressure to remain addiction free,
and mass education about potential problems of addiction
may soon lessen perceived vulnerabilities there.

<u>Characteristics seen in geriatric deaf populations which
may predicate addiction:</u>

People who have gradually become deafened, especially
late in life, may be more vulnerable to alcoholism due to
depression and feelings of isolation than are people fully
ensconced in the Deaf community. It has been cryptically
noted that elderly hard-of-hearing and newly deafened
people don't really "fit" into the Deaf community, but they
see themselves increasingly unable to function in the
hearing society. Deaf Life Magazine (1989) states:

People who are losing their hearing usually go through the same psychological process; the 'stages of adjustment' to a loss: first comes denial, then anger, then guilt, and finally, some level of adjustment. But many are afraid of deafness because they don't know how to confront it. Understandably, they may have negative feelings about deafness, and feel bitter and depressed about their own deafness and loss of identity.[236]

Presbycucis, a hearing loss which is frequently noticed after age 60, is a form of nerve deafness. Presbycucis and other disorders in which auditory acuity is lost are frequent in geriatric populations, and are the occasion of much distress. Powers and Powers discuss the hearing problems of elderly persons and the social ramifications of these, citing the increasing sense of isolation as a primary pathological sign. Happily, their subjects sought out more contact and did not report feelings of loneliness any more than did the controls, non-deafened elderly people.[237]

Contributing to the psychology of hearing loss, Rousey focused on psychological defenses, such as denial and projection, which are frequently used to cope with hearing loss. He observed instances of mourning, shame and lowering of self-esteem.[238]

---

[236] Rocky Stone, "America is Getting Older and Deafer," in Deaf Life, 1 (7) Rochester, N.Y.; Jan. 1989) pp. 9-13 at p. 10.

[237] Joyce Powers and Edward Powers, "Hearing problems of elderly persons: social consequences and prevalence." American Speech and Hearing Association, 20 (2), February, 1978. pp. 79-83.

[238] Clyde L. Rousey, "Psychological Reactions to Hearing Loss," Journal of Speech & Hearing Disorders, 36 (3) August 1971, pp. 382-389.

McCartney and Nadler noted that feelings of isolation and depression are often caused by hearing loss in the geriatric population. They discuss possible medical aids and offer some suggestions for their patients with hearing loss, e.g. "Initiate conversations rather than waiting for others to speak to you first."[239]

Stevens sought to identify psychological problems in middle-aged and elderly people with hearing loss, and to determine whether or not hearing-aids would ameliorate these. The feeling of social isolation was the principal psychological problem noted, and although the use of an hearing-aid helped, there remained a residual sense of loss which kept the people from resuming their former active, social lives.[240]

Cooper et. al. re-examined the association between acquired deafness and paranoia in the elderly. After taking into consideration the possibility that selection and age factors might have skewed the results, they were still able to draw a few tentative conclusions regarding the observed phenomenon that patients with paranoid psychosis showed more severe hearing loss than did patients with affective illness. They believed that the long interval between the onset of deafness and the emergence of psychosis offered hope in the area of opportunity for prevention of paranoid psychosis in elderly deafened people.[241]

---

[239] James H. McCartney, Ph.D. and Gay Nadler, MSW, "How to help your patient cope with hearing loss." in Geriatrics, 34 (31) March, 1979, pp. 69-71 & 75.

[240] John M. Stevens, "Some Psychological Problems of Acquired Deafness" in British Journal of Psychiatry, 140 (1982) pp. 453-456.

[241] A.F. Cooper, A.R. Curry, D.W. Kay, R.F. Garside, & M. Roth. "Hearing Loss in Paranoid and Affective Psychoses of the Elderly," The Lancet, 2 (7885) October 12, 1974. pp. 851-854.

Jones et. al. interviewed a random sample of 657 patients, aged 70 and over, from a general practitioner's clientele. These people were asked about their hearing difficulties and also about problems in other areas of their lives. Standardized measures were used to survey the subjects' levels of anxiety, depression and memory loss. Hearing loss was associated with both depression and anxiety, both of which are high risk factors in the incidence of alcoholism. But other physical disabilities of the subjects may have weakened the statistical significance shown in the link between age and vulnerability to addiction.[242]

A notable exception to the bulk of studies showing increased amounts of depression, a sense of isolation and a sense of deep loss in the deaf geriatric population is Thomas et. al's, in which 259 healthy people between the ages of 60 and 89, who lived independently, stated that their (moderate) hearing loss did not cause them to feel depressed; in fact, they sought out additional contact with their families.[243]

Other Deaf Populations Viewed in terms of Addiction Risk:

Adults deafened suddenly, as in accidents, and people who are moderately hard-of-hearing all their adult lives may also be without peer groups for comfort. Dana

---

242 D. Jones, Christina Victor, and Norman Vetter, "Hearing Difficulty and its Psychological Implications for the Elderly," Journal of Epidemiology and Community Health, 38, (1984), p. 75.

243 Paula Thomas, William Hunt, Philip Garry, Richard Hood, Jean Goodwin & James Goodwin, "Hearing Acuity in a Healthy Elderly Population: Effects on Emotional, Cognitive, and Social Status," Journal of Gerontology, 38 (3), May, 1983, pp. 321-325.

Mulvaney, a deaf social worker who took her first sign language class when she was 22, tells of feeling ignored by agencies serving deaf people. She discusses the difficulty of learning to sign adroitly as an adult and the abdication of hope of being able to "keep up" with a hearing world that is implied in transferring one's attention to communicating primarily with other deaf people. She relies heavily on written communication, and speaks of the frustrations of such methods. Overall, she conveys a sense of loss, of feeling out of place, and of not being adequately understood.[244]

A social worker, Luey, discussed problems of deafened adults, which she perceived as being different from those of people who were born deaf. She notes problems in communicating, social functioning, and in self-acceptance.[245] Similar in its conclusions, but differing in vantage point is Cornforth and Woods' study on the effects of sudden or progressive deafness on people. They state that in both sudden and progressive deafness, results are traumatic to the individual experiencing the loss. The individual feels isolated and unable to sustain relationships they had nurtured throughout their lives.[246]

It is understandable that people who feel overwhelmed by changes they do not understand, and people who feel that control of their lives is slipping away from them, might seek help. Some turn to alcohol or chemicals to numb their

---

[244] Dana Mulvaney, "Not Quite Deaf, Not Quite Hearing," The Glad News, Fall, 1988, p. 18.

[245] Helen S. Luey, "Between Worlds: The Problems of Deafened Adults," Social Work in Health Care, 5 (3) Spring, 1980, pp. 253-256.

[246] Anthony R. Cornforth and Marie M. Woods, "Progressive or Sudden Hearing Loss," in Nursing Times, 68 (7), February 17, 1972, pp. 205-207.

awareness of all that is unpleasant in their circumstances. It would appear that this group of deaf people, who may be experiencing multiple losses, due to other mixed causes, are quite vulnerable to substance abuse. Factor analysis studies of deaf people who develop alcoholism or drug addiction could develop a scale, similar to the common *stress* index, which would isolate and take into account such variables as age, general health and life situation.

In addition to the above surveyed populations of deaf people, studies have been done on multi-handicapped deaf people, psychiatric deaf populations, black and Indian deaf people, and deaf children, some of which were cited in the second chapter. To review these here would unnecessarily lengthen this work, but a few summary statements can be deduced. Where psychological implications were offered, the same range of emotions, beliefs, attitudes and value systems as obtain in the larger society were demonstrated. We can excerpt a typical summation, to amplify this concept. Altshuler (1974) wrote:

Early parent-child communication is a traumatic issue between hearing parents and their deaf children. Although the hearing parents talk to and in front of the child, they can only guess at his level of understanding . . . We have laid the special difficulties of the deaf child to the fact that he does not hear the emotionality transmitted by sound, that he does not learn verbal language at the optimal times, and that the presence of his handicap is the starting point of a vicious circle of maladaptive influences, as parental reaction influences him, and his responses in behavior evoke further concerns.[247]

Such a child's prospects are certainly less than optimal, and would encourage every precaution in nurturing and instilling internal resources. In a world where people frequently feel over-extended and inadequate to fulfill their responsibilities, however, offering what might be perceived as "extra" care may not seem probable.

Referencing specific populations of deaf people in terms of their vulnerability to alcoholism may help to avoid blanket generalizations and absurd characterizations, and provide selection criteria for the most vulnerable people, when limited resource allocation of treatment funds and facilities are also relevant.

Finally, regarding the hodge-podge of theories, explanations and interpretations of the available research results, let us introduce the *slot-machine theory,* offered by Kinney and Leaton. To become an alcoholic, using the analogy of this theory, one must receive the equivalent of three "cherries" in life. Some individuals may be born with physiological predisposers or tendencies toward physical problems which would constitute one cherry. The environmental and cultural interactions he experiences may provide a second cherry. The personality, with its unique interactions with the first two areas, may be the third cherry. Any one "cherry" (major drain on one's resources) may become interwoven with another. With the presence of three major forces contributing to the drain on one's resources, alcoholism or drug addiction is most

---

[247] Kenneth Z. Altshuler, M.D. "The Social and Psychological Development of the Deaf Child: Problems, their Treatment and Prevention," in <u>Social and Psychological Development.</u> 119 (4) august 1974, pp. 365-376, at p. 374.

probable, although not inevitable. The combination of two major forces (cherries) may constitute a sufficient drain on the individual's resources and self-esteem to pull him into alcoholism. One lone cherry, e.g. deafness, is not in and of itself an accurate predictor of who becomes alcoholic.[248]

We have not seen conclusive evidence that deafness, per se induces alcoholism. Deaf people, however, due to cultural factors such as isolation may not have acquired adequate preventive information regarding the dangers of alcoholism. People are, across other variables, all vulnerable to addiction to alcohol or other substances. The very real dangers of alcoholism can threaten anyone, and research literature, cited in this chapter, offers a number of insights which might serve us: 1) Despite much and varied research on alcoholism, we still do not understand all of the medical and neurological implications of what research has shown in the process of alcohol addiction and degeneration. We do not even know if the disease finds access to its assorted victims in the same physiological way consistently or if a variety of paths, weak links, and/or inter-related factors are involved, with personalized fitting to the individual occurring in the process of degeneration. Thus, open-minded continuing examination of all facts available is essential. 2) Certain characteristics of people have been identified which may be either (or both) predisposing and/or resulting from alcoholism, and among these characteristics and sociological situations, a number of close parallels can be seen in certain deaf people. 3) The disease of alcoholism is so destructive that concerns about possible vulnerability may overshadow more usual concerns and urge us to err on the side of caution and early intervention. And, 4) Showing a correlation is not demonstrating a cause and effect

---

[248] Kinney and Leaton (ibid.) p. 78.

relationship. Even if the characteristics of alcoholics and deaf people matched perfectly, some outside "cause" could be operative; both phenomenon could be effects, symptoms, or coincidental events.

Regardless of the fact that stereotypes about groups of people die hard, they do ultimately yield to honest examination of the facts. So, as hearing and deaf people together endeavor to perceive each other respectfully and to identify the various needs of our shared world with clarity, it is hoped that factors such as mis-diagnosis, the halo effect or its converse and labeling-to-avoid-encountering are likely to decrease. Then, it is hoped, such destroyers of people as alcoholism and substance abuse may be straight-forwardly addressed, remediated and ultimately prevented from ensnaring people.

CHAPTER IV

SUBSTANCE ABUSE AND DEAF PEOPLE

This chapter will review the literature regarding substance abuse as it relates to the deaf population of the United States. We will survey 1) basic information, such as names (some brand and some generic) and classifications of assorted drugs, controlled substances and chemicals under discussion; 2) differentiation of psychological dependence, habituation and physical addiction; 3) assorted physical effects of various drugs, both individually and in combination, synergistically; 4) estimates of incidence and prevalence of substance abuse, including substance abuse among deaf people; 5) various hypotheses regarding the etiology of drug abuse; 6) research regarding any predisposing factors involved in addiction; 7) characteristics of addicts and of addiction, with special implications for deaf people; 8) prognosis of substance-abuse prevention and treatment among the deaf population and 9) literature summaries and opinion regarding prerequisites of effective drug treatment.

Classification and Identification of Terms:

Within the realm of drugs and chemical substances commonly abused, there are three broad classifications: They are 1) stimulants, 2) hallucinogens, and 3) depressants. Stimulants (also commonly called *uppers* and *speed*) are common and include both prescription and non-prescription drugs. Some are legal and ubiquitous, such as coffee, others are illegal and less common; some are controlled substances, i.e. legal with strings attached. Common stimulants are caffeine, amphetamines (and similar chemicals such as MDA, DMT, MMDA, DCM, and PMA), cocaine and crack.[249]

Hallucinogens are commonly referred to as psychedelic substances. LSD is the drug most people think of when hallucinogens are mentioned, yet psychedelic mushrooms, peyote, mescaline and other hallucinogens proliferate. The most dangerous hallucinogen is PCP, used either singly or dusted into other drugs.[250]

Depressants are also commonly abused. There are many, many depressant drugs, including tranquilizers, sleeping pills, narcotics and alcohol. Barbiturates include such well known names as Phenobarbital, Seconal, Nembutal, and *reds* and *yellow jackets*. Narcotics include such major destroyers as heroin, morphine, opium and codeine. Pain killers in prescription form, e.g. Darvon, are also depressants. Even such things as airplane glue fumes, fingernail polish remover, hair spray, gasoline, shoe polish, charcoal starter and paint thinner, however, have been abused, and these also fall into the category of depressants.[251] Alcohol, of course, is a depressant, as has been discussed in the preceding chapter.

Adding to the confusion, many drugs are better known by their *street* names than by their chemical or brand names. Catherine O'Neill (1988) notes that there are hundreds of slang terms for drugs—e.g. snow, horse, witch,

---

[249] J. Woodward; Signs of Drug Use; silver Spring, MD.; T.J. Publishers; 1980. p. 3.

[250] Linda Cherry. "The Good Life: A Smart Choice" prepared by the Bay Area Project on Disabilities and Chemical Dependency. Institute on Alcohol, Drugs & Disability. 1988. p.3.

[251] Ibid. p. 4.

blue dots, angel dust and weepies.[252] The National Institute on Drug Abuse reports that marijuana, alone, has more than 150 *street* names, and cocaine is known by over 100 different appellations.[253]

We shall use the term *drug* to include alcohol, medicines and other chemical and naturally occurring substances which affect human beings by changing the way they think, act and feel. *Addiction* is defined as resistance to efforts to control usage, and is characterized by 1) compulsive, 2) repetitive use, in spite of adverse effects. In a treatment-book designed for reading-limited clients, the Addiction Intervention with the Disabled Agency asks the question, "What are drugs?" and offers these guidelines for a definition: 1) People take drugs to change the way they feel; 2) Drug abuse is using medicine when you are not sick; and 3) Taking more medicine than is directed on the bottle is drug abuse.[254]

Psychoactive and psychotropic drugs, uniquely, affect the brain directly, altering blood chemistry to affect sensation, perception and the neurotransmitters, themselves; these are usually prescription drugs. Stimulants, such as amphetamines, include such brand names as Ritalin, Preludin, Dexedrine, Benzedrex and Voranil. Anti-depressants include such brand names as Elavil and Tofranil.

---

[252] Catherine O'Neill. "Slang and Reality" in the Health tabloid of The Washington Post. December 27, 1988. p. 21.

[253] National Institute on Drug Abuse handout: staff information sheet. n.d.

[254] Patricia Callahan, & Alexander Boros. Looking at The Treatment for Alcoholism; A.I.D.; Kent State Univ. Press; Kent, OH. 1988. pages unnumbered.

Antipsychotics include the entire family of phenothiazines–e.g. Thorazine and Stellazine, and as well as such pharmeceutically complicated drugs as Haldol.

Tranquilizers include everything from the classic Miltown, Librium and Valium to Xanax, Atarax and Inderal. Sedative hypnotics, i.e. sleeping pills, are primarily barbiturates, e.g. Tuinal, Seconal and Mebaral. Non-barbiturate sedatives include such much abused drugs as Quaaludes.[255]

Regarding the more commonly abused drugs, marijuana is a weed-drug, derived from dried hemp leaves and flowers. The narcotic is commonly smoked, but may be used other ways also.

Cocaine is considered by the government to be a drug with small recognized medical value and much potential for abuse. Cocaine comes from the coca plant. Its botanical name is *erythroxylum coca*, and it grows in the Andes Mountains of South and Central America. The history of cocaine use is a colorful story, but it is sufficient here to note that the drug was cited in 1906 by the FDA to have significant problems attendant with its use, and it became a controlled substance in the U.S. Cocaine is consumed any/all of three ways: it can be sniffed, smoked or injected. Smoking and injecting the drug cause the most rapid absorption into the bloodstream and, thus, to the brain.[256]

Heroin comes from opium, as do morphine and codeine. These narcotic drugs are prepared from the juice of the

[255] Essie Lee. Breaking the Connection: How Young People Achieve Drug Free Lives. N.Y.; Julian Messner Publ.; 1988. pp. 173-185.

[256] Mark Gold. The Facts about Drugs and Alcohol.; N.Y.; Bantam Books. 1987. pp. 29035.

unripe seed capsules of the opium poppy, which contains a number of alkaloids.[257]

<u>Differentiation between Psychological Dependency and Chemical Addiction:</u>

Between psychological dependence and physical addiction a differentiation is often made. Diagnostic discrimination is gradually being refined into terminology which may reflect such distinctions. Kinney and Leaton (1983), identify a substance-abuse disorder category. They note, "In general, the feature that distinguishes abuse from dependence for this group is the presence of demonstrated tolerance and withdrawal syndromes with the latter."[258] They admit that the medical profession is not satisfied with the diagnostic criteria, but they believe that the variables proffered are definitely pointed in the right direction. Certainly, chemical analysis of someone physically addicted will show more of the drug in the bloodstream than would analysis of someone using the drug for the first time. However, that is not the only criterion; the lines are not clearly drawn, since even first-time use of some substances alters brain cells. At this point in drug research, the terms are used not so much for qualitative demarcation as to identify incremental, quantitative degrees in the addictive process.

The term *habituation*, additionally, is sometimes used to refer to primary stages of addiction, but many writers and

---

[257] Noah Webster <u>New World Dictionary of the American Language: College Edition.</u> Cleveland, OH. The World Publishing Co. 1964. "heroin" & "opium" entries.

[258] Jean Kinney, and Gwen Leaton. <u>Loosening the Grip: A Handbook of Alcohol Information.</u> 2nd ed. St. Louis, MO.; The C.V. Mosby Company. 1983. p. 254.

therapists use all these terms interchangeably. Marijuana is often cited as a drug which creates a psychological dependency, but which may not be shown to be chemically addictive.[259] The usual trend of marijuana usage is: tolerance, dependence, and then the inability to stop using the drug. Semantic precision would discriminate between this trend and the addictive pattern of other drugs, but to the lay-person, the processes are indistinguishable.

Physical Effects of Drug Abuse:

Each type of drug affects users in identifiable, deleterious ways. Rather than include precise medical terminology, since there are so many drugs under consideration, we shall generalize regarding the main effects noted in the literature of the commonly abused chemicals. Stimulants accelerate the heart's rate of pumping and increase the load on the lungs. They interfere with normal physiological signaling of the body to the brain, e.g. hunger pangs, fatigue and sleepiness are more easily ignored, and they cause sensitivity to certain kinds of pain to significantly decrease.[260]

Hallucinogens affect cortex processes and alternately speed and retard metabolic processes. The most dangerous hallucinogen, PCP (commonly called *angel dust*) is often fatal because it inhibits pain sensitivity, distorting people's awareness. e.g. under the influence of PCP, individuals may think they can fly or breathe under water.[261]

Depressants are often called *downers*, because they decelerate brain function significantly, and the CNS, in

---

[259] Mark Gold. ibid. p. 59.
[260] Linda Cherry. ibid. p. 2.
[261] ibid. p. 3.

turn, slows down other body processes.[262] Depressants also include tranquilizers and the sedative hypnotics.

Even singly, these powerful drugs can destroy people; in combination, they are often lethal. People taking one prescription drug, e.g. for pain, and another for another problem, e.g. sleeplessness, may be unaware of the various aspects of their medicines which act synergistically. Often families and loved ones find themselves woefully surprised when the combined effects of depressants nearly claim the lives of the drug user.

Some research has been completed regarding the brain centers which are affected by various drugs, especially psychotropic drugs. Regarding the various methods drugs attack the brain, Larry Thompson writes:

> Drugs reach the brain most quickly when smoked. The path is the most direct and drug concentrations are highest:
> 1. From the mouth, drug passes down the trachea to the lungs.
> 2. Drug quickly saturates the huge surface area of the lungs.
> 3. Highly concentrated drug speeds directly to the heart.
> 4. Major arteries leave the left side of the heart and proceed directly to the brain.
> This entire process takes about eight seconds.[263]

---

[262] ibid. p. 4.

[263] Larry Thompson. "How Drugs Attack the Brain" in Health, a magazine insert in The Washington Post. December 27, 1988. pp. 12-14.

Drugs such as cocaine work directly on the brain's *pleasure centers*, which are chemical systems within the brain. The key chemical messenger which transmits stimulation impulses in the brain is dopamine. One nerve ordinarily *signals* another nerve by squirting a chemical, such as a neurotransmitter like dopamine, into the space between the two nerves. Then *up-take pumps*, in the membranes of the sending nerve cell, suck the chemical back out of the space, recycling the dopamine. If dopamine isn't vacuumed again and is left remaining in the space between the nerves, the receiving nerve is continuously stimulated.

When cocaine enters the body, it blocks the *up-take pump* from reclaiming dopamine, which keeps the receiving nerve stimulated until both the sending and receiving nerves are exhausted. Over time, larger and larger amounts of cocaine are needed to give the stimulated feeling, and, in the process, the body's CNS is severely damaged. both nerve receptors, on the receiving end, and initiators, or senders, deteriorate. Other drugs may follow slightly different neurological paths, but achieve the same consequences. Cocaine and morphine, e.g., although quite different chemically, have both been found to "turn off the cortex," an area of the brain controlling consciousness, so it becomes evident that much remains to be explained in the area of chemical reactions and CNS interactions.[264]

In addition to understanding physiological processes, particularly in the intra-cranial area, with ancillary ramifications of such things as variations from the usual blood circulation patterns upon the brain, an understanding of the various powerful ways drugs affect the body carries some urgency. "Despite progress in understanding the

---

[264] ibid. p. 14.

biochemistry of addiction, researchers remain a long way from linking the effects of different drugs on specific nerves to the behaviors they see in the addicts," says Larry Thompson.[265]

Drug abuse has been cited in malfunction of all the body's vital organs. Research has concentrated mostly upon the brain, heart and cardiovascular system, but all vital organs, including the liver and pancreas also show diminished function after heavy drug usage. Even the skin (the largest human organ) shows dramatic evidence of damage by chronic drug abuse. Mark Gold notes that chronic abuse of cocaine also results in a variety of other physical problems. These include: stress, high blood pressure, possible damage to the body's auto-immune system, dental problems, malnutrition, throat and larynx problems, diminished drive and ambition, heightened paranoid tendencies, reduced appetite and diminished sexual drive.[266]

(See Table III regarding drug classification and common effects.)

---

[265] ibid. p. 14.
[266] Mark Gold. 800-Cocaine. N.Y.; Bantam Books. 1984. p. 34.

Table III

Names, Classifications and Primary Effects
of Commonly Abused Drugs

TYPE OF DRUG	COMMON EFFECTS

Stimulants:

amphetamines	* Stimulate and over-
anti-depressants	stimulate the heart and
anti-psychotics	brain.
mood elevators	* Overload lungs, pancreas,
caffeine	liver and other organs
cocaine	with demand for
crack	speedier functioning.
MDA, BMT, MMDA, DCM,	* Damage / cause
PMA, etc.	deterioration of
	specific tissues, e.g.
	nose membranes.
	* Decrease sensitivity to
	sensation, e.g.
	diminishes appetite,
	lowers awareness
	of fatigue, pain, and
	nausea.
	* May cause psychotic
	episodes.

Depressants:

sedative hypnotics	* Decelerate brain
pain-killers	function.
narcotics, e.g.	

codeine, morphine, & heroin barbituates household substances, e.g. glue marijuana alcohol	* Retard metabolic functions. * Damage organs. * Cause severe withdrawal symptoms, including possible psychosis.

Hallucinogenics:

LSD psilocybin (magic mushrooms) peyote angel dust	* Distorts sensory input. * May intensify psychotic tendencies. * Contributes to panic neuroses.

All Table III information is taken from: Mark Gold's The Facts about Drugs & Alcohol and Essie E. Lee's Breaking the Connection: How Young People Achieve Drug Free Lives.

Estimates of Incidence and Prevalence of Drug Abuse:

It has been estimated that there are millions of people in the United States addicted to something–alcohol, chemical substances or even unhealthy relationships. Experts are naturally reluctant to offer precise estimates, since certain particulars of the scant data available are confidential rather than publicized, e.g. since use of some drugs is illegal, people are not forthcoming about the use of those drugs. Information on drug use often relates to prevalence, rather than incidence, and it usually comes from treatment center populations, thus a certain percentage of recidivism must be taken into consideration. Individuals who do not come to the attention of the law and/or medical treatment units are also not included in those estimates. Mark Gold (1987) states that each year more people die from prescription drugs, which may have been obtained legally, but used improperly, than from all illegal substances combined.[267] Most treatment therapists will venture generalizations, with caveats, as did Rosenthal (1988).

Although there have been positive changes in drug use by American adolescents–fewer youngsters, for example, now smoke marijuana–overall drug use by teenagers remains extremely high, the highest of any industrialized nation. Moreover, youthful drug abuse has become more life-threatening. Use of cocaine stands at record levels, and the number of frequent users has been increasing.[268]

---

[267] Mark Gold. The Facts about Drugs & Alcohol. Ibid. p. 2.

[268] Mitchell Rosenthal, in Essie Lee's Breaking the Connection: How Young People Achieve Drug Free Lives. p. ix.

We do not know the extent of substance abuse among deaf people, for several reasons. 1) Professionals in the substance-abuse field are not, routinely, alert for signs of hearing impairment, and may not recognize or diagnose it accurately. 2) Deaf people with substance-abuse problems may not seek help because, a) they do not recognize that they need help, b) they fear the stigma substance abuse might carry, c) difficulties such as distance and expense seem prohibitive, and d) they have had frustrating experiences in their previous attempts to gain help from the mainstream society. 3) Limited reporting systems also may undermine attempts to estimate substance abuse among deaf people.

By extrapolation of statistics provided by the U.S. Census Bureau, NIAAA and the National Institute of Drug Abuse, Miller & Cisin (1979) and Zinberg (1980), suggest that there may be 73,000 deaf alcoholics, 3,500 deaf heroin users, 14,700 deaf cocaine users, and some 110,000 deaf people who regularly use marijuana.[269]

Mark Gold (1984) states that some 25 million Americans report having used cocaine at least once.[270] Other researchers, such as Thomas Dixon, also report significant incidence of drug use among the deaf.

In 1989, the California attorney General's Commission on Disability issued a report stating, "There are reliable estimates on the incidence of alcohol and drug abuse among people with disabilities; indications are that it is at least

---

[269] J.D. Miller, & I.H. Cisin, Highlights from the National Survey on Drug Abuse: 1979. Rockville, MD. NIDA print-out. 1980. p. 1.

[270] Mark Gold. ibid. p. 2.

double that of non-disabled people."[271] Laura-Lynne Powell (1992) estimates that at least 35% of deaf and hard-of-hearing people are substance abusers.[272]

In addition to the prevalence of people abusing one specific drug, there are a number of people who abuse drugs indiscriminately and/or in combination. Polydrug use includes simultaneous use of different drugs and also sequential use of assorted drugs. Kinney and Leaton note that different patterns of multiple drug use might be identified. One they discuss in detail involves naive *recreational fruit-salad*, in which teenagers, e.g. attending a party, would each bring and contribute whatever pills could be gleaned from the family's medicine cabinet. In a sort of chemical roulette, the bowl would be passed around, and each person would take a handful of pills, indiscriminately, to *turn-on* for the evening. This practice became known to the larger society as more and more teenage party-attendees wound up as victims in emergency rooms, having ingested unknown drugs with unknown effects in unknown quantities.[273]

Sometimes, just as one disorder can mask another, and make diagnosis difficult, one substance abuse can cover another and shield it from scrutiny. In their book, *Dual Disorders: Counseling Clients with Chemical Dependency and Mental Illness,* Daley, Moss and Campbell state, "Possibly 70% of hospitalized alcoholics have experienced one or more episodes of another substance abuse or

---

[271] Linda Cherry. CommPre: Alcohol, Drugs & Disability: 5 Case Studies. ibid. p. 6.

[272] Laura-Lynne Powell. "Deaf advocates call substance abuse programs" in Silent News. July, 1992. p. 1.

[273] Kinney & Leaton, (Ibid). p. 262.

psychiatric diagnosis in their lifetimes."[274] Certain drugs, e.g. marijuana and tobacco, also are reputed to have a *gateway effect*, leading toward the use of more dangerous, life-threatening drugs.[275] In 1990, the New York Times carried a front-page alert regarding the growing incidence of multi-drug users who have no idea of the ways the various drugs combine, exacerbate each other's effects, or act synergistically. The trend of cocaine users to expand to crack and then to heroin, especially was noted as an alarming and dangerous trend.[276]

Another form of polydrug abuse revolves around sequential, rather than simultaneous use. Often, for people abusing drugs in this manner, the aim is not to get high, but merely to cope. People under a great deal of stress but with access to ameliorative prescription drugs may get into the habit of taking stimulants, such as amphetamines, in the morning, to "get going," then other drugs throughout the day, e.g. to counteract fatigue, and sleeping pills to help them sleep at night. Using chemical assistance to operate at super-human achievement or proficiency levels, however, carries a high physical price tag, and drains emotional capacities as well.

---

[274] Daley, Moss & Campbell. Dual Disorders: Counseling Clients with Chemical Dependency & Mental Illness. quoted by Swan, Kristen in "Dual Disorders in Chemical Dependency Treatment." a publication of the Minnesota Chemical Dependency Program for Deaf and Hard of Hearing Individuals. August 1992. p. 1.

[275] Gold. ibid. p. 60.

[276] Joseph B. Treaster. "Cocaine Users Adding Heroin to their Menus. The New York Times. July, 21, 1990. p. 1.

The Etiology of Drug Abuse:

A number of researchers have pondered the *whys* of drug abuse. From hypotheses regarding inherent characteristics of certain people, to musings about social contagion and peer pressure, theories abound regarding why people get hooked on drugs.

Why, then, do people abuse drugs? There are many answers, depending on the type of drug, the type of population, and the life-circumstances of the abusers. Clearly the *getting high* phenomenon, which has been seen as analogous to joy-riding of the previous generation, but with more extreme consequences, can be seen as quite different in character and scope from the drug use of an elderly person who has gradually become deaf and grieves, inappropriately, by abusing prescription pain killers and sleeping aids. All drug abuse, however, can be construed attempts to escape from reality. Some drug abuse may be seen, additionally, as a misguided coping mechanism.

David LaChar, director of the Psychological Assessment Laboratory of the University of Texas Medical Sciences Institute in Houston says, "There isn't one personality associated with substance abuse, and there isn't one path that leads to substance abuse."[277] Indeed, there are many; anyone can be vulnerable. Addiction is multifaceted, and anyone who uses a drug can become addicted to it. The demographics of drug abuse are also fairly inclusive in terms of economic status, age, education level, and geographical region of the U.S.

---

[277] Sally Squires quoting David LaChar. "The Personality Factor." Health, a supplement of The Washington Post. December 27, 1988. p. 10.

Focusing on prevention of chemical abuse problems, Seppala (1977) posits several psychological theories, all of which have in common the factor of deficits in self-esteem and consequenting disturbances in personal functioning, as markers which may predispose people toward addiction. She says,

> Since 1966, research has suggested that the *causes* of chemical use problems are related to the lack of development of healthy personal functioning. Two significant research results suggest preliminary indications of a casual relationship between development of chemical use problems and deficiencies in personal functioning.[278]

She reviews and summarizes the work of Dr. Ardyth Norem-Hebeisen and Dr. Andrew Ahgren of the University of Minnesota, and also the research conducted by Drs. Cohen, White and Schoolar. These studies suggest that specific traits, such as autonomy and anxiety-free confidence are lacking in drug addicts. The backgrounds of subjects repeatedly revealed patterns of deprivation of parental intimacy. Self-esteem levels of these clients tested at far below average. They conclude that low self-esteem has led to, or has been associated with, the beginning of drug abuse with many people.[279]

People with hearing-impairment experience the same stresses and frustrations that people in the larger society do, and may experience additional ones related to difficulties of functioning in a hearing world. After

---

[278] Theresa A. Seppala. <u>A Primer on the Prevention of Chemical Use Problems.</u> Center City, MN. Hazelden Press; 1977. p. 5.
[279] ibid. p. 6.

enumerating disadvantages people with disabilities face in interacting with other people, the Resource Center on Substance Abuse Prevention and Disability says,

These stresses may predispose people with disabilities to choosing an escape through the use of alcohol or other drugs. Due to medical needs such as pain, spasticity, seizure control, or breathing difficulties, people with disabilities also have more ready access to prescription drugs. It is well documented that medical personnel, attendants, and family members sometimes enable the use and abuse of alcohol and other drugs by a person with a disability, to alleviate their own guilt, provide a perceived pleasurable diversion, or simply avoid conflict.[280]

The staff of the Resource Center point out that approximately 43 million Americans meet the Americans with Disabilities Act disability criteria, and that, although the specifics of their disabilities vary vastly, all of these 43 million people are at increased risk of developing chemical dependencies. In addition to the reasons why anyone might abuse drugs, additional reasons, related to their disability, are relevant. Some of these additional factors include: decreased tolerance for mind-altering drugs (due to the probability of taking medication regularly), atypical childhood experiences leaving a lack of shared cultural values with people in mainstream society, lower resistance

---

[280] Resource Center on Substance Abuse Prevention & Disability. An Overview of Alcohol and Other Drug Abuse Prevention and Disability. Washington, D.C.; Information packet prepared by the Resource Center on Substance Abuse Prevention & Disability. 1992.

to peer pressure (since their peer groups may be different from those of the larger society), overprotection by family members and usual caretakers, and long-term use of medications, (which may encourage a casual attitude about taking drugs or offer the possibility of stock-piling drugs). Increased frustrations due to miscommunication or inadequate communication, stresses on family life, fewer social supports, and even such things as excess free time were all listed as contributory factors which place disabled persons at higher than average risk in developing drug dependence.[281]

The September / October 1992 issue of *Prevention Pipeline* carried a staff-written review of treatment focus on substance abusers with assorted hearing impairments. They note that for deaf people, access to information and education about alcohol and drug dependency and relevant treatment programs is inadequate. The authors state, "The nature of deafness tends to isolate affected individuals from the general community, further compounding the problems of alcohol and other drug abuse and domestic violence."[282] Because such ideas may not have been directly addressed, preventively, some deaf people may not realize the great difference which exists between taking medication and in using alcohol or other drugs to deal with emotions and difficult situations.

---

[281] ibid. p. 1.

[282] "Breaking the Silence" About AOD Abuse and Domestic Violence in the Deaf Community." Conference report in Prevention Pipeline. 5 (5) September/October 1992. p. 30.

Possible Pre-Disposing Factors Toward Dependency:

Some scholars have speculated about a general proclivity toward addiction, including possible genetic predisposition, and others have outlined hypotheses regarding a non-specific substance abuse pre-disposing personality profile. Research, at this point, is not definitive, but some encouragement is given to the view that there may be a slight genetic factor in addiction. Goleman (1990) hypothesized certain chemical imbalances which may pre-dispose some people toward addiction, writing,

> Researchers are beginning to identify the particular imbalances associated with addictions to particular drugs like cocaine, heroin or alcohol. Because scientists believe many of these imbalances are inherited, they are seeking to identify genetic markers and other evidence, such as behavioral signs that indicate a person is vulnerable.[283]

Of course, identifying brain lesions in drug addicts does not imply these lesions preceded drug addiction. Since drug abuse itself causes and contributes to brain lesions, no assumptions may be made regarding significant genetic predilection from such scant evidence. With more modern technology, future research may yield further information.

---

[283] Daniel Goleman. "Scientists Pinpoint Brain Irregularities in Drug Addicts." in The New York Times. June, 26, 1990. p. C1.

<u>Characteristics of Drug Addicts and of Addiction, with
Implications for Deaf People</u>:

As we observed in our survey of the emotional
characteristics of alcoholics, cause and effect are hard to
separate, since they often form a circle; thus it may be
impossible to assert, e.g. that people with poor impulse
control are at greater risk of abusing drugs than are people
with average impulse control. We can note that poor
impulse control is evident, progressively, in substance
abusers, but we can not at this point deduce or separate
original causes from their cyclical effects. Denial, blaming
others for one's circumstances, and rationalization also are
typically noted as characteristics of drug addicts, including
alcoholics. But whether it is the case that people who are
likely to reveal such traits (denial, blaming others and
rationalization), are the ones most likely to also turn to
drugs, or whether chronic drug abuse creates these
personality traits has not been adequately addressed. Most
psychotherapists and long-term observers of people who
abuse drugs, maintain that each end of the equation
exacerbates the other. Thus a circle is created, whereby
certain personality traits "feed" drug abuse, and, in turn,
drug abuse flattens a colorful, variegated personality into a
diminished profile that only allows those personality
characteristics to thrive which maintain drug dependency.

Several adult children of alcoholics and drug addicts
have written compellingly regarding the emotional climate
in a home torn by chronic substance abuse. Jim Trotter
says that growing up in such a home urges the children to
learn how to avoid conflict, at all costs. He notes that
family members of the alcoholic or drug abuser strive so
hard, in trying to ward off the despair which surrounds
them that they develop a reactive weakness in their frantic

159

desire to try to please everyone.[284] Such overly-placating behavior stems, inferentially, from the escalating excesses of the family member abusing drugs or alcohol. along with the classic symptom of denial, the characteristics of widely swinging moods (alternating from grandiosity, megalomania and euphoria to deep depression) and of increasingly-demanding interactive behavior are noted consistently by researchers and casual observers alike, as traits of substance abusers.

Mark Gold compiled a profile of the typical cocaine user, after counseling some 100,000 callers to his 1-800-Cocaine hotline. He identified certain commonalties, both demographically and psychologically. Five hundred chronic cocaine users, chosen at random from among the first one hundred thousand people calling the hotline, were surveyed to yield this information. In close-up, these 500 people averaged age 30, with most of them between ages 25-40. The age range, however was from 18 to 78. They averaged about five years of chronic cocaine use. About 1/3 of this 500 were female. Some 85% of these 500 were Caucasian. They were overwhelmingly highly educated and economically somewhat above middle-class. Almost 2/3 of these 500 callers resided in New York, New Jersey, California or Florida.[285]

Despite a number of physical health problems these people had experienced, connected to their cocaine use, nearly all of these people reported that economic considerations were the primary limiting factors in their drug use. Even though they had experienced adverse

---

[284] Jim Trotter. "The Fatal Pursuit of Happiness." in West a
    Sunday Supplement of the San Jose Mercury. San Jose, CA.
    February 28, 1993. pp. 18-20.
[285] Gold. 800-Cocaine. ibid. p. 9.

effects of cocaine, most of these 500 respondents reported that they continued to use the drug. When the *high* wore off, some 80% of them said they felt severely depressed and fatigued, and approximately 70% reported using alcohol, heroin or other drugs, also, in attempts to re-gain the feelings of euphoria they desired. These respondents reported physical side-effects such as insomnia, chronic fatigue, severe headache, nasal problems and poor or decreased sexual performance. Significant numbers of these addicts additionally reported seizures, loss of consciousness and even such things as nausea and involuntary vomiting.

In the psychological realm, an ever narrowing, mutually-reinforcing, cycle of cause and effect pattern of flattening personality traits is also visible. More than 80% of these addicts admitted to experiencing psychological problems including: severe depression, chronic anxiety, increased irritability, paranoia, and loss of interest in other things (besides drugs), difficulties in concentration and comprehension. Some 53% of these people said they had gotten so desperate and low they had seriously considered suicide as a way out of their difficulties.[286]

Psychological profiles of marijuana users, stereotypically include such descriptors as: un-ambitious, lethargic, deficient incomprehension, paranoid tendencies and showing diminished interest in activities other than taking drugs; presenting a consistent picture of the crumbling ego. By contrast, the novice cocaine user is often achievement-driven. But even though marijuana users typically have not been noted for productivity, and cocaine users have, progressive, chronic use of either drug leads to the semblance of similarity of presenting problems, a narrowing

---

[286] ibid. pp. 10-11.

and extinguishing of perceivable personality traits, so that after a period of time the personality, regardless of the drug used, is muted and the person's emotional affect is flat. With chronic abuse, Mr. Gold says, this trend progresses so that ultimately the control of the drug makes disinterest in things, other than taking drugs, become the most visible characteristic of abusers of either drug.

In terms of identifying personality characteristics of substance abusers, this phenomenon would seem worthy of at least cursory attention, as it may help to explain the multi-drug use and sequential drug use, cited earlier in this chapter. An increasing number of therapists are calling attention to the phenomenon of substitute addictions. When one addiction is dissolved, another frequently takes its place. This implies that some fundamental, underlying lack remains which has not been perceived or treated.

Regarding this phenomenon, Kavanaugh (1992) says:

Substitute addictions develop when only one expression of the addictive energy is addressed, because hidden feelings only manifest as another addiction. I have seen this frequently at 12-Step meetings where members report attendance at several different 12-Step groups simultaneously-attending one group for alcohol abuse, another for cocaine, another for codependency, etc. Their addictions move sideways, and the addictive energy that has its source in dysfunctional beliefs continues to be expressed in unhealthy ways.[287]

---

[287] Philip Kavanaugh. Magnificent Addiction: Discovering Addiction as Gateway to Healing. Lower Lake, CA.; Aslan Publishing Co.; 1992. p. 134.

This theory is quite consistent with thoughts, previously introduced, of researchers hypothesizing a lack of self-esteem, a deficiency in the emotional area, as the common factor which might predispose a person to abuse substances. Contributing to poor self-esteem, of course, may be a multitude of life experiences which have in common the clue or suspicion, upon reflection, that one is valueless, or that one handles most situations inadequately or improperly. When piled upon each other, multiple condemning messages reinforce the self-labeling of inadequacy or even *badness*. Researchers, educators, and psychotherapists almost universally point to such experiential factors in the developing psyche to explain personality disorders, including alcoholism and drug addiction, which are characterized by a poor self-image. Improving the self-image is, thus, seen to be the number one task of psychotherapy, both remedially and preventively, and this is relevant, as we shall demonstrate, in the area of substance abuse among deaf people.

Research regarding deaf people, as we have repeatedly seen, cumulatively notes that deaf people are as much, if not more, at risk in these psychological areas as are people in the larger society. Such factors as isolation, frustration, social stigma and inadequate education contribute to this increased risk of deaf people.

Elaine Walker reports that for some deaf people, using drugs may be a way to feel more a part of the hearing world. She speaks of the need to belong to the greater society, felt by deaf people, as a pull toward antisocial behavior. One deaf person she cited believed that buying friends with drugs would prevent others from rejecting him because of his deafness. Of course, such rationalizations don't affect the reality of the situation that the person hoping to buy acceptance has actually become drug dependent and is no longer able to function or plan his life objectively.[288]

Whether or not the type of incident Ms. Walker reports is typical, there are additional burdens felt by the deaf, which have been explicated in a previous chapter, which may put them at additional risk of drug addiction. Communication difficulties and frustrations in dealing with the hearing world are seen by many researchers as primary areas of vulnerability for deaf people, inducing some of them to fall prey to substance abuse. For a deaf person, trying to communicate with hearing people may be inexplicably and consistently frustrating and unsatisfying, inducing at least discouragement.

The National Information Center on Deafness information service states that more than 90% of parents of deaf children are hearing people with no previous contact with or knowledge of deafness.[289] The developmental years of these deaf children may be laden with frustrations, isolation, a sense of perhaps being unwanted and cumulative evidence of being unacceptable to the larger society.

Larry Stewart wrote very movingly of special needs and problems of deaf substance abusers. He noted that substance abusers with hearing loss constitute a cross-section of the general population, with the same traits as everyone else. "Their only common denominator is impairment of hearing and consequent loss of ability, in varying degrees in the communication area."[290]

---

[288] Elaine Walker. "After 20 years of addiction, deaf man finds sobriety, helps others." in Silent News. March 1993. p. 17.

[289] NICD "Educating Deaf Children: an Introduction." Gallaudet Univ. Wash., D.C.; 1986-87. p. 1.

[290] Larry Stewart. "Hearing Impaired Substance Abusers" Gallaudet Univ. Wash., D.C. n.d.

The impact of substance abuse on the emotional facilities of deaf people is not a pretty picture. Stewart identified four overlapping areas of damage:

1. Substance abuse further complicates the deaf person's adjustment in all areas of life. Personal, family, work, social, and other relationships are jeopardized. The social isolation of the deaf person in the community is increased, particularly when his status as a substance abuser becomes known in the deaf community. Severe loneliness is a result, which increases the need for resort to substance use.

2. The inability to function in a variety of areas has an input on the deaf person's economic self-sufficiency. The need to buy substances may force the deaf individual into criminal activities, which in turn eventually lead to involvement with law enforcement and all the problems that brings.

3. The loss of coping skills attending substance abuse in leading the deaf person to unemployment, also quite often results in the individual becoming reliant upon public assistance. This becomes an added burden to society and further erodes the deaf person's confidence and motivation for rehabilitation.

4. The problems brought to a deaf person by substance abuse inexorably lead toward mental health problems, the breakdown of the family, and dependency.[291]

---

[291] ibid. p. 5.

Therefore, with such massive and debilitating problems being established as associated with substance abuse among the deaf, addressing problems of vulnerability to substance abuse among deaf people, via education and adequate treatment programs is substantially overdue.

Prognosis of Substance Abuse Prevention and Treatment for Deaf People:

At present, prevention, via education is just beginning to be recognized as needed, and has not made significant inroads to reach clients who most need the information. If low self-esteem is seen to increase vulnerability to drug abuse, reaching pockets of society in which self-esteem is at risk would certainly be an obvious preventive aid. Yet, lack of personnel, inadequate funds, resistance within the deaf community and other factors have kept this and other such steps from being taken. Clearly, when demand consistently exceeds supply of drugs, one entire area of access to remediation of social ill is being inadequately utilized. The following chapter elaborates on prevention guidelines, as well as citing effective program efforts for creating a drug-free society.

At present, it is much easier to get drugs than it is to get treatment for drug abuse. And even if treatment is available, there is no certainty that treatment will cure addiction. Dennis Moore (1992) reflects on the total picture for therapists regarding the hazards of working with substance abuse people who have other disabilities. He notes that the act of labeling a person *handicapped* or *disabled* leads people to focus on that label rather than other salient factors, and often makes diagnosis and implementation of treatment difficult. He also cautions therapists about problems of substance abuse after therapy.

"Even among patients with no previous history of substance abuse, the chances of abuse appear to increase following rehabilitation."[292] The person apparently becomes habituated to ingesting or injecting a substance in his/her body, as a first-choice method of dealing with a difficult situation. High-profile advertising of over-the-counter drugs adds to this trend.

Some communities of deaf people still deny the need for drug and alcohol abuse information. The Resource Center on Substance Abuse Prevention and Disability summarizes the research of Boros (1981) and others and suggests that one reason deaf communities have resisted dealing with the problem of addiction is that deaf people have long labored under social stigma, due to being perceived as different, and they see admission of problems with substance abuse as constituting another negative label, which would further isolate them from mainstream society.[293]

Therapists and drug treatment centers are uniformly overwhelmed and inadequate; the need for help far surpasses help available. Still, progress is being made. Successful treatment of addiction may seem incremental and may take diverse forms, but the treatment programs surveyed have in common certain features. Among these features are: detox or withdrawal from the addictive substance, restoring a perception of the ideal (what could be) for the person, building hope and providing assistance in developing alternative living patterns and habits. Hitting bottom, after years of denial, and admitting the

---

[292] Dennis Moore. "Substance Abuse Assessment and Diagnosis in Medical Rehabilitation." in NeuroRehabilitation. 2 (1) 1992. p. 7-13, at p. 7.

[293] Resource Center on Substance Abuse Prevention & Disability "A Look at Alcohol and Other Drug Abuse Prevention and Deafness and Hearing Loss." Wash, D.C.; 1992.

need for help have been almost universally proclaimed as inherently necessary in order for help to proceed in the treatment of addiction. In each of these, as well as subsequent recovery steps, mutual communication is mandatory; a monologue from the helping professional is inadequate in that it may not elicit co-operative effort.

In order for successful treatment to occur, creating whatever is necessary for real encounter dialogue is the obvious second step, with full recognition that treatment is needed being the first step. In the case of deaf people, the language of meaningful dialogue in the U.S. will probably be ASL. In order for dialogue to exist between the person seeking help and the helping professional, certain basic ingredients are needed, to create and maintain at least a threshold of a therapeutic environment. Many therapists have written exhaustively about the therapeutic emotional climate, conducive to psychological healing and growth, and summarizing that vast body of literature is not the present task. But the variables identified as inherently therapeutic in interpersonal communication hover first around unconditional acceptance, which includes, among several other things, at least a respect for the humanity and instincts of the persons involved.

The person who is to receive the *help* is the ultimate judge of how helpful the proffered help actually is. Various features of the proffered treatment may be evaluated from the end of those receiving the treatment. With deaf and hard-of-hearing clients, ease of communication with the helping professionals is a basic need, not a luxury. This means that for deaf people, basics such as deaf therapists or therapists who are fluent in ASL, or at least consistently available, discreet, unobtrusive interpreters are prime requisites for therapy to begin.

Effective drug treatment must become individualized and open-ended, with the needs of the individual client dictating the personnel, strategies, methods and materials of therapy, if the effort expended is not to be wasted. Every therapeutic aid available should be considered, from immediate detoxification of the physical system to having telephones adapted so that deaf people may use them, from unending reassurance that the drug abuser has reason to hope for a better life, to presentation of clear information and offering of specific aids toward achieving a better life. All these things are clinically indicated, and all steps of the therapeutic process are interwoven tightly together, with some vacillating back and forth among the stages of progress.

After detoxification and stabilizing the physical system, establishing emotional rapport between the therapist and client is the next important step. Many approaches may be used in this effort.

Kavanaugh (1992) says:

> Emotional addictions are chronic disorders eventually producing symptoms that result from beliefs that we have learned in childhood. Once these chronic symptoms are adequately treated through a combined program of medication (when indicated), uncovering and desensitizing buried feelings, and addressing the beliefs underlying emotional addictions, our healing journeys can successfully continue.[294]

He advocates treating the whole person, rather than focusing solely on the particular addiction which is

---

[294] ibid. p. 134.

currently manifesting. Other therapists are likewise recognizing the practicality and long-range efficiency of such concerted approaches. Why treat one addiction only to treat its replacement later, if underlying needs haven't been met? Addressing the belief system which allowed the toxic condition power to control the person next becomes salient.

Many drug treatment centers now operate in the U.S., with a variety of results and recidivism rates. These treatment centers treat thousands of addicted people every month; periodically treatment personnel *burn out*, and periodically long-term planning is required to circumvent the problems, flaws, and patterns of ineffectuality which become visible. Out of these evaluation and re-evaluation sessions, real help may emerge.

In May, 1992, the first national conference was held to address such issues as the isolation of deaf people, their up-to-now inadequate educational/information disseminating facilities for such topics as substance abuse, and other elements which may pre-dispose deaf people toward substance abuse. This conference, held in Minneapolis, Minnesota, involved input from over 200 professional people who work with deaf people in drug treatment centers. Their concerted effort was called "Breaking the Silence," and it focused in-depth on these critical issues. Lectures and many specific workshops addressed strategies to overcome substance abuse among people with hearing impairments. Such professional conferences, including the *Next Step* Conference, held in Denver, CO, on July 5-8, 1992, are springing up nationwide, with enthusiastic, hopeful participation. Participants believe that such meetings of the minds of people in the helping professions, as occurs in these sessions, will aid the effort already in progress in the existing treatment centers, by clarifying special needs of the deaf population for such services, and by generating expertise, facilities and motivation to address these needs.[295]

Summary of Opinion Regarding Pre-Requisites for Effective Drug Treatment:

By analogy, curing the drug infestation in our society has been compared to going to war, i.e. the prevalence of phrases as the "war on drugs" show such a comparison. *Gearing up* to meet the challenge is now in progress; recognition that there is a problem is the first step in preparation. We can also see that drug use is, additionally, a business–a very profitable one for the sellers, with demand always available for the supply. Decreasing the demand via education may be the best preventive action. Because chemical abuse affects many facets of society, and deterioration of a system is interwoven in all interacting areas, treatment is necessarily complex and convoluted.

Certain elements of our society descry the lack of scientific exactness in the realm of substance abuse treatment programs, pointing to such handicapping factors as vagueness in terminology. e.g. The criteria for establishing "abuse" of a drug, as differentiated from "use" of a drug, such as with prescribed medicines, varies. In the realm of illicit drugs, however, any use whatever is officially considered abuse, per se. Refusal to get beyond preoccupation with trivia such as variation in dependency criteria, however, only translates, in consequence, into a delaying tactic and avoidance gesture; it does not address the larger problem. Gradually pragmatic definitions and

---

[295] "Breaking the Silence about AOD Abuse and Domestic Violence in the Deaf Community." Prevention Pipeline. 5 (5) September/October, 1992. p. 30.

therapeutic goals need to emerge, subsuming minor differences in favor of efficacy. Here, our perspective is prerequisite to drug treatment programs, considering infrasystems of society, suggesting the need for deeper reflections regarding the ways society as a whole continues to generate societal problems such as substance abuse.

Swan (1992) writes of the current trend of preferably treating the total person, when drug treatment is requested. She says that this ideal doesn't often happen, because of a limited number of professionals trained and experienced in both chemical dependency treatment and other needed psychological and psychiatric areas. She says:

> Within the deaf community we are currently in the pioneering stages of providing appropriate treatment for clients with hearing impairment. It is a big challenge to find people with expertise in deafness and train them in chemical dependency counseling and vice versa . . . This emphasizes the need for team approaches and consultation from other professionals since the availability of individuals with training in all three skills may be limited.[296]

[296] Kristen Swan. "Dual Disorders in Chemical Dependency Treatment." Steps to Recovery. Minnesota Chemical Dependency Program for Deaf and Hard of Hearing Individuals. August, 1992. p. 2.

[297] Mitchell Rosenthal. introduction to Essie E. Lee's Breaking the Connection. N.Y. Julian Messner 1988. p. x.

[298] Abigail Trafford "Beyond the Reach of Medicine." in Health, a Weekly supplement of The Washington Post. Dec. 27, 1988. p. 22.

In addition to creating or adapting adequate training programs, society, as a whole, must involve itself with the philosophical implications of the problem of substance abuse. Regarding society's apparent ambivalence and lack of clear demarcation in the area of chemical substance abuse, Rosenthal (1988) states that until society resolves some larger questions and adapts some higher standards about what constitutes a good life, what is entertaining, and what enhances health, we will not progress in ameliorating problems such as drug abuse:

What has handicapped efforts to confront drug abuse in this country has not been the lack of adequate treatment resources so much as ambivalent public attitudes. We have been unwilling to use all our muscle–informal sanctions as well as drug laws–to reduce demand for drugs. Rather, we have taken a narrow view of drug prevention, one that has allowed us to tolerate what misguidedly came to be considered "social" drug use.[297]

Responding to the hue and cry for drug treatment centers, Trafford (1988) is hopeful, but cautious. She cites statistics which show that only some 20% of drug addicts get any treatment at all. She applauds the increasing interest in treating drug abuse, however, she points out that drug abuse is not only a physical disease, but it reflects problems in other areas as well. We may spend millions of dollars on rehabilitation centers and still not faze the drug abuse problem, she notes. Realistic expectations of chemical dependency treatment should include recognition of, and help in, these other areas.[298]

These viewpoints are included, not in an attempt to be negative, but to present a more realistic, total picture. Charles R. Schuster, director of the NIDA said, "I am most concerned about the public feeling that we are capable of a quick fix. My fear is that because we are looking for a quick solution, any failure in that regard will lead to disillusionment."[299] With disillusion, comes lowered motivation toward subsequent effort. So, getting an accurate overview of the scope of the entire problem area first, may be disheartening, but it may preclude self-deception regarding the ease of addressing these issues and prevent later burn-out of staff and dropping out of clients from the remedial process.

At one rehabilitation clinic in Washington, D.C., a cocaine hotline has been available for some four years. Staff records show that of all the people who phone in asking for help, less than half will make an appointment, and of those, only one half will show up. Clinical psychologist Ronald Wynne, who runs the hotline says, "Anything is easier to deal with than with crack addicts. They make you feel so impotent."[300]

As people look beyond the allure of a *quick fix* in the realm of drug rehabilitation, and realize the enormity of the problem, certain parameters, basic principles and guidelines begin to emerge. Beyond being immobilized and overwhelmed, therapists now are taking hard, realistic looks at the magnitude of work to be done. Some are beginning to tackle the work at various access points within their expertise. We will next summarize and discuss these

---

[299] A. Trafford quoting Charles R. Schuste ibid. p. 22.

[300] Ronald Wynne. quoted in staff written article, "The Medical Side of the War on Drugs." in Health a weekly supplement of The Washington Post. Dec. 27, 1988. p. 5.

efforts. The next chapter shall focus on drug prevention and treatment programs, specifically those which are most accessible to deaf people.

CHAPTER V

PREVENTIVE AND TREATMENT EFFORTS

AND DEAF PEOPLE

In the two previous chapters, after surveying the problems of alcohol and drug abuse, respectively, we have gathered a few general principles and guidelines and noted some specific suggestions regarding what characteristics of treatment for alcoholism and substance abuse are most important and relevant for the deaf population of the United States. This chapter will: 1) examine current preventive efforts in the substance abuse field; 2) provide an overview of drug and alcoholism treatment programs in the United States 3) discuss specific centers, as they relate to and meet the needs of deaf and hard-of-hearing people; 4) consider additional criteria for effective prevention and treatment of substance abuse in deaf populations, and 5) offer the gleanings of prognostic implications available thus far in the area of substance abuse prevention and treatment for people who are deaf.

It may be seen that there is a qualitative difference in a small portion of the material surveyed for this chapter from that of previous chapters. Overview of literature in earlier chapters included substantial references to articles in professional journals, expert opinion from clinical experience, excerpts of conference proceedings, research studies and scholarly dissertations. While some of the studies may have been out-dated, not clearly representative in terms of population selection or size, or were liable to criticism for other methodological shortcomings, they nevertheless passed scrutiny of some professionals in the field in order to be included in their respective formats.

There is a small amount of material included in this chapter which consists of promotional packets, leaflets and brochures from treatment centers. Leaflets, fliers and brochures designed to "sell" a facility to possible paying customers may be seen as self-serving, and thus, the objectivity of such offerings is compromised. Phrases like "fully accessible to the deaf" may not be adequately defined, nor may they mean what the proposed clientele might assume they would mean. Feedback from clients using the service, treatment center or resource is not yet universally available. These listings are included so that deaf people may be aware of the availability of these services and to enable future assessments of these services.

For the most part, information has been taken from journal articles, compendium-style books, catalogues and indices of networks or resources. Outcome-of-therapy studies of the projects, facilities and methods presented here are generally not yet completed, although therapists and researchers now, presumably, keep records and notes for such eventual use. With that caveat, we shall survey the comparative literature and materials which are available.

<u>Overview of Current Efforts in the Field of Substance Abuse Prevention:</u>

Effort, time, money and other resources spent in prevention are seen, in most analyses, as significantly more effective than those given to remedial treatment. Treatment given after the fact of addiction often entails documenting losses in terms of the health or potential of the individuals seen for treatment. Some trauma to the CNS is considered irreversible, and the cost of such damage is incalculable. Many needless problems to both the individual and to society could be obviated, if prevention rather than remediation could be the primary line of defense. Such tangential factors as time lost from the work force and accidents caused by people operating vehicles under the influence of a mind altering substance constitute major burdens to society. In 1985, 50% of all fatal vehicle accidents were attributed to alcohol and/or drug involvement.[301]

Costs of addiction also include human-potential losses, since people fully obsessing with addiction are unable to give fully of themselves in such things as self-development or intimate relationships; e.g. the example a parent might wish to offer a child about how to form loving relationships is severely hampered when the parent is visible primarily as an addict. Further costs to society for substance abuse include the costs of quality control remediation, since people who are unable to adequately do their jobs because of addiction, are also unlikely to be able to recognize the inadequacy of their work, resources of manpower fighting crime, since drug-related violence is prevalent, higher insurance rates, and imbalanced allocation of resources, if society's energies and economic means are spent intervening in drug-related crises rather than on life-enhancing facilities and projects, e.g. art education. Washton and Boundy further delineate the costs to society of drug addiction.

There are also more hidden, yet far reaching ramifications of our addictions epidemic: some $200 billion is drained from our economy each year, the

---

[301] Silent Sobriety Foundation; statistics from the Better Hearing Institute; CA State Dept. of Social Services & the National Council on Alcoholism. Dec. 1985.

result of lost work productivity, addiction-related medical care, and crime. And the amount of money spent on our drugs directly is mind-boggling ($150 billion a year on cocaine alone). This epidemic may even jeopardize our national defense, for the rates of drug and alcohol use among those who enter our armed forces are thought to be substantial.[302]

Because the problem of drug and alcohol abuse is crucial to the health of the Deaf community, people are understandably concerned. The Silent Sobriety Foundation notes that 40% of all male admissions by deaf people to state mental hospitals are listed as alcoholics or drug addicts.[303] We do not, at present, know the full extent of this problem. Dr. Dennis Moore, as recently as July 1992, said:

No sufficiently large populations with deafness have been sampled. Specific epidemiologic data regarding drinking or drug use is difficult to locate on this population, chiefly because it is difficult to conduct substance use studies among the deaf.[304]

Education looms as the most effective preventive tool available. Seppala (1977) offers insight on both medical

---

302 Arnold M. Washton & Donna Boundy, Willpower's Not Enough. N.Y. Harper & Row 1989. p. 18.

303 The Silent Sobriety Foundation; "Some Sobering Facts." California. Dec. 1985.

304 Dennis Moore, Ed. D. "Substance Use Patterns of Persons with Hearing Impairments: A Regional Survey"; Paper presented at: "The Next Step: A National Conference Focusing on Issues Related to Substance Abuse in the Deaf and Hard of Hearing Population" July 5-8, 1992; Denver, CO.

and psychological conceptual models of prevention, with several basic guidelines.[305] The St. Paul, MN Substance Abuse Prevention Program, of which Seppala speaks, offers activities which may be seen as divided into five broad areas: 1) enhancing social competencies; 2) providing chemical-specific information; 3) promoting alternative ways of feeling good; 4) providing training for people who are influential in the lives of the persons at risk, and 5) influencing social policy in areas affecting substance abuse treatment.[306]

Focusing specifically on the area of enhancing social competencies of the clientele at the St. Paul program, there are six main issues addressed. These are a) trust, b) self-confidence, c) directionality or sense of purpose and clear goals, d) integrated and coherent sense of identity, e) the ability and willingness to see another person's point of view, and f) the development of specific interpersonal skills to build and maintain fulfilling relationships.[307] Content and methods of approaching these objectives were developed after much consideration of the gravest lacks of the clientele served. There is not yet any longitudinal research showing the effectiveness of this project, but the project bears watching. The essence of prevention is such that if it is effective, it obviates problems which might otherwise happen, so assessing the effectiveness of preventive programs is necessarily complicated.

Distinguishing prevention services from treatment services, including early intervention efforts, may appear

---

[305] Teresa A. Seppala, M.A. A Primer on the Prevention of Chemical Use Problems. Center City, MN; Hazelden. 1977. pp. 7-9.

[306] ibid. p. 8.

[307] ibid. p. 9.

arbitrary and artificial, but precise description of services is required by funding bureaucracies. So, working definitions of preventive services have evolved: prevention services are an aggregate of community programs of many kinds, social, educational, and even physical. These are explicit in the delivery of information to the people served, even though the activities may be directed toward people who have not been singled out as experiencing problems of addiction. Early intervention programs, to differentiate along the continuum between the two points of effort, are directed specifically to people who have been identified as at risk and are experiencing early-stage chemical dependency symptoms.

Gallaudet College has implemented a student-wellness program, which qualifies as both primary and secondary prevention (or early intervention), in which student helpers are used as peer counselors. Mihall, Smith and Wilding state that "the key to Gallaudet's proactive and rehabilitative substance abuse services is the use of student para-professionals," implying that there has been some measure of success noted therein.[308]

Furthermore, Gallaudet University Center sponsors, each October, an educational effort called STRIDE. This University program consists of a series of workshops focusing on drug education. It is open to all students, but is especially used as a training tool for the student para-professionals who will be used as peer counselors.[309] It is

---

[308] John B. Mihall, Emily Smith & Melanie Wilding. "Gallaudet's Student Development Approach to Substance Abuse Education and Identification/Treatment. Paper presented at 2nd Natl. Conference of the Habilitation & Rehabilitation of Deaf Adolescents. Afton, OK. Apr. 28-May 2, 1986. p. 333.

[309] ibid. p. 334.

thought that "airing" information about drugs and alcohol dependency will decrease inadvertent, gradual overuse of prescribed drugs as well as urge caution regarding street drugs. If more deaf people learn to view substance abuse as an unfortunate affliction, which can be treated, rather than a shameful secret to be hidden, progress may occur in reducing drug dependency.

As Gallaudet educators have realized, schools have an important potential role in the socialization process of children. Therefore, the school is a natural place to invest maximum substance abuse prevention efforts. Carol Kusche et al offer strategies to generalize and replice their PATHS project, used among deaf adolescents as a preventive tool.[310] The objectives of the PATHS Project relate primarily to development of emotional maturity and social skills, which, presumably, would obviate vulnerability to drug abuse.

SARDI, the substance Abuse Resources and Disability Issues, is a demonstration and training pilot program operating in Kentucky, Illinois, Indiana, Michigan and Ohio under the auspices of Dr. Dennis Moore and Dr. Harvey Siegal. In prevention efforts, SARDI has been attempting to sensitize professionals in disability-related agencies and service fields to the risks and problems associated with substance abuse for people with disabilities. The SARDI training manual provides objectives to:

---

[310] Carol A. Kusche, Mark Greenberg, Rosemary Calderon & Ruth Gustafson "Generalization Strategies from the PATHS Project for the Prevention of Substance Abuse disorders" Section Six: Strategies of Enhancing The Social and Emotional Development of Deaf Adolescents. Proceedings of the 2nd Nat.l Conference of the Habilitation & Rehabilitation of Deaf Adolescents; Anderson & Watson (Ed.s) Afton, OK. April 28-May 2, 1986.

1. Sensitize professionals working with youth who experience disabilities about substance abuse risks.
2. Provide training to a select group of professionals from a variety of disciplines and evaluate the impact of this training.
3. Develop printed training and intervention materials.
4. Disseminate the materials and findings of the project regionally and nationally.[311]

After noting several special considerations regarding drug abuse by people with disabilities, the SARDI staff note:

> Substance abuse prevention is particularly important in special education settings. For these youth, the prevention focus should be on precursors of substance abuse which often accompany the disability (i.e. poor school performance, lowered self-esteem, limited social outlets, vulnerability to peer influences, and lack of knowledge about drug effects and consequences.)[312]

Factors which may increase vulnerability of disabled persons to substance abuse, which were reviewed in the previous three chapters, need to be directly addressed by everyone concerned. These include psychological as well as physical aspects of disability and addiction. As previous

---

[311] Dennis Moore, Ed.D. ibid. & SARDI Training Manual; ibid; p. ii.

[312] ibid. p. 3.2.

chapters noted, things such as atypical childhood experiences, isolation, increased peer pressure due to the relatively small number of peers, chronic pain, frustration in communication attempts, and even excess free time may put a deaf person at risk of becoming dependent on drugs.[313]

In a thorough prevention program strict confrontation of such lingering attitudes as *entitlement* is crucial. The phenomenon of a strong sense of entitlement survives when, through a series of unsatisfactory social interactions, with complex mixing of feelings of guilt on the part of people interacting with a disabled person, a disabled person may be tacitly allowed to ignore the consequences of his/her actions to compensate for the injustice of having a disability.[314] Such expectations must be acknowledged and dealt with honestly by all the people involved in perpetuating the non-productive behavior. The ease of obtaining medicine by persons with disabilities also needs to be confronted, the SARDI staff say. The SARDI training manual, however, goes beyond addressing societal attitudes toward the disabled person in its attempt to create guidelines for preventive therapy:

---

[313] Deborah R. Waltzer, "A Sobering Tale: Drug & Alcohol Abuse & Recovery in the Deaf Community" Focus; Drug Prevention Programs in Higher Education. U.S. Dept. of Education. p. 18. & Douglas Watson. (Ed.) Readings on Deafness. Deafness Research & Training Center, N.Y. University School of Educ. 1973. pp. 91-105.

[314] Debra Guthmann "Saying 'No' in College: How to Deal With Substance Abuse among Deaf and Hard of Hearing Students" Minn, MN; MN Chem. Depend. Prog. Publ.; 1990. & Wm. McCrone "Serving the Deaf Substance Abuser" J. Psychoactive Drugs. 14, Jul-Sep, 1982. pp. 199-203. p. 12.

A multiple systems approach to prevention should be adopted. In addition to persons with disabilities, families, policy makers, community leaders, the business community, and other significant parties must be included in prevention efforts. Prevention activities can include: multiagency trainings or staffings, providing accurate information about drug effects, training policy makers and community leaders, involving the media in information dissemination, creating positive alternatives to alcohol and other drug use within the community, and instituting policies relating to substance use and abuse within the community (i.e. school policies, workplace policies, policies relating to legal consequences for AOD related crimes, etc.).[315]

These stated intentions largely duplicate the previously listed aims of the St. Paul, MN prevention program, which is reasonable, since professionals are addressing the same problem. Indeed, most prevention programs focus on education and dissemination of information as their primary venues, some also mention the importance of attractive role models and the availability of alternative activities. Packaging education alluringly, e.g. via films or videos, enhances the probability of reaching the targeted population with the message of the joys of addiction-free living and coping. "Tobey's Tales," e.g., a colorful, widely marketed video for deaf children, and produced by deaf people, in concert with the Southeast Council on Alcoholism and Drug Problems, particularly *Awakenings*, a California based group, was created and directed by Bobbie Beth Scoggins, a deaf administrator. The helpful video has been

---

[315] Watson. ibid. p. 3.3.

awarded the Silver Apple, from the National Educational Film & Video Festival.[316] The Minnesota Chemical Dependency Program for the Hearing Impaired's "National Information Catalog" lists other videos/movies as well as a number of books and pamphlets focusing on substance abuse and deafness.[317] Wide dissemination and discussion of these in schools, community groups, churches and other organizations which serve deaf people would accelerate the rate of time necessary to permeate the deaf community with the knowledge that drugs can be harmful.

In psychosocial paradigms for viewing the problem of addiction, personality characteristics of people at risk are given much stress. In the case of alcohol and drug addiction, most therapists and community prevention workers focus on the umbrella term *self-esteem*, or self-image, and have identified a cluster of personality variables which place a person at risk of addiction, as was discussed in chapters three and four. Primary characteristics noted include: 1) perfectionism and being unduly self-critical, 2) hunger for power, to compensate for feelings of powerlessness, 3) denial/self-delusional tendencies, due to lack of adequate feedback opportunities 4) limited view of alternatives (either-or perceptions), 5) ego-centricity, due to isolation, 6) feelings of inner emptiness, 7) having no sense of purpose or meaning of life, 8) excessive concern with others' approval, due to perceived powerlessness, 9) trouble managing anger, 10) trouble with authority figures, and several other traits.[318]

---

[316] Bobbie Beth Scoggins, "Tobey's Tales" Downey, Ca. Awakenings Substance Abuse Recovery Programs for Deaf and Hard of Hearing Persons. Apr. 1991.

[317] MN Chem. Depend. Program for Hearing Impaired "National Information Catalog" Minn. MN. Deaconess Press. n.d.; p. 10.

[318] Washton & Boundy, ibid. pp. 70-71.

Teachers, community leaders, coaches, and other people who are in a position to observe people are key in identifying people at risk of substance addiction. They are urged to become proactive in this role.[319] Beyond identifying people at risk, substance abuse prevention programs involve themselves in promoting alternative ways for individuals to meet needs and feel good about themselves.[320]

More educational tools which specifically reach the target population need to be created. This entails making learning easy and fun, or at least to be perceived as better than other alternatives offered. Printed materials are often inadequate because 1) they are not written at the level the people for whom they are intended can easily read, 2) they are not interesting, or 3) the target population just doesn't read, but receives most input from television or social contact. Oral teaching methods are not appropriate for people who have trouble hearing, either, so hands-on activity methods with generous inclusion of sign language becomes an obvious method when working with deaf people who sign. Cartoon/film media could also be more effectively explored as preventive tools as they become more affordable. Electronic bulletin boards for networking purposes, and computerized bibliographic databases are becoming available, and these could expand to become available to more people.[321] It seems to this researcher that

---

[319] Suzanne Wetlaufer "Teen-age drug use: Personality traits can predict abusers" The Daily Breeze, March 5, 1986.

[320] Seppala; ibid. p. 10.

[321] The Combined Health Information Database (CHID), a computerized bibliographic database is funded by the Federal government, and available to recognized agencies. CHID presently serves people in the helping professions. The NIDCH Clearinghouse recently developed a sub-file on CHID

basic computer keyboard literacy would help to compensate for any perceived imbalance in communication skills of deaf people communicating with hearing people.

It is necessary to involve key community leaders regarding aspects of disability and provide awareness to these leaders of groups of people at high-risk by all means available. Easily-read printed media and easily-absorbed films, e.g. "J.R.'s Story: The Disability of Chemical Dependency" are most likely to reach these people.[322]

Building a strong drug-free support system for people seen as vulnerable has been seen as a vital need in preventing substance abuse. Since families are no longer seen as the primary emotional support of individuals, other supports must emerge. AA has been supplying "sponsors" or "buddies" in self-help groups with ancillary support services for some 50 years, and AA spokesmen claim significant success in prevention, as well as treatment, with such groups as Al-Anon and Ala-Teen working from the connection of a loved one with an addiction. AA has put together a special packet for deaf people offering aids to prevention and treatment, including a translation of the Twelve Steps that simplifies concepts which might otherwise be too abstract. Additionally, AA is now working to promote sobriety in black and Hispanic communities.[323]

The buddy system, similar to AA's sponsor-mentor system is seen as a help in prevention as well as in

---

regarding hearing, and hearing impairments among other things from the National Institute of deafness and Other Communication Disorders, of the National Institutes of Health.

[322] SARDI Training manual; Ibid. p. 1.9.

[323] Barbara Yoder "Alcoholism among the Deaf" The recovery Resource Book. N.Y.; Simon & Schuster, Inc. 1990. pp. 82, 74-75.

remediation.[324] *The Recovery Book* lists quite a few agencies and "clubs" primarily for treatment, although some offer preventive features. Some of these groups, such as Rational Recovery and Secular Organizations for Sobriety (SOS), offer non-spiritual support services for people who find the proffered avenues of spirituality unhelpful. Again, their literature lists preventive features, but their primary thrust is remedial.[325]

Helping people become aware of all the options available is another high priority of both early intervention and prevention efforts. Teachers, writers and other caring people who want to be of help may write pamphlets and offer catalogues and indices of services indefinitely, but until people who *need* the information receive it and take the time to read it, it remains useless on the page. People caught up into addiction do not ordinarily list reading as a high priority in their lives. Alexander Boros, with Patricia Callahan and others, from a two-year study at Akron, Ohio, developed a largely pictorial educational text called, *Looking at Treatment for Alcoholism.*[326] They offer this work for people who do not have highly developed reading skills. The work shows ordinary people finding ways to deal with anger, hurt and other emotions in ways which do not hurt them, and offers information about drug abuse in easily understood terms. The James Learning Method offers a wide variety of educational and diagnostic services, including easily understood written materials such as six

---

324 AA. General Service Office: box 459; Grand Central Station; N.Y., N.Y. 10163. June 1, 1992.

325 Al J. Mooney, Arlene Eisenberg & Howard Eisenberg. The Recovery Book. N.Y. Workman Publ. Co. 1992. pp. 42-43.

326 Patricia Callahan, Alexander Boros & Julie Ewrin. Looking at Treatment for Alcoholism. Akson, OH. Kent State Univ. Press. 1988.

different low-vocabulary booklets on alcohol and drug related topics, an educational table game, workbooks, picture-cards, and other such educational tools. More of such booklets with wider dissemination among the deaf population is needed.

Swaying public opinion, so that peer pressure discourages taking drugs, rather than encourages it, is likewise necessary, and this again requires the strong role-model influence of people willing to devote energy to people who are at risk in the area of substance abuse.

Seppala notes:

> Accordingly, this model proceeds on the hypothesis than an effective prevention program must be holistic in approach; that is, it must affect the individual on all cognitive, affective, and behavioral levels and in all phases and settings of his/her life . . . The existence of this mass of theory and research on the prevention of chemical use problems has little meaning until it finds application in the communities of our state. It is in the interaction of the meaningful social institutions and systems (family, church, peers, school, criminal justice system, etc.) that many of our chemical use patterns are developed and changed.[327]

The VIP Peers in Rochester, N.Y., and Klein and Acevedo, speaking of the New York Society for the Deaf Substance Abuse Program, shared their insights regarding preventive efforts in this area. They have written:

---

[327] Seppala. Ibid. p. 22.

Outreach to schools, recreation programs, community clubs and social groups is a vehicle to reach "at risk" adolescents. These efforts begin the process of providing information and understanding of the problems of substance abuse. The goal is to pave the way toward changing attitudes and views, thus leading to an understanding that a substance abuse is a disease. These programs can be an effective way to bridge the gap between professionals and the deaf community in a productive way.[328]

Mooney, Eisenberg and Eisenberg place some educational responsibility on doctors who see patients in the beginning stages of alcoholism, to recognize the breadth and scope of the problem and to communicate the seriousness of the health hazard to their patients. They include this note to physicians:

It's about time we acknowledged that the drinkers and druggers who wind up on Skid Row show up in our offices first; often–and it's up to us to recognize it–at a highly teachable moment.[329]

Additionally, they make the point that doctors encounter few chronic diseases other than alcoholism, in which early intervention, by a person whom the patient respects, can be so decisive in helping patients to avoid massive function deterioration or decline of general health.[330]

---

[328] Klein and Avecedo.; ibid. p. 328.

[329] Mooney, Eisenberg & Eisenberg; ibid. p. 578.

[330] ibid. p. 578.

Education does not imply coercion or legislation, however. Prohibition, as tried in the United States, did not work. Left to their own devices, a certain number of people would gladly interpret temperance, regarding alcohol beverage consumption, to mean abstinence for everyone, and make even aspirin a prescription-only drug. To legislate away other people's right of choice, in the name of helping people, robs people of their own decisions and may backfire, anyway, in the long-range view. Alcoholism and substance abuse have come to be seen as physical and psychological dependencies needing treatment rather than as moral lapses to be censured. Communicating this concept throughout the deaf community might relieve the strong stigma and sense of shame related to identifying oneself as in need of help.[331]

Preventive services seek to reduce the demand for drugs, rather than focusing on remediation. To most analysts, this implies addressing non-physical areas. Help in the area of spirituality is offered by AA and other self-help groups which usually are sought out only after the fact of addiction, and thus are primarily remedial. Preventative emotional and spiritual inoculations might help individuals avoid vulnerability to addiction, but many perceived avenues to spirituality have been seen as inadequate, and one common symptom of people with addiction problems is emotionally impoverished homes.[332] The person at risk of addiction has limited awareness of resources in those affective areas, almost by definition. Preachiness and an

---

331 Steve Thomas "Introduction" Interpreting Signs of Recovery. Visalia, CA. State of CA Dept. of Alc & Drug Programs; Tulare Co. Alc. Council, Inc.; 1988. p.3.

332 Washton & Boundy. Willpower's Not Enough: Understanding & Recovering from Addictions of Every Kind. N.Y. Harper & Row, Publ.; 1989. p. 85.

authoritarian manner on the part of formal religious systems often discourage two-way communication rather than open it. Thus the people who might most benefit from emotional or spiritual growth often see no effective models or access to the "inoculation" such a buffer might create.[333]

In a position paper presented by the Disabilities / Substance Abuse Task Force, Inc., a number of recommendations were made. Among these were mandates for on-going efforts to aid Centers for Independent Living, and other agencies providing frequent help to people with disabilities, to see the need for early intervention via identification of their clients who have substance abuse problems.[334] Other groups and organizations are emerging with their own conferences, status reports, networking aids and position papers. Schowe, a deaf analyst and writer, says, "Evidence of the prevailing trend to 'programs and services' today is all around us, too comprehensive for detailed listing."[335]

The truism that "An ounce of prevention is worth a pound of cure," is recognized as valid for people wanting to make inroads on the emotionally wrenching and statistically significant problem of substance abuse among deaf people. Education, consisting of information, either delivered directly person-to-person or through appropriate, interesting materials available both to read and to view, plus more strong role-models embodying positive attributes

---

[333] ibid. p. 85.

[334] Disabilities/Substance Abuse Task Force, Inc. "The Forgotten Minority" a position paper; n.d.; p. 7.

[335] B.M. Schowe, Identity Crisis in Deafness, Tempe, AZ. The Scholars Press; 1979. p. 140.

and emotional support have been noted as primary needs in this area.[336]

Overview of Substance Abuse Treatment Resources:

Treatment resources include residential in-patient treatment centers, out-patient treatment centers, treatment referral and networking services, self-help support groups, aftercare and follow-up materials, self-reinforcing methods and councils or study groups, such as the Resource Center on Substance Abuse Prevention and Disability and the National Council on Alcoholism, which has over 200 local affiliates. Some facilities offer more than one service, e.g. National Council on Alcoholism centers were established to offer information, but they also unofficially often provide impromptu counseling and diagnostic services in their communities.

A basic concern about substance abuse treatment efforts, in general, is that they have not proven effective. While a pragmatic outlook may be inadequate and insufficient, it is at least necessary. Recidivism rates outpace recovery statistics, as was covered in the preceding chapter. The perceived lack of efficacy drives therapists into apathy and burn-out. Jack Gorey says, "I have avoided discussing specific statistics on client recovery rates."[337] Reasons for ineffectiveness include multiple intrapersonal

---

[336] Chuck Norris of the Kick Drugs Out of America Foundation, offers martial arts and several programs, including "Helping Hand Initiative" in which at-risk individuals have one-to-one contact with well known role models, such as movie stars, the President of the U.S., musicians, and other heroes. This program operates out of Houston & Galveston, TX. 1992.

[337] Jack Gorey. "Rational Alcoholism Services for Hearing Impaired People" J. Rehab & Deaf. Dec. 1979. p. 7.

and interpersonal factors and their interaction, and blaming doesn't accomplish anything. However analysts do study inadequate treatment programs in efforts to improve upon them.

In addition to major problems in the area of efficacy, many alcoholism/drug treatment centers do not, at present, offer auxiliary aids which would make treatment available for most deaf people, so if they can adapt their facilities/services so that they can comply with the law and serve everyone, we can consider them. Some renowned alcoholism treatment units and drug clinics are currently inaccessible to the deaf because they lack direct methods of access, e.g. "hotlines" are often developed and provided for people who abuse alcohol, yet many deaf people, unable to use ordinary telephones, cannot reach the proffered help. Social services are just beginning to offer TDDs. These factors are gradually changing, and facilities and staff are being updated continually to comply with federal access laws.

A significant number of substance abuse treatment centers do not yet have deaf personnel on staff, or offer anyone who is fluent in ASL, or even have a full-time interpreter available. Some treatment facilities, which may hire an interpreter infrequently, may have scheduling problems, asking people who have endured inconveniences traveling to the treatment center to return at another time, when they may receive help. Treatment personnel may not as yet be sensitive to the additional problems the factor of bringing in another person, not intimately involved in the healing process, such as an interpreter, may bring to the treatment process, (e.g. confidentiality and inhibition.[338])

---

[338] Betty Miller, "Interpreters & the Recovery Process" Project: A Second Chance. July, 1991.

Overall, present treatment facilities are rated as inadequate to deal with the special needs of deaf substance abusers. Dr. Dennis Moore says:

> Professional awareness about substance abuse and persons with disabilities also is quite low. For example, disabled services providers in colleges frequently have reported to us that substance abuse problems among their students is minimal. Our research has suggested that this is not the case. In addition, these same professionals are not aware that treatment and intervention resources generally are not accessible or appropriate for persons with a serious disability.[339]

Attention now being focused on the needs of deaf people in substance abuse treatment may provide remediation for the deficiencies observed. Bowe, Watson and Anderson state that comprehensive rehabilitation for deaf people is in beginning stages. They have attempted to isolate particular needs for that effort:

> A model for delivery of services to a given target population generally must meet certain criteria before it can be considered effective. Criteria frequently utilized in the development and evaluation of social service programs include, among other requirements, the necessity for 1) a wide range of services encompassing many of the needs of the population, 2) an acceptable level of quality in the

---

[339] Dennis Moore, Ed.D. "Research in Substance Abuse and Disabilities: the implications for prevention and treatment. Paper presented at 3rd Nat.l Prevention & Training Conference: People with Disabilities. Apr. 4-7, 1990. p. 9.

services delivered, 3) some provision for continuing delivery of services on a permanent basis, 4) economy, and 5) adaptability for meeting the needs of similar populations in other geographical areas. Designing and implementing a model for delivery of community services to a deaf population requires that additional factors be considered. In addition to the criteria listed above, provision should be made for meeting the special needs presented by persons who cannot hear. Examples of such provisions may include interpreting or related communication services, specialized information-referral services, and modified outreach techniques.[340]

The primarily negative assessment of substance abuse treatment centers not specifically designed to include the needs of deaf people hovers around the mandated area of communication. In order for a facility to be considered accessible to deaf people, one necessity is a common language, in order for communication to occur. It is incumbent upon people in the helping professions to meet the people they wish to help at the present circumstance of those people seeking help. This simply and unequivocally means that people attempting to help deaf people who sign need to learn sign language; professionals working with deaf people who do not sign, need to ascertain and use that clientele's most comfortable method of communicating, etc. Written information provided to a client should be well within the client's ability to read and comprehend.

---

340 Frank Bowe, Douglas Watson & Glenn Anderson. "Delivery of Community Services to Deaf Persons." in Douglas Watson (ed) Readings on Deafness. N.Y., Deafness Research & Training Center. N.Y. University School of Education. 1973. p. 70.

As one newspaper article points out, it is a shame that drug dealers have bothered to learn sign language, and to recruit deaf people to work under them to promote sales of drugs in the deaf community, while people with more humane motives have not. Drug dealers actively try to develop and enhance a sense of rapport with deaf people in order to offer debilitating addiction, while people offering more worthwhile services and products often have not expended that effort.[341] Bothering to learn a person's language creates a sense of shared experience and connotes respect for that person's traditions and culture. In the arsenal of tools for education and prevention of such serious problems as addiction, caring enough to learn the language of the people addressed should rank as a high priority and basic requirement for professionals. Thus, communication assessments and determining the preferred method of communication of each client should be a preliminary part of intake, evaluation and admission to treatment programs.

Since communication is not therapeutic if it is only one-way, care must be given to structuring therapy so that clients not only have the opportunity to respond but that they have every encouragement to respond and participate in recovery/health enhancement.

Regarding the numerous problems of alcohol and drug treatment centers, Rowan notes five specific areas which typically need addressing. The first challenge she perceives is networking, and making use of existing materials, personnel, and other aids. She says,

> Professionals and programs have tended to
> isolate themselves, investing time, energy and

---

341 Lisa Holewa. "Drug dealers said learning sign language" Silent News. Jul., 1993. p. 10.

money to re-invent the wheel. Because of this tendency to isolate, many programs have experienced and suffered the same problems previous programs have experienced–resulting in eventual reduction in or termination of services.[342]

This researcher has noted that tendency and suggests wider dissemination of ongoing clinical insights, including more agencies and schools serving the deaf in conferences focused on substance abuse treatment and airing proceedings of such conferences in all agencies and resource bases to elicit feedback and expanded future participation in substance abuse deterring activities.

Douglas Watson, after listing needs for networking, deaf peer-counselors, and more precise diagnostic effort, voices a theoretical consideration:

> The field has yet to generate vigorous examination of various theoretical approaches in treatment of deaf clients. We use whatever theory we use with all our clients, not because it has been demonstrated to also be effective, feasible, and successful with deaf clients, but because it is the theory we practice. Yet, the lack of supporting evidence–for the efficiency of our particular theoretical base–can undermine our confidence in its use, thereby influencing the way we implement it in treatment of deaf clients. Such insecurities and self-doubt are undoubtedly reflected in our "counseling," reducing our own level of comfort and confidence–

---

[342] Roanne Rowan. Chemical Abuse & dependency. MN. 1988 in introductory pages.

and thereby the quality and nature of our theoretical assumptions with deaf people.[343]

Previous chapters have cited informed opinion that family therapy, or at least strong family involvement in therapy for deaf substance abusers might be efficacious. Moore concurs:

Significant others, including family members, friends, and attendant staff need to become involved in any chemical dependency treatment program. It is very important for individuals with limited resources and alternatives to receive consistent feedback from sources of support. Involving family and friends in treatment is particularly salient when these persons may not fully understand the degree of risk or problem than an individual is facing.[344]

Regarding deaf people who have been induced into drug abuse from peer pressure, several therapists believe that the most effective method to change behavior is to change the attitudes, often using peer pressure from counseling groups. The theory is that group counseling is best equipped to influence the development of values, and much time in group sessions is spent focusing on expanding and

---

[343] Douglas Watson. "Substance Abuse Services for Deaf Clients: A Question of Accessibility." p. 13-16.

[344] Dennis Moore. "Research in Substance Abuse and Disabilities: The Implications for Prevention and Treatment" paper presented at the Annual Meeting of the Nat.l Prev. & Training Conf.: People With Disabilities (3rd, April 4-7, 1990. p. 13.

crystallizing values superior to the ones which brought the participants into treatment.[345]

When information has permeated the Deaf community and is made available, via service agencies to isolated people undergoing hearing impairment regarding the dangers of drug abuse and the vulnerability of people to its subtle methods of addiction, perhaps the demand for drugs will abate. There already exist a wide range of organizations, newsletters, task forces, and study groups to carry out the task of reaching the deaf community with this objective.

Since every person needing treatment may not be able to afford private, individual psychotherapy or a treatment program's fees, mutual self-help groups have emerged. Alcoholics Anonymous, listed in most phone books, provides self-help support groups in almost every city, and affiliates of AA, such as Al-Anon, are readily available to everyone, regardless of financial resources. Written helps, provided by AA, to deaf people, have been re-written to convey the needed information in concepts within the average deaf person's reading vocabulary, as noted before. Other self-help support groups often emulate AA both in this and in the use of a "sponsor" for the newcomer.

These insights, garnered from researchers, therapists, and community leaders concerned about substance abuse, comprise some general guidelines regarding treatment centers for people with alcohol and drug abuse problems. We propose, now, to review literature on a number of such

---

[345] Martin L. Sternberg. "Group Counseling with the Non-Communicating Deaf:" in The Use of Group Techniques with Deaf Persons. N.Y.; The Deafness Research & Training Center. n.d.; p. 33.

facilities which offer programs at least minimally accessible for deaf and hard of hearing people.

<u>Survey of Alcohol and Substance Abuse Treatment
Programs Accessible to Deaf People:</u>

Among the alcohol treatment programs which offer access to the deaf, a San Francisco based group represented a first step in treatment. Originating in 1975, the Alcohol Project for the Deaf used the facilities of existing organizations and agencies, cooperatively in mainstreaming efforts to meet the individualized needs of deaf substance abusers.[346] Now nearly every state offers a substance abuse program available to deaf people. Not all of these programs or facilities, however, are "user friendly" enough to overcome the tendencies toward discouragement of both the populations of people who abuse substances and of deaf people who find attempts at communicating with a hearing world wearying.

The Minnesota Chemical Dependence Program, directed by Debra Guthmann, M.A., was the first program available to deaf people ages 16-25. Started in 1988, the treatment program expresses caring for the clientele, beginning with a thorough evaluation. It requires, among other things, that a patient record his own drug use history, to get beyond the very difficult stage of denial, so that treatment may proceed. It further employs a *feelings collage* to assist clients, who may not have experience in articulating feelings, to accurately identify and accept responsibility for their own feelings. Beyond evaluation, referral meetings may be held, involving other family members and other concerned people. Most of the treatment is based on the

---

[346] Jack Gorey, ibid. p. 6.

traditional 12 step plan AA developed. Counseling sessions include both group and individual sessions, each day, and aim at a consistent pace of emotional work with frequent evaluations of progress.

The Minnesota Chemical Dependency Program offers additional services such as occupational therapy and academic tutoring. Follow-up, aftercare and a *Relapse Prevention Guide* and referral program is also offered in many states, when the client leaves the residential unit at Fairview Riverside Medical Center.[347]

Treatment efforts have multiplied in the past ten years. In 1983 there were only ten treatment centers for deaf substance abusers in the entire United States. Here are a few additions to that number, using their statements about their capabilities:

Project AID (Addiction Intervention for the Deaf), which identifies deaf people in need of substance abuse treatment and prepares them for in-patient programs in existing treatment facilities in the Northeast Ohio area, also providing follow-up services for the deaf substance abuser upon his/her release from the treatment program.[348] Dr. Alex Boros, out of the Department of Sociology at Kent State University, and Sue Adams, a consultant on the project, state they provide specifically designed materials for learning-impaired or language-impaired people on the drug treatment topic. Although their work is with people who are substance abusers, in the area of remediation, they believe their work is primarily educational. specific

---

[347] Debra Guthmann. "An Innovative Substance Abuse Program for Hearing Impaired Youth." Minn, MN. The MN Chemical Dependency Program for the Hearing Impaired. Oct., 1990.

[348] Katherine Lane. "Substance Abuse among the Deaf Population: an Overview of Current Strategies, Programs & Barriers to Recovery, Vol. 22 (4) Apr., 1989. p. 82.

references to their educational projects have been noted earlier.[349]

Cape Cod Alcoholism Intervention & Rehabilitation Unit Project for the Deaf, offering both residential and outpatient services in Massachusetts, relies on a program with much structure, which may be necessary for people steeped in denial. This is a mainstreaming program, offering involvement in area AA chapters, as well as individual counseling at least twice a week. The center keeps a 24-hour TDD hotline, with a deaf counselor always available. Much after-care is offered to help keep the person from slipping back into addiction.[350]

The Rochester Institute of Technology, a leader in the field of treatment for deaf substance abusers, has created a multi-faceted networking and referral service called the Substance Abuse Intervention Services for the Deaf (SAISD), mentioned before in this chapter, which provides both preventive/educational and remedial intervention and support-group services. Working with professionals and agencies, SAISD provides this wide array of information and services with an emphasis on confidentiality.[351]

Signs of Recovery, Inc. offers deaf-to-deaf alcoholism recovery support services in cooperation with the Clare Foundation, in Santa Monica, CA. This in-patient center offers explicit rules, policies and expectations of participants, including no outside passes for the first 30 days, to keep the recovering addict's attention focused on preliminary recovery issues. The treatment program is

---

349 Alex Boros "Addiction Intervention with the Disabled Resource Center" Kent, OH. Kent Univ. Press. Dec., 1992.

350 ibid. p. 82.

351 S.A.I.S.D. information packet, brochure, resource list and video tape list. Rochester, N.Y. Dec., 1992.

divided into three levels, and people work through levels and complete assignments, learning to accept responsibility for their own actions.[352]

In December, 1992, the New Bridge Foundation announced the opening of two recovery programs for deaf people. One is a six-month residential treatment program, available for people who cannot enroll in the regular eighteen month program, and the other program is an outpatient program offering daytime care. The New Bridge Foundation was the first residential treatment program in the Bay Area of California which offered treatment accessible to deaf people with addiction problems. Their literature states that sliding scale fees are available for people who do not have adequate resources for treatment services. With offices in Berkeley and San Leandro, The New Bridge makes a sincere attempt to reach deaf people in need of their services.[353]

The John L. Norris Alcoholism Treatment Center offers in-patient treatment for up to 44 deaf people over age 18 whose communication skills are adequate to participate in group process, and it has a rigorous screening policy. The center offers a full spectrum of professional services and much effort has been made to assure complete accessibility to deaf adults. e.g. They boast adequate TDD lines for enrolled deaf people have been revised using only words accessible to most deaf readers, and the agency has counselors fluent in ASL. The center includes a "Concerned

---

[352] "Signs of Recovery" Alcoholism Recovery Support services. Info. sheet. 1991.

[353] New Bridge Foundation information packet: admission policies, aims & facilities list. Dec. 1992.

Others Program" to work with people close to the identified patient, and offers after-care guidelines.[354]

The program director for the Antelope Valley Council on Alcoholism & Drug Dependency, located in Palmdale, CA, states that their services are broader and wider than drug abuse focus. e.g. their program offers employee assistance programs as outreach services to business and industry for early intervention. They state that they have some 60 deaf clients at present. Discussion groups form the mainstay of their supportive outpatient activities.[355]

St. Vincent's Hospital and Medical Center of New York has announced that their outpatient treatment program now has services for people with hearing loss and/or deafness. They offer individual counseling upon intake, family counseling, support groups, some teaching regarding the 12-step recovery process, and additional educational aids. They have people on their staff who sign, and the center has TTY phone accessibility.[356]

The New York Society for the Deaf has designed and opened a substance abuse program which aids existing treatment centers in intake and assessment of services needed. Especially formed to be accessible to deaf, deaf-blind and hard-of-hearing people, the staff help to make determinations regarding clients' needs for in-patient or out-patient care and to match existing centers in the geographical area to needs of clients. Their professional staff is fluent in ASL, and the society attempts to offer

---

[354] John L. Norris Alcoholism Treatment Center.
Admission/Information Packet. Rochester, N.Y.; 1992.

[355] Antelope Valley Council on Alcoholism & Drug Dependency
Palmdale, CA. January, 1993.

[356] St. Vincent's Hospital & Medical Center of New York
"Alcoholism Outpatient Treatment Program" N.Y.; N.Y.
Medical College; Dec. 1992.

sensitivity to clients while helping to rid them of addiction. Additionally, the NYSD Substance Abuse Program offers information and resources to area professionals regarding specialized deaf issues.[357]

Belmont, in Philadelphia, Pennyslvania, offers psychiatric help to the deaf with both in-patient and out-patient treatment programs. The focus is not solely on addiction treatment, but upon improving the self-image and functioning patterns of participants. In addition to the usual services available to their hearing participants, Belmont offers a support group which uses ASL for deaf people. The Woodside Hall group therapy adjunct for persons with addictive disorders functions under the 12-Step program rubric. No information was provided regarding costs.[358]

In the area of Milwaukee, Wisconsin, the Keystone residential Services for Deaf and Hard of Hearing Chemically Dependent Adult Men & Women offers individualized recovery services. The program lasts between six months and one year, and offers structured, intensive residential therapy. Aspects stressed are motivation to become involved in one's continued awareness/education and willingness to work. Their aim, regarding staff credentialing, is to obtain Wisconsin AODA certification for both the clinical managing therapist and the chemical dependence counselor. Aftercare services are

---

[357] N.Y. Society for the Deaf. "NYSD Substance Abuse Program" Info. packet. N.Y., N.Y.; Oct. 1992.

[358] "Belmont Center for Comprehensive Treatment" brochure. Philadelphia, PA. n.d.

available to provide a smoother transition back into the larger community.[359]

In Nebraska, Lincoln General Independence Center states that they provide both in-patient and out-patient treatment programs for adult deaf substance abusers, with interpreters available. It is unclear whether this is a mainstream or deaf-only program.[360]

Fairbanks Hospital, in Indianapolis, Indiana, began treating deaf patients in its substance abuse treatment program in 1984. Deaf clients are mainstreamed with hearing clients via the use of interpreters, TDDs and television decorders. The in-patient program lasts approximately one month, and referrals for aftercare are available. Financial criteria for acceptance into the program include covering both the cost of the program itself and the cost of an interpreter, however sliding scale fees are available.[361]

Awakenings was the first facility of its kind to operate for and by deaf. It was started in August, 1988, as a program of the Southeast Council on Alcoholism and Drug Problems, Inc., located in Downey, California. Using services of the large National Chapter on alcoholism in L.A. County, this program received an infusion of tax money, due largely, to the efforts of Dr. Betty Miller, toward the achievement of accessible treatment and recovery for deaf people. With input from the deaf community, including

---

[359] DePaul Keystone: Residential Services for Deaf and Hard of Hearing Chemically Dependent Adult Men & Women. Program/admission packet. Milwaukee, WI. 1992.

[360] NICD "Programs & Resources for Deaf Alcoholics & Substance Abusers" Washington, D.C.; Gallaudet Univ.; n.d. p. 8.A.

[361] Fairbanks Hospital; Substance Abuse Treatment Program. Info. packet. June, 1988.

efforts of GLAD and a grant written with attention to detail, the *Awakenings* Program now serves addicts from the 150,000-200,000 deaf people in Los Angeles County, and is highly visible in the deaf community as a treatment resource.[362] Using a private home, within a suburban setting, *Awakenings* offers residential care to up to 20 adults, focusing on the acquisition of healthful living skills. That home in Whittier, California "graduated" 10 people in the first year it opened.[363] A drop-in center is also available, as is a more formal out-patient service accommodating up to 19 people. The Awakenings Intervention/Education Program (mentioned earlier in this chapter) provides training to educators. Deaf community spokesmen recommend that methods and insights gained by the deaf staff be replicated in other treatment efforts.[364]

The Silent Bridges program at the Manors, in Tarpon Springs, Florida, accepts deaf adults and adolescents for substance abuse treatment; it also accepts deaf people whose primary diagnosis is mental illness or behavioral disorder. Additionally, Hispanic deaf persons are accommodated with their tri-lingual communication needs. The program offers complete medical/psychiatric diagnostic, orientation and treatment services, a private psychiatrist for each patient, sign language interpreting, group counseling, after-care including a relapse prevention support group, and referral. Staff and personnel include

---

372 "Awakenings Substance Abuse Recovery Programs: The Concept" Downey, CA. The Southeast Council on Alc. & Drug Problems, Inc. 1989.

363 Tina Daunt "special Help for Deaf Drug Abusers" Los Angeles Times. Dec. 31, 1989. pp. J1, J6.

364 "Awakenings Subst. Abuse Recovery Programs. Ibid. p. 3.

both deaf and hearing professionals who sign. Costs of the program are not included in the information brochure.[365]

The Heritage Center is a free-standing, long term residential treatment facility for teenagers located in Orem, Utah. It has recently expanded its service to offer psychiatric treatment to deaf adolescents. In their self-contained treatment program for deaf teens, 60 beds are available for long-term care, and a short term (up to 90 day) program of intensive treatment is also available. The diagnostic period involves a 10-30 day evaluation phase, focusing on psychiatric/psychological assessments, but offering other clinical services. The staff respect traditional Deaf culture and employ American Sign Language in their treatment and relationship building efforts. Professionals working with deaf youth are either deaf themselves or certified as proficient in ASL, and focus on bi-lingual, bi-cultural approaches. While this program does not focus primarily upon treating substance abuse, teens who may have emotional, behavioral or academic problems, may also display substance abuse problems. Educational potential of the program for participants is stressed in the facility. In addition to impressive medical coverage, including 24-hour nursing services, and the promise of sufficient TDDs in residential units to meet the needs of the population, the residential treatment programs follow traditional phases, including elaborate aftercare follow-up attention. With all these thorough provisions comes an equally thorough intake application form which seeks the patient's detailed history and adequate promise of insurance or other ability to pay the center's fees. The facility offers many extras such as a

---

[365] The Manors. The Silent Bridges Program: a mental health program for the hearing impaired. Tarpon Springs, FL. Oct. 1992.

swimming pool, riding stables, many athletic options, and referral/placement services; the cost for all this, however, is $250. per day for long term clients, and $325. per day for short term participants. Even with scholarships and aid, not every youth who would benefit from this center will find it accessible.[366]

Lastly, the Benny McKeown Center of San Jose, California offers a co-educational recovery home which mainstreams hearing and deaf people. For deaf residents, staff interpreters, closed caption T.V., TDDs and a light alarm system are provided. The treatment program lasts between 90 and 180 days, depending on individual progress, and is modeled after AA's 12-Step program. The program also offers occupational and transitional helps.[367]

In the area of out-patient services, also, a number of facilities offer special programs for deaf people or offer deaf people access to mainstreamed programs. These, also are nation-wide. A few of these include licensed day-care and daily individual consultation with a credentialed therapist. Most, however, feature initial assessment and referral services and networking information regarding such things as self-help support groups. A case in point is The Program: Alcohol and Drug Services of San Mateo County, based in San Mateo, California. Referral services are available from the San Mateo office to the San Francisco Center on Deafness, Alcohol & Drug Project for San Mateo County. This is a County facility offering diagnostic services during

---

[366] Heritage Center Information Packet. Provo, UT. Mar, 1993.
[367] Benny McKeown Center info. sheet. San Jose, CA. Oct. 1992.

normal business hours 5-day a week, with appointments necessary and interpreters available by pre-request.[368]

Genessee County, Michigan, offers a number of out-patient services through the Commission on Substance Abuse. Genessee County has a high per capita concentration of deaf people, and the Hearing Impaired/Deaf Substance Abuse Support Services offer a collaborative effort in the county in areas of seeking grants for education/prevention, early intervention, treatment, and peer support groups. The commission also intends to train community lay persons to be peer support volunteers to provide aftercare and follow-up resources.[369]

St. Elizabeth's Hospital, in the Washington, D.C. area, although not offering residential treatment programs specifically for deaf people with substance abuse problems, offers high-quality, multi-faceted traditional care for psychiatric patients with impaired hearing, and makes referrals to AA groups or area drug treatment programs. Back in 1973, the treatment staff of the combined in-patient and out-patient resource won a coveted Gold Award for excellence. They offer additional features such as psychodrama.[370]

---

368 Alcohol & Drug Services Directory of San Mateo County. Publ. by the San Mateo County Alc. & Drug Program: Human Services Agency. 1992.

369 Nat.l Clearinghouse for Alc. & Drug Info. "The Fact Is" Office for Substance Abuse Prevention. Rockville, MD. July 1988. p. 2.

370 Luther D. Robinson "A Program for Deaf Mental Patients" in Hospital & Commun. Psychiat. Vol. 24 (1) 1973 pp. 40-42. And "Gold Award: Mental Health Services for the Deaf: St. Elizabeth's Hospital, Wash., D.C." Hospital & Commun. Psychiat. Vol. 29 (10) 1978. pp. 674-677.

Many other facilities such as the Helen Keller National Center, New York, The International Center for the Disabled Chemical Dependency Services of New York, The National Captioning Institute, in Virginia, and the University Affiliated Center for Developmental Disabilities at West Virginia University state that they offer materials, resources or services for deaf people.[371] Evaluations of the adequacy of their services for deaf people will emerge from the clientele and from recidivism records.

John De Miranda, of San Mateo, California, and director of the pioneering CALADD study, interviewed staff at many disability service agencies in California, attempting to assess the extent of problems of such things as access to drug treatment centers by people with disabilities. He found that almost 54% of the people he surveyed responded "Yes" to questions regarding difficulties in receiving help from these service agencies. The CALADD study offers recommendations and proposes a systematic policy for state agencies dealing with people with disabilities that they declare such populations as high-risk groups. This comprehensive project has enjoyed high-visibility within the Deaf community, and that factor may enable DeMiranda's findings to assume an impetus in advocacy programs for services for deaf people.[372]

Catherine Wilson and Beth Benedict report a pilot study, called STAMP, or Stop Teenage Abuse of Marijuana Program, which generated much enthusiasm and cause for

---

[371] "The Fact Is." ibid. pp. 1-5.
[372] John DeMiranda, CALADD Study. San Mateo. Sep., 1989 & "Drugs and drinking takes toll on disabled" in The times. San Mateo, CA. Oct. 9, 1989.

hope.[373]   Working under the auspices of Gallaudet
University, the researchers designed the study using deaf
teens in the Washington, D.C. area. Explicit criteria were
offered, including mandatory attendance at lectures,
regular urine analysis, and the completion of quizzes, one
as a pre-test, and one as a post-test. Although the project
was not an unqualified success, lessons for future treatment
projects may be inferred, such as the importance of
consistency in the application of rules.[374]

Table IV offers some comparison information regarding
various treatment centers.

In the area of non-residential treatment resources, AA
and other self-help support groups help millions of people
by use of the 12-step plan, or variants of it, to increase
participants' insight into their behavior and its
ramifications upon both themselves and other people.
Methods of treatment which accomplish these aims merit
continual consideration for future use.

While outcome research and recidivism studies for all
these programs are not yet widely available, researchers
are optimistic about proactive efforts to eliminate the
demand for harmful substances. Intensive treatment
centers and after-care programs which maintain copious
notes regarding methods, frequency of staff interactions
with clients, etc. contribute to eventual discernment of
therapeutic patterns.

A wide array of indices, foundations, organizations,
publications, directories and resource lists are available for
additional information or contact access. Published by

---

[373] Catherine Wilson & Beth Benedict "Stop Teenage Abuse of
    Marijuana Program" Wash. D.C.; Gallaudet College Press.
    n.d.
[374] Ibid. pp. 1-3.

organizations, task forces and resource study groups of deaf people or of people treating substance abuse, or both, these materials serve people throughout the U.S. and some other countries. Since it is not the aim of this work to duplicate existing resources, these listings will not be offered here. However, Appendix B, consisting of names of several primary resources for comprehensive listings, follows this work, providing elementary contact information.

With these in-patient and out-patient treatment centers and the additional resources listed, finding help may not be the discouraging task it once was for deaf substance abusers. While there remain concerns about confidentiality, ease of communicating and other salient points, treatment should be soon available to anyone who seeks it.

Auxiliary materials are now becoming available to individuals now, such as the "Relapse Prevention Guide," referenced earlier which the Minnesota Chemical Dependency Program uses. Such helps are written using an elementary level English

Table IV
Comparison of Substance Abuse Treatment Programs

Facility	Length of Program	Age	Location	Service	Deaf on Staff	Interp/DDD or ASL
Antelope Valley		all	California	out-pt	yes	
Awakenings	1 year	adult	California	in & out pt	all deaf	
Belmont		all	Phil, PA	full serv	yes	yes
Benny McKeown	90-180 days	adult	California	in-pt	yes	yes
Cape Cod	40+ days	adult	Mass	in & out pt	yes	yes
Fairbanks	3-5 weeks		Indiana	in-pt		yes
Heritage	90+ days	adult	Utah	in & out pt	yes	yes
Keystone	60 days	18+ yrs	Wisconsin	in-pt		yes
Lincoln		20+ yrs	Nebraska	in-pt		yes
MN Chem Dep Prog	40+ days	16+ yrs	Minnesota	in & out pt	yes	yes
New Bridge		adult	California	in & out pt	yes	yes
Norris	42-60 days	16+ yrs	New York	in & out pt		yes
RIT (SAISD)	ongoing	all	New York	out-pt	yes	yes
Signs Recovery		adult	California	in-pt	yes	
Silent Bridges		16+ yrs	Florida	in-pt	yes	yes
St. Elizabeth's		16+ yrs	Wash, D.C.	in & out-pt	yes	yes
St. Vincent's		adult	New York	in & out-pt		yes

vocabulary, and require only minimal reading skills, for people for whom English is not their first language.

The words used in the "Relapse Prevention Guide" are all ones for which ASL signs now exist. Advertising the availability of such helps and making their acquisition easy are seen as reasonable next steps in out-patient aids to recovery.

Fairly comprehensive and complete program proposals now exist and could be replicated for substance abuse treatment to deaf people in regionally targeted areas. e.g. One proposal, submitted as a bid to the governing board of Los Angeles County by the Southeast Council on alcoholism and Drug Problems, outlined a plan to provide residential drug-free and outpatient drug-free services to deaf residents. This complex work, approximately 300 pages of specific objectives and methods concerning both treatment and outreach, offered a contract submitted to the Department of Health Services. Using existing resources, such as The Greater Los Angeles Council on Deafness (GLAD) and the *Awakenings* program, this proposal offers both a comprehensive scope and attention to detail.[375]

In this proposed treatment plan, all the key personnel on the treatment staff are themselves deaf and are well-known and accepted in the deaf community there. This council has some experience in working with both substance abusers and the deaf community in both residential and out-patient programs. Additionally, beyond the treatment program, this proposal offers to hold certain events to highlight community awareness and recruit involvement in three separate populations: the deaf community,

---

[375] S.E. Council on Alc. & Drug Problems; "Proposal to provide residential drug free and out patient drug free services to hearing impaired persons in Los Angeles County." Sections C & D. July 7, 1988.

organizations and other service providers to the deaf, and service providers who serve, at present, predominantly hearing people but whose work would be enhanced if the needs and problems of the deaf were more consistently in their consciousness.[376]

From the early 1970s, scholars have written regarding special issues or methods needed for therapy with deaf people.[377] Salient issues perceived have included: the necessity of visual, rather than auditory communication, concerns of diagnostic accuracy, unexpressed client expectations, strengths of deaf patients, involvement of third parties, and flexibility in both the counseling process and in techniques.[378] Boros discussed issues in treating deaf alcoholics within hospital settings, listing eight issues which he perceived. The questions he raised included: 1) Should deaf clients be treated as in-patients or out-patients? 2) Should we send people who need additional aids, such as staff who sign, to certain facilities or should their proximity to a given treatment center be the determinant? 3) Are triage concerns, regarding available resources and necessary staff preparation in order to accommodate deaf clientele, valid? 4) Should deaf clients be mainstreamed or have separate facilities/efforts? 5) How do deaf clients affect hearing clients in the same treatment groups? 6) How important is it that some staff treatment personnel be deaf? 7) Who is qualified to make diagnoses of deaf clients? and 8) Who should interpret? Is a counseling

---

376 Ibid. pp. 3-15.

377 H.S. Schlesinger, & K. Meadows. "A Conceptual Model for a Program of Community Psychiatry for a Deaf Population" Commun. Mental Health J. 8 (1) 1972. pp. 47-59.

378 Michael F. Hoyt, Ellen Siegelman, & Hilde Schlesinger. "Special Issues Regarding Psychotherapy with the Deaf" Amer J. Psychiat. 138 (6) Jun., 1981. pp. 807-811.

credential necessary for an interpreter? Boros offered clinical observations from the AID program with which he was affiliated.[379] These questions will be discussed further in the next chapter.

Among the criteria of therapy offered in a full-time residential unit is the need that it offer no less than six hours of planned treatment activity, per day, to differentiate itself from a merely custodial facility. The descriptive/marketing materials surveyed for the various programs all have stressed their required activities, frequent client-therapist contact, and high levels of staff involvement with participants.

Among the variables isolated which interfere with therapy, and which, conversely, the absence thereof might be presumed to enhance therapy, loom size and heterogeneity/homogeneity factors. Researchers of NIDA have posited, for several reasons relating to human motivational dynamics, that small and/or homogeneous groups may expect to benefit more from therapy than will large and/or widely variant groups.[380] Regarding treatment modalities, many therapists including Swan favor a cognitive behavioral approach with deaf clientele, finding it helpful in influencing thought processes and beliefs which underlie behaviors.[381]

---

[379] Alex. Boros. "Issues in Treating Deaf Alcoholics within Hospitals" Mental Health, Substance Abuse and Deafness: ADARA Monograph #7. Rochester, N.Y. 1981 pp. 27-30.

[380] Kathleen Carroll & Bruce Rounsaville "Can a Technology Model of Psychotherapy Research be Applied to Cocaine Abuse Treatment?" in NIDA's Research Monograph Series, #104. Ibid. p. 92.

[381] Kristen Swan, "Dual Disorders in Chemical Dependency Treatment" Steps to Recovery, Minn, MN. The MN Chem.

Specific techniques, such as family confrontations of the addict,[382] programs to heal self-image, such as the "Positive Day" program[383] and efforts at the Queen Anne House of L.A., CA's Self Actualizing Institute for the Deaf have been offered in the literature for therapist consideration of usefulness on an individual basis.[384] In the same conceptual area, Owner & Ulissi (1981) offer conflict resolution strategies which they recommend teaching to deaf students presenting behavior problems.[385] Most of these strategies, techniques and suggestions have already proven their usefulness in general psychotherapy, and now are being tried, with documented results, with deaf people.

Additionally some researchers are documenting more specifically their findings and bases for theoretical frameworks, e.g. Whitehouse, Sherman and Kozlowski (1991). They don't attempt to draw broad generalizations from their sample; they posit only the current needs of deaf substance abusers in the state of Illinois.[386] Precise

---

Depend. Program for Deaf & Hard of Hearing Individuals. Aug. 1992. p. 2.

382 Jane M. Adams "Confronting the Addict: When Families Draw the Line" The Washington Post Health Supplement. July 17, 1990 pp. 12-15.

383 Maria Stephens & Frankie Walker. "Increasing Self-Esteem, Decreasing Drug Abuse: A Positive Approach to a Negative Situation" article provided by Gallaudet Univ.; n.d. pp. 5-14.

384 David Risser, "Program Helps Deaf Students Hone Living Skills" Los Angeles Times: Expressions. Aug. 27, 1987. pp. 1, 3.

385 Susan Z. Owner & Stephen M. Ulissi. "Conflict Resolution Training Program: Strategies for Hearing-Impaired Students with Behavior Problems" A.A.D. 126(6) Sep. 1981. pp. 619-626.

386 Adelaide Whitehouse, Richard Sherman & Karen Kozlowski. "The Needs of Deaf

documentation and caution in assuming that localized findings are transferable signals a step upward in research standards in this literature.

Family therapy, among other theoretical frameworks, has been suggested as an ideal vehicle for involving the loved ones of the deaf substance abuser. Family therapy focuses on the dynamics of family interactions and makes explicit how each person's behavior affects the rest of the family, while enhancing awareness of the caring that may exist in the family. Family therapy, in which the therapist communicates easily with both the deaf person(s) and the hearing person(s), (i.e. the therapist, either hearing or deaf, signs adequately to communicate with the deaf signing person(s) and speaks adequately to communicate with hearing people) may be difficult to obtain. But it may enhance communication with everyone involved and increase rapport. This is a more laborious path than working within narrower limits, such as peer-age groups, but it can eliminate, fairly early in its course, the creation of false excuse-facades, denial and game playing, since/if the family members know each other well enough to be immune to each other's avoidance gestures and rationalizations. Family therapy, additionally, may assist inarticulate members of a family to express their caring and thus provide a stronger foundation for future attempts of the addict to remain addiction free.

Shapiro and Harris have developed a co-therapy process which maximizes communication in the therapeutic situation. Shapiro is hearing and Harris is deaf. They report some success with co-therapy, particularly with deaf adolescents and deaf children of hearing parents.[387]

People who offer substance abuse treatment for deaf people are concerned that the treatment offered be effective. To this end, they have studied and assessed the relative merits of having special treatment units for deaf people or for integrating them into existing treatment programs, in which the deaf person would be a minority. Much discussion about the efficacy of both methods is available in the literature. The *Awakenings* staff come down tentatively on the side of free-standing treatment, but are open to changing that stance should future research offer evidence that mainstreamed deaf clients of addiction treatment thrive in that atmosphere.

We feel that, especially in the recovery process, it is critical that the deaf spend a considerable part of the group process and recreational time with others in the deaf community. At the same time we recognize that there is little likelihood that they will be able to return to the external world and remain isolated from the hearing. Upon graduation, clients will need to work with them, may opt to socialize with them, may even live with them. Under these circumstances, we also recognize the need to conduct certain activities in an integrated setting, if only to assist in the "reentry process."[388]

---

[387] Rodney Shapiro and Robert Harris. "Family Therapy in Treatment of the Deaf: A Case Report" Family Process. 15 (1) Mar., 1976. pp. 83-96.

[388] "Special Issues for the Hearing Impaired" Section E3e2 of C Needs Assessment from a proposal by Awakenings. The Southeast Council on Alcoholism & Drug Problems, Inc. Los Angeles, CA. Mar., 89. p. 28.

The mainstream vs. separate treatment question consumes many therapists' attention; in addition other questions, such as the type of therapy offered, whether the therapist should hear or be deaf, the comparative gains of one-to-one over group therapy, and the optimum length of treatment. These questions have not been fully answered. Regarding the advantages of individual and/or group therapy, Schein and Naiman have said:

> There are those who argue that the group may be the more effective milieu in which to treat certain social and emotional disorders. For the client whose principal difficulties arise from his inept management of interpersonal relationships, the group situation may be the better one in which to resolve his problems.
>
> Still other psychologists insist that the pitting of group against individual methods ignores good practice. They would argue that both have their place in counseling and psychotherapy. Under different conditions one or the other may be more helpful to an individual; at some times he may be best served by both approaches in combination.
>
> Whatever their philosophical positions . . . the authors here agree that it is important that group methods be open to deaf persons as an alternative treatment. And they further appear to agree that, to some extent and in at least some cases, group methods can be effective with deaf persons.[389]

[389] Jerome D. Schein & Doris W. Naiman, (Ed.s) The Use of Group Techniques with Deaf Persons, Wash., D.C. Introductory remarks to workshop presented by The New York Deafness Research & Training Center & the

Prognostic Implications Regarding Substance Abuse Treatment for Deaf People:

While some researchers focus on specific needs of disabled clientele for drug abuse therapy, other people in the helping professions are evaluating additional access points of the therapeutic process for possible breakthroughs in healing. The type of addiction, age of onset of addiction, and its duration are among the factors which have been shown to significantly impact effectiveness of treatment and determine the type of treatment which is considered most appropriate.[390] Factors such as therapist-patient rapport have been considered with implications for deaf people. Chough writes of the trust-mistrust phenomenon among the deaf, offering further explanation for the slow development of the therapeutic climate,[391] as has Kannapell.[392]

Whether or not the therapist hears or is deaf was considered as a treatment variable by Langholtz and Heller, in their attempt to examine any perceived differences in

Psychological Association for the Study of the Hearing Impaired. n.d. p. ii.

[390] Al J. Mooney, Arlene Eisenberg & Howard Eisenberg. The Recovery Book. N.Y. Workman Publ. Co. 1992. p. 6.

[391] Steven K. Chough "The Trust vs. Mistrust Phenomenon Among Deaf Persons" Mental Health, Substance Abuse & Deafness. D. Watson et al. (Ed.s) Silver Spring, MD. The Amer. Deafness & Rehabilitation Assoc. pp. 20-22.

[392] Barbara Kannapell "The Trust-Mistrust Phenomenon" Amer. Deafness & Rehab. Assoc. Vol. 7 (1) 1983.

[393] Daniel J. Langholtz & Bruce Heller "Deaf and Hearing Psychotherapists: Differences in their Delivery of Clinical Services to Deaf Clients" in D. Watson et al (Ed.s) Integrating Human Resources, Technology and Systems in Deafness. Silver Spring, MD. ADARA n.d. pp. 34-45.

delivery of clinical services between deaf and hearing therapists.[393] Although this study offers thoughtful scrutiny of a legitimate area of concern, it is limited in method, and is, in this researcher's opinion, useful mostly as an illustration pointing up the need for more careful research in this area. Because this variable is important to many deaf people, more studies focusing incisively on this question are in order.

Other factors which have often been identified as possibly affecting the outcome of therapy include the presence of an interpreter,[394] and the existence, or lack thereof, of a support group for the client, either peers or strong family unit, as has been documented already in this chapter.

Outcome of treatment studies act as feedback in research, offering corrective and prescriptive implications for future drug abuse treatment; thus as more outcome studies are completed, we can make further refinements in more precisely addressing the most important concerns. The National Institute on Drug Abuse has pioneered treatment outcome research, and offers a number of general guidelines for effective treatment. A series of monographs, published by the NIDA consider the impact of such components of therapy as method, therapist, duration of treatment, point and degree of intervention and follow-up services. Michael Lambert notes:

> Those investigating treatment effects have been largely occupied with the nature of the treatment process, while ignoring or focusing on assessment of change as only an afterthought. As a consequence,

394 Thomas L. Dixon "Addiction among the Hearing Impaired". EAP Digest Jan/Feb. 1987. p. 43.

thinking and theorizing about the assessment of change lags behind developments in treatment strategies themselves. Unfortunately, the development of effective treatment for drug abuse, or any disorder, is largely dependent on the accurate assessment of client change.[395]

Has the client really changed if relapse occurs? Alcoholism is generally viewed as a treatable but incurable disease, so that recovering alcoholics need to be continually on guard against relapsing. So rigorous after-care and maintenance programs are absolutely essential.[396] Statistics vary, but some recovery groups report that 60% of their members relapse into drinking. For other addictions, the recidivism rate can be even higher.[397]

Alex Boros, project director at Kent, Ohio, offers guidelines for teaching recovery to deaf abusers. He lists eleven points for working w/deaf person in a 1-1 ration, and eight pointers for counselors in group situations. His suggestions are basic and perhaps obvious, but until their implementation is the norm, they bear stating. e.g. He suggests rephrasing statements which were inadequately understood, rather than merely restating the same words, in case it was the particular combination of sounds of lip movements which were confusing. He also speaks of the necessity of getting feedback from the deaf person who nods a lot, in case the nod doesn't really signify

---

[395] Michael Lambert, Ibid. p. 80.
[396] Mooney, Eisenberg & Eisenberg. Ibid. p. 541.
[397] Ibid. p. 542.

understanding.[398] Gaining client participation, rather than mere intellectual agreement, augurs emotional growth.

Kavanaugh (1992) asks "What is Healing?" and proceeds to answer that the process is far more than the mere removal of disturbing symptoms. "It consists of a combination of methods which address our problems at every level," he says.[399] He notes that it is possible for people to go through therapy, completing all the required steps and remain unchanged and unhealed, in 12-step programs or in any other program. There is no simple formula for growth, and a clear and accurate assessment of change is needed.[400] John De Miranda adds "We as a society are still ambivalent about whether to view alcoholism/addiction as a 'real' disability." He offers the opinion that until cultural attitudes change, recovery efforts are severely hampered.[401]

In 1986 the Second National Conference on the Habilitation and Rehabilitation of Deaf Adolescents was held. The proceedings of that meeting constitute an early progress report on current treatment efforts. The progress reported there, as is much that we have seen in this examination, was primarily in terms of hope on the part of workers in the helping professionals that measures and programs which have been planned, if well implemented, will be effective in eradicating substance abuse among deaf adolescents.

---

[398] Alex Boros "Instructions for Teaching Recovery to Reading-Limited Alcoholics" AID Bulletin 7(3) 1986. pp. 1-4.

[399] Philip Kavannah, Ibid. p. 224.

[400] Ibid. p. 225.

[401] John DeMiranda "The Common Ground: Alcoholism, Addiction and Disability" Addiction & Recovery. Aug. 1990. pp. 45.

In an impassioned book, *Willpower's Not Enough*, Washton and Boundy take a larger look at the many factors predisposing people to addiction in the 1990s, and offer a surprisingly hopeful conclusion ability of the average person to avoid or to get out of an addiction. They repeat the adage that accepting helplessness is disabling.[402]

Research Implications for Preventive Efforts for Deaf Populations:

In the few years since the extent of the problem of substance abuse among the deaf has been glimpsed, a number of therapists have labored to remedy the situation. They have documented their work, and tried to establish network connections with others with similar objectives. If their hopes are rewarded, we should see a decrease in the addictive penchant among deaf people, and educational efforts will aid new generations in building strong, therapeutic support systems and internal defenses against addiction.

Disseminating information regarding the researched effects of alcohol and/or drugs, especially additional loss of hearing, in layman's terms, in films, video-tapes or easily understood written materials is regarded by some therapeutic agencies as a first line of defense. To do this, academic wordings and abstract concepts need to be re-phrased, if at all possible without losing meaning, to allow the thought to be accessible to the clientele. As reported in chapter three, a number of deleterious processes occur in chronic alcoholism, and likewise, in chapter four, drug abuse has deteriorating effects on the brain and CNS; permeating the deaf culture with popularized re-statements

---

[402] Arnold Washton & Donna Boundy. ibid. pp. 47, 73.

of this information is needed. Several of the studies cited in chapters three and four could provide dramatic impact if they were used as preventive data. e.g. Wheeler's (1980) finding linking length of heavy drinking time and loss of auditory acuity and Luterman's (1982) findings while studying evoked responses of human brainstem auditory processes during alcohol intoxication and during recovery. Studies which can clearly be seen to be relevant to concerns of deaf people need to be widely disseminated, perhaps in layman's terms. The physical losses shown by such research might prove to be an adequate deterrent to people who already have some hearing loss and can imagine implications of further handicaps.

Methods of publicizing these research findings include such things as community lectures and/or panel discussions e.g. researchers could explain the implications of their research, dramatizations of case histories by deaf theatrically talented people for town meetings, and other such methods. Because CNS damage of alcoholism and drug abuse is largely irreversible, full use of available methods of publicizing results of such studies (in layman's terms), before people have reached the stage where results of abuse become obvious, may be a method of educating people at risk, and avoiding such problems. Such airing may be seen as a scare tactic, but extreme measures may be required to change substance abuse patterns.

While many scholars, researchers, agencies and programs have offered specific suggestions and guidelines for necessary ingredients for good treatment programs, most have, additionally, at least alluded to certain intangibles, which we wish to further explore.

First there is perceived, almost universally in the literature, a need for common-sense flexibility and judgement in implementing suggested guidelines. The

Americans With Disabilities Act ruled that such entities as government agencies must provide whatever auxiliary aids are necessary to give a deaf person an equal opportunity to participate in and get the advantage of the government service, program or activity.[403] The appropriate auxiliary aid, of course, depends on the type of activity planned and the disability of the person. In the case of counseling sessions or group support meetings, talking is the activity: communication is the vehicle by which change is invited to occur. Thus, adequate communication is a primary concern.

If all of the participants are signing-deaf, signing in ASL is the probable medium, even though ASL is not 100% standard usage among culturally Deaf people. An adult who loses hearing in mid-life and who is not proficient in sign language, however, may not sign well and may need a computer monitor with on-going print-outs of what other people are saying, and a keyboard to be able to offer input on topics while they are still relevant. A shy deaf person who signs very well may not be comfortable revealing innermost thoughts and feelings, especially those which reveal doubts about adequacy, in the presence of a third party, thus an interpreter to translate from a hearing/speaking therapist would not be the most appropriate aid for that person.

So flexibility and a willingness to see individual needs within the larger framework is necessary. Legal Rights of deaf substance abusers are protected equally with rights of everyone else, so the National Center for Law and Deafness asserts that deaf people should not be required to pay for

---

[403] Public Law 101-336, 42 U.S. Code (U.S.C.) 12101 et seq. 28 C.F.R.; #35.160(b) 1989.

"auxiliary aids," but that they should be provided by the agency or resource offering contact with deaf people.[404]

Payette offered a number of grant writing strategies for community based projects offering prevention services to young deaf persons.[405] These might be useful for people trying to fund programs adequately on limited means. Perhaps more mini-workshops on grant writing strategies, offered in conference settings of deaf community centers in large cities, would enable more treatment facilities to use such information and techniques.

Qualified counselors are clearly needed, in sufficient numbers; yet most of the written check-lists tend to assume this basic necessity. Not everyone who possesses adequate credentials or experience in the areas needed, however, is adequately caring or mature enough psychologically to actually be helpful. Some people, possibly those without substantial private incomes, may never see therapists who exude caring qualities conducive to healing. There is a cliche circulating among counselors of dysfunctional families, especially families with histories of overt abuse which states, "Hurting people hurt people." "Hurts" consist of both committed acts and words and omitted ones which were essential. They include physical and non-physical trauma and unseen wounds of neglect which, if not treated, may fester for years.

While we are not equating less-than-cream-of-the-crop counselors with abusive people, we are noting that, in order for therapists to offer optimum help, they should be more

---

[404] Legal Rights: The Guide for Deaf and Hard of Hearing People. Wash. D.C.; Gallaudet Univ. Press. 4th edition. 1992. p. 28.

[405] Bruce A. Payette "Community Based Grantwriting Strategies for Substance Abuse Prevention with Deaf and Hard of Hearing Youth" n.p.; n.d. pp. 109-112.

than merely adequate, psychologically, themselves, and they should possess adequate insights to be able to offer amelioration of the patient's psyche, even if the patient is not articulate and cannot request what is needed.

This may be a special need for disabled people, since often their past history includes one or more factors of omission in the realm of nurturing and inculcation of perceptions toward psychological health. In the realm of deaf children born to hearing parents, for instance, we have seen (see Chapter II), that early parental denial of their child's handicap and sporadic feelings of rejection may color their relationships with that child. We have seen, additionally, that the developmental process which has included many small incidents in which "You are not adequate" is communicated, (usually inadvertently), add up to a strong sense in the developing child, so that by adulthood, that message has been internalized. With the additional factor of addiction of one or more of the people in the family, unseen wounds, in the form of inadequate positive reinforcement, further deter the development of psychological health. i.e. If the parent of a deaf child has been too occupied being an addict, and has not given adequate nurturing to the child, it becomes doubly important that, later, the counselor attempting to be of help be a caring, emotionally stable individual.[406]

It would be optimum if we had pre-hiring screening tools and objective measuring devices which would accurately assess such factors as counselor empathy, but we do not. Therefore it becomes incumbent upon hiring agencies to listen to feedback from clients regarding counselors who are perceived to be helpful. This is not a blank-check for the people receiving treatment to "order" only therapists who

---

[406] Kavannah, ibid. pp. 101-104.

will not tell them anything they do not wish to hear; it is more concerned with insuring caring qualities in the counselor, which are communicated clearly to clients, regardless of whether other things are communicated. The findings we have surveyed regarding substance abuse treatment for deaf people are preliminary, but hopeful in most instances. Washton and Boundy say:

It is the hope for recovery that the 90s hold for both the baby-boom generation and for the larger society. Since we can't successfully arrest addictions without giving up unrealistic expectations and goals and opening ourselves up to receiving help from others, the more people that bottom out in our addictive society, the more society itself will change for the better. But in the meantime, all we can do is change ourselves.

. . . We can practice honesty, stop blaming everyone else for what's wrong in our lives, and start changing what we can. In this way, the *real* War on Drugs will be fought by each one of us, through our own personal recovery.[407]

---

[407] Washton & Bounty, ibid. p. 139.

CHAPTER VI

DISCUSSION

This work has examined a large body of research literature, informed opinion, and statistical material covering the sizable problem of substance abuse among deaf people. Pertinent information about deaf populations, alcoholism, drug abuse and current efforts at prevention and remediation have been reviewed.

In the process of this examination, areas in which opinion is divided have been noted. There are many questions which conclusive evidence has not yet answered. It is not our purpose to offer conclusions regarding these questions, but rather to consider the issues involved and to discuss the implications and ramifications of various viewpoints regarding several basic questions.

Some questions deserving consideration are: 1) Is there a psychology of the deaf, and if there is, can it be useful as a composite profile and not be used to perpetuate stereotypes which would further impede deaf people? 2) Are there specific personality characteristics, which have been identified as being conducive to vulnerability to addiction? If so, are these traits often found among deaf people, perhaps due to their previous isolation and enculturization rather than anything inherent in deafness, which place deaf people at greater risk than the larger society for addictive disorders? 3) In the area of prevention and treatment for substance abuse, including abuse of alcohol, is there one clear-cut superior method to proceed with deaf people or not? 4) Is mainstreaming deaf people into the larger society, in drug and alcohol preventive efforts and remediation, helpful in the long run, or is separate treatment for deaf people superior in terms of both immediate and ultimate benefit? 5) In treatment for substance abuse, including alcohol abuse, are counselors who are a) deaf themselves and/or b) former addicts themselves superior/inferior to hearing and/or non-addict counselors?

TWO VIEWS OF DEAFNESS

Outline by Chris Wixtrom

—DEAFNESS AS PATHOLOGY—

With this perspective, a person might:

Define deafness as a pathological condition (a defect, or a handicap) which distinguishes abnormal deaf persons from normal hearing persons.

Deny, downplay, or hide evidence of deafness.

Seek a "cure" for deafness: focus on ameliorating the effects of the "auditory disability" or "impairment."

Give much attention to the use of hearing aids and other devices that enhance auditory perception and/or focus on speech. Examples: amplifiers, tactile and computer-aided speech devices, cue systems . . .

Place much emphasis on speech and speechreading ("oral skills"); avoid sign and other communication methods which are deemed "inferior."

Promote the use of auditory-based communication modes; frown upon the use of modes which are primarily visual.

Describe sign language as inferior to spoken language

View spoken language as the most natural language for all persons, including the deaf.

Make mastery of spoken language a central educational aim.

Support socialization of deaf persons with hearing persons. Frown upon deaf/deaf interaction and deaf/deaf marriages.

Regard "the normal hearing person" as the best role model.

Regard professional involvement with the deaf as "helping the deaf" to "overcome their handicap" and to "live in the hearing world."

Neither accept nor support a separate "deaf culture."

—DEAFNESS AS A DIFFERENCE—

With this perspective, a person might:

Define deafness as merely a difference, a characteristic which distinguishes normal deaf person from normal hearing persons. Recognize that deaf people are a linguistic and cultural minority.

Openly acknowledges deafness.

Emphasize the abilities of deaf persons.

Give much attention to issues of communication access for deaf persons through visual devices and services. Examples: telecommunication devices, captioning devices, light signal devices, interpreters . . .

Encourage the development of all communication modes including—but not limited to—speech.

Strongly emphasize the use of vision as a positive, efficient alternative to the auditory channel.

View sign language as the most natural language for the deaf.

In education, focus on subject matter, rather than a method of communication. Work to expand all communication skills.

Support socialization within the deaf community as well as within the large community.

Regard professional involvement with the deaf as "provide access to the same rights and privileges that hearing people enjoy."

Respect, value and support the language and culture of deaf people.

These questions will be considered one at a time in terms of implications for present and future action. Rather than return, piecemeal, to the detailed research surveyed in previous chapters of this work, we shall, for the most part, summarize and distill conclusions and opinions from the literature. In some instances, answers are hedged, due to inadequacy of present information. In other instances, it may appear that insights line up as rationalizations for preconceptions, due to perceived inadequacies or distorting implications of the question, itself. I shall, however, endeavor to report, faithfully, the evidence and insights gleaned from the evidence, throughout this discussion.

I. Is there a "psychology of the deaf?"

This question reflects the gestalt of the questioners more than it provides preventive and remedial insights. If, after all the research is tabulated, the term "psychology of the deaf" translates in practical application to prejudicial treatment of deaf people, because of their deafness, it is reasonable to question whether or not it is valid to generalize across a broad spectrum of people with individual differences, with deafness as the only variable presumed to be remaining constant. While researchers may identify similar tendencies and report observed commonalties of behavioral reactions among deaf people, it has not been ruled out that researchers might also report the same or very similar tendencies and observed behavioral commonalties among other populations under similar conditions. This suggests that research standards have not been, up to now, strict enough to enable us to deduce that deafness, alone, is responsible for perceived similarities of personality structure nor of personality dynamics among deaf people.

If, however, researchers document perceived similarities among a given population, so that a more precise "fit" in approach or "handle" for treatment may be fashioned, rather than to isolate that population, it is worth noting carefully all the descriptive data collected.[408] The fact that some of the data may apply, additionally, to other people besides deaf people, i.e. that descriptions of deaf people may be similar to descriptions of other designated populations, then becomes secondary. The effort to use the collected data of similar characteristics to empower the deaf population in combating substance addiction becomes the foreground. So, a "psychology of the deaf" may mean personality characteristics of deaf people which might suggest certain therapeutic approaches, over other therapeutic approaches. The composite profile, then, is not used prejudicially, but as an attempt to focus primarily on salient personality areas for more immediate interactions with deaf people. Within those parameters, and with those caveats it is possible to speak of 'a psychology of the deaf.'

II. Are there specific personality characteristics of deaf people which place them at risk for addictive disorders?

Are there trait clusters, personality characteristics or other observed qualities which deaf people often possess, which make them additionally vulnerable to drug and alcohol abuse? In previous chapters, discussion has

---

[408] Kenneth Z. Altshuler, "Toward a Psychology of Deafness," 1978, ibid.; A.F. Cooper, "The Psychological Problems of the Deaf and Blind." 1979, ibid; Hans G. Furth, "Linguistic Deficiency and Thinking: Research with Deaf Subjects" 1971, ibid; L.B. Jonkees, "Psychological problems of the Deaf," 1983; ibid; McCay Vernon, "Sociological and psychological factors associated with hearing loss" 1969, ibid.

included such factors as enculturization variables stigma and isolation, as well as specific personality variables associated with communication disorders which can be seen to increase vulnerability to substance addiction. Correlation information, citing commonalties between many deaf people and many people who are at risk for alcoholism or drug abuse has been included. It has not been suggested that any quality inherent in deafness is linked causally with these correlative findings, however.

The isolation of the Deaf culture, the prevalence of moral stigmatizing in many deaf communities and overall previous lack of education regarding substance abuse among the deaf have been cited as major contributing factors to deaf people's additional vulnerability to addiction. Frustrations in dealing with bureaucracy and the lack of adequate accessibility to deaf people of the major society's treatment facilities have also been noted as significantly compounding the problem. Increasing awareness of conditions which place people at risk and increasing access to preventive and remediation resources, it is hoped, will have the chosen impact of reducing deaf people's vulnerability to addiction.

III. What Kind of Therapy is Most Effective with Deaf Substance Abusers?

Is there one, overall, preventive or treatment strategy which works best with deaf people? Is the optimum therapeutic method of treating addiction disorders individually determined? Theorists and researchers have stated that optimum therapy for substance abuse and alcoholism is best determined on an individual, case by case, basis. Most workers in the field, however, venture the opinion that such ideal conditions aren't always possible.

When facilities and resources are stretched, program administrators may be inclined to determine what works adequately for the largest number of people, and applying those methods across the board, unless they are clearly contra-indicated. No method of treatment has been found to be 100% successful; recidivism rates and failure rates far surpass cure rates among all populations surveyed.

A pre-requisite for effective therapy is clear two-way communication. Preliminary research has shown that up until the present time, adequate communication between deaf clients and hearing therapists has been lacking. Treatment centers operated solely by deaf people for deaf people are not common, either, but they have, thus far, reported as much success as has any other paradigm. Attempts to comply with the law, regarding access by Americans with Disabilities, are gradually bringing more treatment facilities into consideration. More counselors are also being trained in ASL, attempts to reach deaf people with addiction disorders.

Since all deaf people are not alike in their communication modalities, providing one method of presentation/reception of information to/from deaf people, e.g. signing, is perceived to be inadequate. Likewise, the use of interpreters has been faulted, as has been discussed in detail, for reasons of confidentiality and because rapport between client and therapist is hard to develop via an intervening person. Clear communication must be two-way in order for therapeutic progress to occur. Meeting the client in his/her current condition and communication modality is a pre-condition for effective therapy, regardless of what type of therapy is offered.

In addition to considerations of effective communication, some therapists have suggested that the answer to the question of optimum treatment methods depends on how far along the continuum of addiction the individual receiving treatment has come. People who work closely with addiction disorders often state that the personality profiles of addicts become increasingly, and similarly, compressed toward flatness, overriding many other variables. Amplifying this view, many therapists suggest that while the ability to hear may, similarly, appear as a major variable in beginning stages of addiction, it is much less significant, than is desire to be addiction free, in late stages of addiction.

So, the kinds of therapy which work best with deaf people in advanced stages of deterioration might very well be not measurably different from the kinds of therapy which work well with hearing people. A flattened personality profile, whether the person exhibiting it is hearing or deaf, may not be responsive to many preferred treatment modes, thus only less than optimum methods, by default, remain.

Before remediation becomes necessary, when society is still concentrating on prevention of substance abuse, similar non-discriminatory insights have also been suggested. The values and strengths which will preclude an individual's susceptibility to substance abuse include such qualities as self-esteem, a well developed sense of autonomy, the feeling of being loved or at least appreciated, and confidence in one's abilities, which are not limited to either hearing or deaf people, but are available to everyone.

Therapeutic methods which directly tie behaviors to insights have been shown to benefit people, across the board. Strong cognitive-behavioral therapies, perhaps with measures built in, e.g. urinalysis, to increase accountability, have reported the greatest degrees of success among out-patients. There is still enough variety among competing psychotherapies which meet this minimum criteria, of cognitive-behavioral prerequisites, to encompass personal preference and ease of delivery criteria.

Psychotherapists, as well as preventive workers, often lead from their individual strengths, in their choice of therapeutic method, milieu and frame of reference.[409] As long as core criteria are maintained, this individualistic proclivity cannot be faulted, and indeed may produce spectacular results, due partly to the therapist's degree of passion. It was noted, in chapter five, workers like actor Chuck Norris who focus on the strong physical appeal of action, e.g. karate, to impel his clients toward increased self-esteem, confidence and ability to shape their lives toward chosen goals, to lead drug-free lives. Other role models in the fields of sports and rock music draw young people by their respective specialties, and are able to instill qualities which may "drug-proof" people under their influence.

These special cases of powerful influence are effective partly due to the increased visibility of the leaders, partly because of the degree of commitment which the leaders bring to the effort, and partly because of the natural tendency to imitate what is perceived as successful and valued. Even though special methods, even unorthodox ones, may work for celebrities or people who bring a great deal of passion to their work, they are not necessarily chosen for mass replication. This somewhat obvious conclusion is due to the fact that the qualities which aid the methods in their observable efficacy may have less to do with variables of treatment which can be standardized and

---

[409] Susan Z. Owner & Stephen M. Ulissi, "Conflict Resolution Training Program: Problem Solving Strategies for Hearing Impaired Students with Behavior Problems" AAD, Sep. 1981. pp. 619-626.

more to do with personal appeal and charisma of these outstanding therapists and leaders.

Does this mean that no commonalties regarding efficient and effective treatment have been observed? No. Effective treatment, as reviewed in our survey of the literature, encompasses a number of observed variables. Some factors are diagnostic: a) overall understanding of the present situation, b) clear presentation of contributing variables, and c) joint understanding (by both client and therapist) of project to be undertaken and potential barriers to be subverted. Some factors are dynamic, e.g. maintaining a high level of commitment to the chosen goals. Still other factors address progress behaviorally, providing feedback and corrective impetus. Such specific treatment aids as counselor-client behavior-contracts have been noted as reinforcing of therapeutic commitment.

A strong belief, by the counselor, in the client's potential to change in desired directions, is, of course, a sine qua non of effective therapy of whatever style offered. Counselors who offer clients only their peripheral attention and minimal emotional investment are worse than useless; they reinforce negative self-esteem and perpetuate the client's hopelessness. So, the over-arching characteristic of effective therapy remains a sensitive, caring counselor.

IV. Is Mainstreaming or Deaf-Only Group Treatment The Most Effective Treatment?

After dozens of groups and therapy situations involving both hearing and deaf people, and a similar number of therapy histories with deaf-only clients have been reviewed, this question is still unanswered. While for many Deaf people who sign, deaf-only support groups and treatment efforts are preferred by the clients, there is evidence suggesting that treatment among one's perceived peers does not sufficiently move people beyond their "comfort zones." It may never challenge people to develop their individual potential or to increase their rapport with other individuals who may seem different from themselves.

Is group treatment type best determined for clients on an individual basis? Perhaps. This may be a factor of personality actualization, and it may involve clients' past experiences as well as presently perceived priorities. Examples have been cited in the literature illuminating problems with both mainstreaming and deaf-only approaches for group therapy among deaf substance abusers. Often proponents of one or the other viewpoint argue quite passionately on the basis of one or two examples. Proponents of mainstreaming provide examples suggesting that if the client's previous peer group was composed primarily of other substance-abusing deaf people, insufficient motivation for change, in deaf-only groups, is proffered because the group vision is too narrow and has too low a ceiling. They report increased respect for individual variety-potential and increased understanding of the role of heterogeneous support among mainstreamed groups.[410]

We can question whether or not the various examples seen in the literature, regarding the characteristics of clientele groups, are worthy of generalization, of course, as we can question whether there were, perhaps in the therapies attempted, unexpressed expectations or other subtle variables, such as personality clashes, not identified, which also might have skewed the results. Our safest conclusion remains that we simply do not have enough good

---

[410] Case summaries: Mental Health Assessment of Deaf Clients: Special Conditions; UCSF Center on Deafness. Conference Report: San Francisco, Ca. Feb. 11-13, 1988.

research to conclude that results of therapy may be linked to whether or not deaf clientele are served in deaf-only addiction treatment efforts.

V. Do deaf clients progress in therapy better with deaf counselors? Do substance abusers progress in therapy better with former substance abusers?

In 1989, Palmer wrote a detailed comparison of the opinions of deaf and hearing professional workers regarding priorities of deafness research, which was previously discussed in this work. The Delphi technique of three rounds of questionnaires were sent to 170 "experts," requesting their specific ideas for topics for future research. Ms. Palmer concluded that hearing and deaf researchers diverged significantly in their perception of needs for research on deafness, with deaf professionals citing much more need than did hearing researchers. Deaf people perceived more nuances of deaf people's reality than did hearing people in the helping professions.[411]

Langholtz and Heller also discussed differences in the delivery of services between deaf and hearing therapists. They noted, among other things, a possible ambivalence on the part of deaf clients toward either/both hearing and deaf counselors, as a further impedance to therapeutic results. The rationalization they found approximated this: "Perhaps, because this therapist is deaf, he/she isn't as highly educated as a hearing therapist, and I need the best therapist available."[412]

---

[411] Ursula J. Palmer, "A Comparison of the opinions of deaf and hearing professionals regarding the research needs in the field of deafness." 1989, ibid.

[412] Daniel Langholtz & Bruce Heller, "Deaf and Hearing Psychotherapists: Differences in their delivery of clinical

Yet, Chough and Kannapell both documented the trust-mistrust phenomenon which a deaf substance abuse client may bring to treatment with a hearing therapist, as have several other researchers noted in previous chapters of this work. The essential rapport/transference between therapist and client is difficult enough to develop that, where choice is possible, it seems only sensible *not* to add potential barriers to the development of that trust. If ideal therapeutic situations existed consistently, perhaps deaf clients would be met and initial diagnostic evaluations would be made which would include, in addition to information relating to what needs to be done, recommendations suggesting characteristics of therapists of choice.

Difficulties in making progress in therapy have been noted particularly in instances wherein all the deaf people were clientele and all the hearing people were staff. A "gamey" atmosphere frequently developed in which clients acted in complicity to encourage a "them vs. us" perception and/or the creation of additional secondary gains barriers. These were frequently manifested in increasing group conformity, along deaf-hearing lines.

In these noted situations, regardless of what may have been accomplished in terms of socialization, therapeutic progress did not, overall, meet expectation levels. The hearing staff may have been aware of some manipulative behaviors, but, for whatever reasons, did not choose to confront them. The deaf clientele may have been aware of their hopes for addiction-free living taking a subsidiary role to Deaf solidarity validation processes. For a client to take refuge in perceived inadequacies of the counselor (e.g. to

---

services to deaf clients" in D. Watson, G. Anderson, & M. Taff-Watson, (Eds.) Integrating Human Resources, Technology & Systems in Deafness ADARA reprint, n.d.; ibid.

adequately comprehend clients' unique situations) is not a monopoly of deaf people, of course. Such ulterior agendas undermine treatment effectiveness, and the people who lose are the unfortunate people whose therapy is thereby diminished.

People who advocate deaf-only peer counseling groups assert that only other deaf participants are capable of challenging denial and other manipulations and behavioral crutches the deaf client might employ in efforts to resist giving up excuses. Confrontation by people who know the typical avoidance flailings, but who continue to demonstrate steadfast commitment to the individual's complete participation in recovery from addiction, can be a powerful tool in treatment. If deaf substance abuse counselors can be found and used, deaf people may have greater chances to begin, and to remain in, therapy. The lack of enough deaf counselors to serve all deaf substance abusers, however, cannot be allowed to serve as an excuse for an addict's not attempting to change addictive and abusive habits.

Whether or not it is inherently preferable that a deaf substance abusing client be seen by a deaf recovering substance-abusing counselor is still being hotly debated, with opinion occasionally switching from one side to the other. e.g. People who believe that, all other things being equal, deaf counselors are more acceptable to deaf clients, also note that in the research and teaching fields there are remarkable exceptions to this generalization. They cite examples of highly motivated, caring individuals, such as McCay Vernon, who seem to be able to explicate viewpoints which deaf people had formerly assumed hearing people could not understand.

When we push the theory to extremes, (that only deaf substance abusers can adequately understand other deaf substance abusers), then no individual can completely understand anyone other than himself or herself, since no two people's experience is completely congruent in every detail. e.g. If only a person who has abused a drug can understand and ameliorate a current drug abuser's situation, a person who takes one drug can say that a counselor who took another drug in the past cannot adequately help him, since the "pull" of one addiction may be different from that of another, or that things have changed since the counselor left the drug scene. Ultimately, such a line of argument becomes ridiculous and is seen as just one more avoidance gesture resisting treatment.

Intuitively, we know that people can learn from vicarious experience, and not have to experience everything completely for themselves. Such basic insights form the basis of preventive efforts and intervention therapy itself. The old aphorism, "Experience is a dear (expensive) teacher, and some will learn by no other," may have arisen for its prescriptive, rather than descriptive properties.

Factors alternative to experience may substitute for experience—for instance, the degree of caring. It is quite often true that a recovering alcoholic is filled with missionary zeal and has much more motivation to help other alcoholics than would a person for whom alcoholism's scary depths never showed their threatening probabilities. But vicarious experience allows civilized societies the hope to avoid every person having to experience every despair and pain.

Likewise, even though the human race is expressed in multiplicity, e.g. some people are deaf and some people hear, we all have the same capabilities emotionally; we all love, fear, etc., and we all hope to fulfill our individual potentials. Feeling at times isolated, alone, misunderstood, under-appreciated and unfortunate is universally experienced.

Effective therapy meets each individual's feelings of abandonment, anger, fear, loneliness and grief, and counters these with parallel insights of self-worth and hope, while, at the same time, effective therapy provides teachings and behavior blocks of incremental progress toward our innately human potentials.

CHAPTER VII

CONCLUSIONS AND RECOMMENDATIONS

Within the consideration of substance abuse among deaf people, this researcher has investigated research literature relevant to multiple and interweaving facts about drug abuse among deaf people. Specifically, a) the nature of deafness, causes of deafness and characteristics of various deaf populations; b) alcoholism, its causes and effects on people's lives and specifically how alcoholism further impedes a significant number of deaf people; c) salient facts about other substance abuse, epidemiology and recidivism rates for drug abuse treatment, examining the literature with special consideration regarding drug abuse among deaf people; d) efforts and prevention and treatment of substance abuse, including alcoholism treatment centers and programs has been considered. This survey has included various community resources as they serve deaf people toward education, prevention and remediation of drug abuse problems, and summary information on a number of treatment facilities, both in-patient and out-patient, with reference to services for deaf people has been provided.

Chapter six discussed questions which had been shown to be germane to the optimum care of deaf and hard of hearing people using the services of these preventive and rehabilitative programs and resources. This researcher has offered insights for improving the lives of deaf children, via education, to preclude pitfalls of drug ignorance, and in areas of treatment, to assist deaf people afflicted, at present, with drug abuse or habits which leave them vulnerable to drug abuse.

This work has carefully delineated a number of interweaving factors which place deaf people at increased vulnerability to addiction, not necessarily because of deafness, per se, but because of socio-cultural and communication variables. The public health model, especially, focuses on the interactions between the agent, the host and the environment, with emphasis in both prevention and remediation on integrated models which include all affected areas. We have offered overwhelming opinion suggesting that potential substance abusers among the deaf population need additional support and preventive attention. We have relayed pleas for more accurate diagnostic and support services, additionally, as we have considered what special features these services might contain to best serve deaf clientele.

The paucity of both excellently designed and executed research and of caring, qualified therapists/teachers and other helping professional people to implement treatment programs has been noted. This researcher has consistently recommended that agencies and resources seeking to serve given populations meet those people at their present circumstance, which, in this work, primarily has focused on communicating in the language of the people addressed, but could have even further implications. This writer specifically recommend wide-spread cross-training of professional workers in these fields.

It is further noted that the number of facilities emerging to meet needs of deaf substance abusers is increasing and existing resources are gradually attempting to make their services accessible to deaf people. The increase in attention being given to preventive efforts is applauded, and it is hoped that more and expanded focus in this area will continue. This writer also applauds efforts to grapple with the problem of substance abuse among deaf people by community and public advocacy groups. Public health care models of prevention, treatment and aftercare have shown much promise in this area, as have community efforts, e.g. John de Miranda's work and the several IADD's conferences and publications. The integration of a community models and public health concepts offers a promise of a wider perspective, a more comprehensive paradigm perhaps, for addressing problems of addiction.

This work has recommended increasing further the networking efforts among helping professions and social resources to avoid duplication of efforts and to use each other's strengths. The appendix following this chapter provides contact information, in the form of addresses, for a number of resources, service providing agencies and resource materials. Each of the entities listed, in turn, offers much information in its category. e.g. the Alcohol and Drug Services Directory of San Mateo County presents detailed information regarding sixty-eight subsidiary programs, such as the Center on Deafness' Alcohol and Drug Project, operated out of the University of San Francisco, which provides diagnostic services, referrals, community training and outreach services for deaf chemical abusers in the county. It may be that the sheer mass of agencies and facilities which seem to be involved, may add to the bewilderment of a person seeking to redress his problems.

It is not the purpose of the present work to duplicate existing reference resources nor, primarily, to compile a comprehensive cross-index of currently viable projects aimed at helping deaf people with substance abuse problems, although this work has surveyed some of these, so only the basal resources are listed in Appendix A. Much subsidiary and ancillary information is subsumed in appendix entries, and may be gathered by contacting the agencies or resources.

Conferences such as "The Next Step," a nation-wide attempt to focus on substance abuse treatment issues which have an impact on deaf people, and deafness concerns which may affect substance abuse treatment, help to spread the insights and experience of concerned people in the helping professions. They also provide ample material for imitative efforts, increasing the effectiveness of each approach. The public health perspective, again, offers much in its models for collaboration and methodology.

Efforts to share knowledge on this topic should not be limited to the United States; indeed the problem is international in scope, as the World Federation of the Deaf has recognized. The WFD has asked the World Health Organization to offer special psychiatric services worldwide for deaf people. Although researchers in various countries primarily work independently, a few efforts have been made and are being made to circulate publications and to establish venues for sharing information.

Satellite TV conference hook-ups could be provided to enable researchers from the world's universities to confer. Conference hook-ups could also more frequently be used among helping professionals in such situations as difficult diagnosis, finding follow-up and aftercare resources for clients going from one geographical area to another and with other concerns involving national access of one area's resources or expertise, by another area.

Overall the electronic media have thus far been significantly underused in the effort against drug abuse among the deaf. Technology has provided ways to by-pass deaf people's lack of access to the common telephone, in the computer's modem. Only vague fears of technology and lack of enabling physical resources now prevent the Deaf community from fully using electronic communication to end the isolation from mainstream society which has been a limiting factor for deaf people.

The electronic highway provided by such tools as universities' communication access, e.g. Internet, has been under-explored among deaf people. We specifically recommend a massive effort to promote telecommunication and computer literacy among deaf people, to discount any communication handicap which might have been previously experienced, and to open new vistas of information and educational resources. Even non-technical arenas, such as on-line chats, which are used primarily to socialize, can boost the confidence of deaf individuals who find they are easily able to maintain the pace and add their own cleverness, with no handicapping factor or communication difficulty.

Additional funding for treatment projects could also be sought by the writing of more grants. Grant writing strategies are finally being recognized as worth learning and are being offered as inservice training to some health care professionals.[413] We recommend more consideration of grants as sources of funding and additional and wider access to grant writing coaching sessions.

An over-arching recommendation, toward the eradication of substance abuse in deaf populations, is for the instilling of hope in the designated population that such a goal is indeed possible, even probable. This is such an important factor that without the hope that substance abuse is a conquerable problem, even if financial resources and treatment facilities were unlimited, efforts would be

---

[413] Bruce A. Payette, "Community Based Grant Writing Strategies for Substance Abuse Prevention with Deaf and Hard of Hearing Youth" p. 109, ibid.

futile. Educational efforts, acquainting people with both affective and cognitive elements of addiction-free living offer reasonable prognosis for this goal.

Continuing present avenues of research, including doing more longitudinal studies, is also strongly suggested. Longitudinal studies offer reassurances of reliability which short-term studies cannot, and help to discount the effects of other present factors of inadequate research. Upgrading the quality of research, overall, might attract other serious researchers to the field. Objective measures (e.g. not sole reliance on self-report questionnaires) and more well-designed research studies, including double-blind studies, focusing precisely on hypotheses relevant to the Deaf community are also highly recommended for long-term accurate information.

One obvious problem has concerned the present inadequacy of research literature. Conscientious researchers of the future will need to be more selective regarding inclusion of research materials in the area of deaf literature. For instance, Seidmon, in 1979, examined the effects of group therapy techniques in a deaf population, as was mentioned in a previous chapter of this work. Skewing the applicability of the study is the fact that it involved only five people, who were all welfare recipients rated by their caseworkers as extremely low in motivation. With ASL as their first language, they differed from the mainstream further in that English was not, as a whole, their second language, but their third. They tested at no higher than a third grade reading level in English, and may not have fully understood the therapist. If this is not typical of a deaf population, how can it represent the deaf in deaf studies?

Even such reputable scholars as Dr. Dennis Moore have had to work with less than optimum research conditions. In 1992, e.g. he reported on a research study which has been viewed as salient to treatment of drug abuse among people with hearing difficulties. He was forced, however, to weaken his assertions with the following caveat:

> This study was not originally intended to focus on persons who are deaf or hard of hearing, and therefore has significant limitations in regard to making generalizations to the larger deaf community.[414]

Researchers cannot speak with authority about issues central to or crucial to deaf populations when such limitations of research continue to exist. The unfortunate aspect we note is that this study is not atypical for its era.

Multiples of studies using small or skewed samples do not add up to conclusions which are applicable to the mainstream population of people with hearing and communication disorders. However, some tentative observations have been drawn from even research such as this, and stricter research has been able to build upon it.

While even a decade ago, such studies may have been all that was available, tighter standards are now becoming possible for inclusion criteria, as more research focuses on problems deaf people experience. Skewed, and/or otherwise inadequate studies will be able to be quietly relegated to oblivion when enough adequate studies provide relevant information for scholarly digestion. Replicability, objectivity and overall relevance need to assume a larger portion of our attention regarding criteria of research.

Beyond the desirability of more and better research, in the area of taking responsibility for our lives, other factors

---

[414] Dennis Moore, "Substance Use Patterns of Persons with Hearing Impairments" 1992, p. 2; ibid.

may be noted as necessary. Acknowledging the existence of our addiction problems, individually, is a big step forward, as most treatment plans point out. Barriers deaf people face when seeking help from programs geared to the larger society have been detailed in previous survey chapters, but alleviating those barriers has just begun. Future research should address both psychological and sociological aspects of addiction disorders among deaf people.

Accepting people who dare to bare their perceived imperfections, communally, is a step which is just as important. The Deaf community is gradually daring to admit the degree of vulnerability and inroads drug abuse has made into their midst, and this admission has not made the larger society impugn the Deaf. Instead, the bravery in such an admission has been admired, and a link of acceptance to the larger society is forged. This step may even act as an enabling tool, freeing other people, either deaf or hearing, who fight the tremendous battle with addiction to avoid additionally feeling insecure about their adequacy within their own peer groups.

Beyond the approaches to self-help thus far recommended, we need to get well beyond the fear of rejection which might come from admitting to the hearing world any difficulties in handling addictions. Plain speaking is required, with no place for denial or evasion to remain. Courageous pioneers like Dr. Betty Miller have shown us this much and more.

The point was made in our fifth chapter that the larger society needs to be more acceptant of diversity. As Meyerson spoke of deafness, "In our culture, individuals who have such impairments may be placed more frequently in special kinds of psychological situations. It is with these situations that the psychologist must be concerned, rather than with the degree of physical impairment directly."[415] Perhaps the larger society would do well to examine the persistent trend to pathologize cultural differences, and not be so easily led to interpret what is different as being abnormal, deviant or dangerous.

Recommendations optimally come in the form of step-by-step prescriptions for ameliorated functioning, not vague general "wishes" however lofty or ideal those might be. Such specific issues are being addressed in national workshops and conferences such as the workshop sponsored by the New York University Deafness Research and Training Center, focusing on the use of group techniques with deaf people. From 1971 continuing to the present, concerned people have focused on the specifics of each "next step."[416] We need to work together to implement the steps we've already envisioned.

When concerned people view what is needed from the viewpoint of what would be ideal, it is evident that we need more excellent role models with whom deaf people can identify, who offer qualities worth imitating.[417] We need supplementary education and prevention efforts in the area of health maintenance, so that people will not be tempted to become addicted to substances which harm them. Removing the demand which fuels substance addiction will

---

[415] Lee Meyerson, in Identity Crisis in Deafness, Schowe. Ibid. p. 49.

[416] Jerome D. Schein & Doris W. Naiman, "The Use of Group Techniques with Deaf Persons" a Deafness Research & Training Center Publication, 1971, ibid. and Kay Fulton, "Alcohol & Drug Abuse among the Deaf: Collaborative Programming for the Purposes of Prevention, Intervention and Treatment." Gallaudet College. Washington, D.C. ibid.

[417] Christine Giombetti, "Alcohol abuse counselor needs skills in many areas" Silent News: (18) Sept. 1992.

make the supply irrelevant, so education remains the primary avenue of conquering addiction.

In the area of therapy, more insightful, caring counselors, intake personnel, therapists and other helping professionals are needed. We need public support, both monetarily and in less tangible areas such as morale. Overall commitment on the part of everyone involved in the therapeutic process, is needed, on both giving and receiving ends, to enable people to bring their best to the process of ridding the Deaf community of the scourge of alcoholism and substance addiction.

BIBLIOGRAPHY

101st congress: "Public Law 101-336" Americans with Disabilities Act of 1990; Wash. D.C.; July 26, 1990.

Adams, Jane M. "Confronting the Addict: when families draw the line" Washington Post: Health. July 17, 1990.

Adler, Edna P. "Vocational Rehabilitation as an Intervenor in Substance Abuse Services to Deaf People" in Mental Health, Substance Abuse, & Deafness. Watson, et al (eds) pp. 10-12.

Alcohol & Drug Services Directory. San Mateo, CA. Peninsula Library System Comm. Information & San Mateo County Alc. & Drug Program; Human services Agency. The Program. n.d.

Alcoholics Anonymous. The Little Red Book Center City, MN; Hazelden Publ.' 1970.

AA "A Deaf Newcomer Asks AA" Center City, MN; Hazelden, n.d.

AA "AA. Chapter 5 in American Sign Language" Center City, MN; Hazelden, n.d.

AA Twenty-Four Hours a Day. Center City, MN; Hazelden; 1975.

AA "AA Groups & Contacts for Hearing Impaired Alcoholics" Center City, MN; Hazelden Publ. n.d.

ADARA. "Mental Health, Substance Abuse, and Deafness." Readings in Deafness. Monograph #7. n.p. 1983.

"Addictions" Program leaflet for the hearing impaired person. Santa Rosa, CA. 1992.

AID Bulletin inserts. P.S.A.s. Sociology Dept.; Kent State, Univ. n.d.

Alcohol & Drug Services Directory. San Mateo County, CA.; Alc. & Drug Program; Human Services Agency. n.d.

Alcoholics Anonymous. 3rd edition. N.Y.; A.A. World Services, Inc. 1976.

Alexander, Robert N. "The Law and Reasonable Accommodation of the Handicapped in Federal Government: Focus on Deafness." Journal of Rehabilitation of the Deaf. Vol. 20 (2) October 1986. pp. 24-26.

Allphin, Lisa "Harlan Lane: Psychology of the Deaf: Dangerous Stereotypes?" Deaf Counseling, Advocacy and Referral Agency. May 1988. p. 1.

Alterman, Arthur L. "Language & the Education of Children with Early Profound Deafness" AAD. 115(5) Sep., 1970. pp. 524-521.

Altshuler, Kenneth Z. & Rainer, John D. "Observations on Psychiatric Services for the Deaf" Mental Hygiene; Vol. 54, (4) Oct. 1970, pp. 535-539.

Altshuler, Kenneth Z. M.D. "Sociological & Psychological Development of Deaf Children: Problems, their Treatment & Prevention." Social & Psychological Development. (119) Aug., 1974. pp. 365-76.

Altshuler, Kenneth Z. M.D. "Studies of the Deaf: Relevance to Psychiatric Theory" American Journal of Psychiatry; (127):11, May 1971. pp. 1521-1526.

Alshuler, Kenneth Z., "Toward a Psychology of Deafness" Journal of Communicaiton Disorders; Vol. 11. (4) 1978. pp. 159-169.

Anderson, G. & Bowe, F.; "Racism Within the Deaf Community." American Annals of the Deaf. 117(6) Dec. 72. pp. 617-619.

Anderson, Pete. "Networking – The Forgotten Minority. Paper presented at 2nd Nat.'l Conf. on the Habilitation & Rehabilitation of Deaf Adolescents. Afton, Oklahoma. Apr. 28-May 2, 1968.

Andersson, Yerker J.O. "A Cross-Cultural Comparative
    Study: Deafness." Ph.D. dissertation; University of
    Maryland, 1981. pp. 115-123.
Andrews, Jean & Conley, Janet. "Beer, Pot, & Shoplifting:
    Teenage Abuses" American Annals of the Deaf. 122
    (6) Dec. 1977. pp. 557-562.
American Deafness and Rehabilitation Assoc.; Mental
    Health Substance Abuse & Deafness. Readings in
    Deafness: Monograph No. 7. Proceedings from the 1st
    National Conference on Mental Health, Substance
    Abuse & Deafness, at Rochester, N.Y. 1981.
Antelope Valley Council on Alcoholism & Drug Dependency.
    Palmdale, CA. information packet, 1993.
A.P.A. Diagnostic & Statistical Manual of Mental Disorders
    3rd ed. Wash., D.C. '80.
"Arresting Alcoholism" Mill Neck, N.Y.; The Christopher D.
    Smithers Foundation; 13th printing; 1985.
Atkins, Dale V. (Ed.) "Families and their Hearing-Impaired
    Children." in The Volta Review. 89 (5) Sep. 1987.
Austin, Gary Ph.d. (compiler) Bibliography: Deafness.
    Silver Spring, MD.; National Association of the Deaf.
    1976.
Awakenings Substance Abuse Recovery Programs: "The
    Concept" Downey, CA. The Southeast Council on Alc.
    & Drug Problems, Inc. 1989.
Baldessarini, Ross "Chemotherapy" The Harvard Guide to
    Modern Psychiatry. Cambridge, Mass.; Belknap Press
    of Harvard Univ. 1978. pp. 429-432.
Bannowsky, Alfred Wm. "Personality Factors, Job
    Satisfaction, and Long-Term Employment of
    Prelingually Profoundly Deaf Adults" Ph.D.
    dissertation; California Institute of Integral Studies,
    1983.

Becker, Gaylene, "Coping with Stigma: Lifelong Adaption of Deaf People," Social Science & Medicine. (158) Jan., 1981. pp. 21-24.

Belmont Center for Comprehensive Treatment: brochure. Philadelphia, PA. n.d.

Bell, Peter & Evans, J. Counseling the Black Client: Alcohol Use and Abuse in Black America. Center City, MN.; Hazelden Press. 1981.

Benedict, Beth, Parker, Jerry, Saunders, William, & Wilson, Catherine. "Stop Teenage Abuse of Marijuana" pilot program for the Model Secondary School for the Deaf, Washington D.C., Gallaudet College, n.d.

Berard, Yamil "The new (and deadly) drug of choice" Press-Telegram May 31, 1993.

Berg, Paul, "Teens in Trouble." in Health, 4 (52) Dec. 27, 1988. p. 15.

Best, Patrick K. "Psychological Differentiation among the Deaf." Doctoral dissertation. Detroit, MI.; Wayne State Univ.; 1974.

Bevan, Marlene A. "The effects of hearing aids on interpersonal perceptions: credibility, employability, and interpersonal attraction." Doctoral dissertation. Univ. of CT.; 1980.

Black, Claudia Double Duty. N.Y.; Ballantine Books; 1991.

Bodner-Johnson, Barbara, "Professional Preparation of Parent Educators: A Survey & Recommendations," AAD. (125) October, 1980. pp. 931-936.

Bolger, Robert W. "DAMN is Born" DAMN Austin, TX. Vol. 1(1) n.d.

Bonham, H.E., Armstrong, & Bonham. "Group Psychotherapy with Deaf Adolescents." American Annals of the Deaf. 126 (7) Oct., 1981. pp. 806-809.

Bonvillian, John D. "Effects of Signability & Imagery onWord Recall of Deaf and Hearing Students;" Perceptual & Motor Skills; vol. 56; 1983; pp. 775-791.

Bonvillian, John D. Charrow, V.R. & Nelson, Keith E. "Psycholinguistic and Educational Implications of Deafness;" Human Development; 16, 1973; pp. 321-345.

Booth, Wm. "Crack Cocaine's Lock on Synaptic Space" in The Washington Post, March 19, 1990. p. A-3.

Boros, Alex. "Activating Solutions to Alcoholism among the Hearing Impaired." in Schecter, A.J. (ed). Drug Dependence and Alcoholism: Social & Behavioral Issues N.Y.; Plenum Press. pp. 1007-1015.

Boros, Alex. "Instructions for Teaching: Recovery to Reading-Limited Alcoholics" AID Bulletin. Vol. 7 (3) Spring 1986. pp. 1-7.

Boros, Alex. "Alcoholism Intervention for the Deaf," Alcohol Health & Research World. Special Issue: The Multi-Disabled; 5 (Summer 1981) 2; pp. 26-30.

Bowe, Frank G. "Crises of the Deaf Child and His Family" in Readings on Deafness. Watson, D. (Ed.) N.Y.; N.Y. Univ School of Educ, Deafness Research & Training Center. 1973. pp. 38-44.

Bowe, Frank, Watson, Douglas & Anderson, Glenn. "Delivery of Community Services to Deaf Persons" in Readings on Deafness. Watson, Douglas (Ed) N.Y. Deafness Research & Training Center N.Y. Univ. School of Education; 1973. pp. 77-90.

Bowe, Frank G. "Non-White Deaf Persons: Educational, Psychological, & Occupational Considerations" AAD 116(3) Jun. 1971. pp. 357-361.

Bowyer, L.R. & Gillies, J. "The Social and Emotional Adjustment of Deaf & Partially Deaf Children" Brit. J. of Educ. Psychiatry. Vol. 42 (11) 1972. pp. 305-308.

Brandsma and E. Mansell Pattison, "Homosexuality and
   Alcoholism," in Pattison & Kaufman, Encyclopedic
   Handbook of Alcoholism N.Y., Gardner Press; p. 740.
"Breaking the Silence about AOD Abuse and Domestic
   violence in the Deaf Community" Conference report in
   Prevention Pipeline. 5(5) Sep/Oct, 1992. pp. 30-31.
Breindel, Tina "Drug or Alcohol Problems? You are not
   alone." DCARA News. Mar-Apr 1991. p. 11.
Brewster, Ghisdin The Creative Process. Berkeley, CA;
   Univ. of CA Press; 1952. p. 19.
Burke, Florrie. "Self-Esteem in Children who are Deaf"
   Impact-Hi Newsletter. 2nd Quarter 1990. pp. 5,16.
CA Dept. of Social Services. "Some Sobering Facts" CA.
   Silent Sobriety Foundation. Dec. 1985.
C.C.C.D. "The Psychology of Deafness." Ottawa, Ontario,
   CAN Press. 1983. pp. 1-9.
Callahan, Patricia, Boros, Alexander & Erwin, J. "Looking
   at Treatment for Alcoholism" Addiction Intervention
   with the Disabled release. Kent, OH. Kent State Univ.
   Press; 1988.
Calvert, Kathryn A.S., "A Comparison of therapy methods
   with a hearing impaired geriatric population."
   Doctoral Dissertation. Ft. Hays, KS.; Univ. of KS.
   1976.
Carmel, Simon J. "Aspects of sociolinguistic segmentation
   in an American urban deaf community." Master's
   thesis. Wash. D.C.; The American Univ.; 1980.
Carney, Edward C. "Deaf People in the World of Work," in
   Readings on Deafness. Watson, D. (Ed.) N.Y.; N.Y.
   Univ. School of Educ., Deafness Research & Training
   Center. 1973. pp. 134-136.
Carroll, Kathleen & Rounsaville, B. "Can a Technology
   Model of Psychotherapy Research be Applied to

Cocaine Abuse Treatment?" in NIDA's Research Monograph #104. Rockville, MD. 1990.

Case Summaries: Mental Health Assessment of Deaf Clients: Special Conditions. UCSF Center on Deafness, Conference Report. S.F., CA Feb. 11-13, 1988.

Cherry, Linda "The Good Life; A Smart Choice" S.F., CA; The Bay Area Project on Disabilities & Chemical Dependency; Oct. 1988.

Cherry, L./DeMiranda, John et al "CA Alcoholism, Drugs & Disability Studies" 1988.

Cherry, Linda "Review of Literature Related to Alcohol & Drugs; IADD, 1991.

Cherry, Linda. "Beyond Ramps: A Guide for Making Alcohol & Drug Treatment Accessible" compiled by the Bay Area Project on Disabilities & Chemical Dependency. Belmont, CA. Oct. 1988.

CHID: Combined Health Information Database: NIH. Oct. 1992. Federal computerbase.

Children of Alcoholics Foundation. Info Packet. N.Y. n.p., n.d.

Chough, Steven K. "Perspectives on the need and acceptance of counseling services reported by deaf college students." Doctoral dissertation. Columbia Univ. 1978.

Chough, Steven K. "The Trust vs. Mistrust Phenomenon Among Deaf Persons" American Deafness & Rehabilitation Assn. vol. 7; 1983. pp. 17-19.

Cohen, M.J. (Ed) Drugs and the Special Child. N.Y.; Gardner Press. 1979.

Cohn, Victor. "Where Doctors Fail." in Health, 4 (52) Dec. 27, 1988. p. 19.

Colburn, Don. "Undoing the Damage." in Health, 4 (52) Dec. 27, 1988. p. 6.

Cole, Charles B. "Social Technology, social policy and the severely disabled: issues posed by the blind, the deaf, and those unable to walk." Doctoral dissertation. Berkeley, CA.; Univ. of CA; 1979.

Cole, Debbie. Sign Language and the Health Care Professional. Malabar, FL. Robert E. Krieger Publ. Co. 1990.

Conner, Karen K. "A Curriculum schema to provide an in-service program to promote socialization of post-secondary deaf students." Doctoral dissertation. Buffalo, N.Y.; State University of N.Y. at Buffalo. 1982.

Consequences of Deafness, a fact sheet n.a.; n.p.; n.d.

Cooper, A.F. "Psychological Problems of the Deaf & Blind" Scottish Medical Journal. Vol. 24(2) Apr. 1979. pp. 105-107.

Cooper, A.F., Curry, Kay, Garside, & Roth. "Hearing Loss in Paranoid and Affective Psychoses of the Elderly," The Lancet, 2 (7885) Oct. 12, 1974. pp. 851-854.

Cooper, A.F. & Garside, R., & D. W. Kay. "A Comparison of Deaf & Non-Deaf Patients with Paranoid & Affective Psychoses. Brit. J. Psychiat. 129 Dec. '76. pp. 532-8.

Cork, R. Margaret. The Forgotten Children. Toronto, CAN. Paper-Jacks Press, 1969.

Cornforth, Anthony & Woods, Marie. "Deaf People in Psychiatric Hospitals–Why Loss of Hearing?" Nursing Times. Jan. 27, 1972. p. 101-103.

Cornforth, A. & Woods, M. "Deaf People in Psychiatric Hospitals: Disturbed & Deaf" Nursing Times. 68(5) 3 Feb. 1972. pp. 139-141.

Cornforth, Anthony & Woods, M. "Progressive or Sudden Hearing Loss" Nursing Times. Feb. 17, 1972. pp. 205-207.

Cosmos, Carolyn "Breaking the Chain of Substance Abuse
    and Hearing Loss" SHHH Journal July/August 1992.
"Council Line" newsletter for L.A. County Awakenings;
    alc/drug treatment center for Deaf. 1989.
Critchley, E.M.; Denmark, J.; Warren, F. & Wilson, K.
    "Hallucinatory Experiences of Prelingually Deaf
    Schizophrenics" Brit J. of Psychiatry. Vol. #138; 1981.
    pp. 30-32.
Cunningham, Glen Cocaine & the Body Builder: a scientific
    perspective. monograph from physical education
    department; McGill University. n.d.
Daley, Moss & Campbell. Dual Disorders: Counseling
    Clients with Chemical Dependency & Mental Illness.
    quoted by Swan, Kristen in "Dual Disorders in
    Chemical Dependency Treatment." A publication of
    the Minnesota Chemical Dependency Program for
    Deaf and Hard of Hearing Individuals. Aug. 1992.
DAMN Publ. of the Deaf Atheist Materials News; Austin,
    TX. Vol. 1, #1. Summer, n.d.
Danek, Marita McKenna "Rehabilation outcomes and
    caseload management as a function of counselor
    expertise in hearing impairments." Doctoral
    dissertation Univ. of MD.; 1979.
Darmsted, N. & Cassell, J. "Counseling the Deaf Substance
    Abuser" report on workshop; n.p.; n.d.; pp. 40-41.
Daunt, Tina "Special Help for Deaf Drug Abusers" Los
    Angeles Times. Dec. 31, 1989.
Davis, Sherry "The Deaf Substance Abuser: Awareness,
    Needs and Services Conference; Talladega, Alabama,
    April 15-18, 1991." Prevention Pipeline. 4 (4) 1991.
"Deafness: A Fact Sheet" Gallaudet University Press.
    Washington D.C.; n.d. pp. 2-3.
"Deafness & Mental Illness" n.a.; The Lancet; Vol. 7990 (10)
    1976. p. 837.

Deafness: The Invisible Handicap. The Canadian Co-Ordinating Council on Deafness. Ottawa, Ontario Canada. n.d.

Deafness Research Foundation (DRF). Info sheet. N.Y. n.d.

Deafpride, Inc. "Alcohol & Chemical Dependency Services, Goals & Objectives; Wash. D.C.; Project Access; n.d.

Deaner, Guy E. "A Survey of Graduates from a Program of Rehabilitation Counseling with the Deaf." Doctoral dissertation. Tuscon, AZ. Univ. of AZ. 1978.

DeCaro, James J. "A hierarchy of skills as an organizational aid in a programmed instruction sequence with deaf persons" Doctoral dissertation. Syracuse N.Y.; Syracuse Univ.; 1977.

DeFord, Cecile. "A descriptive overview of service delivery to persons with impaired hearing inselected industrialized Western societies since World War II." Doctoral dissertation. Claremont Graduate School. 1980.

Delgado, Gilbert L. (ed) The Hispanic Deaf: Issues and Challenges for Bilingual Special Education; Washington, D.C.; Gallaudet college Press; n.d.

Delgado, Gilbert L. "Report on Activity of the Media." Wash. D.C.; Gallaudet Press. n.d.

De Miranda, John Ed. M. "Alcoholism, Drugs & Disability: What are the Connections?" San Mateo, CA. IADD Conference Announcement. Jul., 1991.

De Miranda, John "The Common Ground: Alcoholism, Addiction, & Disability." Addiction & Recovery. Aug. 1990. pp. 42-45.

De Miranda, John "Working with Disabled Clients" CALADD fact sheet. n.d.

De Miranda, John Alcohol, Drugs & Disability: Five Case Studies. Alameda County, CA. Community Resources for Independent Living. 1990.

De Miranda, John Student Use of Drugs & Drinking Takes Toll: CALADD paper. n.d.

Denmark, John C. "Mental Illness and Early Profound Deafness;" British Journal of Medical Psychology; vol. 39; 1966; pp. 117-124.

Denmark, John C. "Mental illness & early profound deafness" Brit. J. Psychiat. 39(2) Jun. 1966. pp. 117-24.

Denmark, John C. & Eldridge, R.W., "Psychiatric Services for the Deaf" The Lancet. Vol. (614)2 Aug., 1969. pp. 259-262.

Denmark, John C., "A Psychiatric Unit for the Deaf." British Journal of Psychiatry. 120 (557) Apr. 1972. pp. 423-428.

Denmark, John. "Psychiatry & the Deaf" Current Psychiatric Therapies; 2; 1971; pp. 68-71.

DeView, Lucille S. "Disabled are finally seen via Hollywood" LA Life 3 Dec., 1990. p. 2.

Dillaha, Alton R. "A needs assessment study of the deaf in North Texas region." Doctoral dissertation. East Texas State Univ.; 1976.

"Directory of programs and services for the deaf in the United States" AAD. Apr. 1973. pp. 337-358.

"Disabilities/Substance Abuse Task Force" Information, Research & Resource Center. CA State Univ.; Long Beach, CA.; 1984.

Disabled and AOD Abuse, The.; The Office for Substance Abuse Prevention's National Clearinghouse for Alcohol & Drug Information. Rockville, MD.; n.d.

Dixon, Thomas L. "Addiction among the Hearing Impaired" EAP Digest. Jan./Feb. 1987. pp. 41-44.

Dodd, Judy E. "Overcoming Occupational Stereotypes Related to Sex & Deafness" AAD. (122) Oct., 1977. pp. 489-91.

Dolnick, Edward "Deafness as Culture" The Atlantic.
272(3) Sep. 1993. pp. 37-53.

"Drug Abuse – Worse Now Than Ever Before" World
Around You. Sep. 1986. p. 10.

DuBow, Sy. & Geer, Sarah (eds) Legal Rights: The Guide
for Deaf and Hard of Hearing People. Wash. D.C.;
National Center for Law & Deafness. Gallaudet Univ.
Press; 1992.

Dulfano, Celia. Families, Alcoholism & Recovery: Ten
Stories. Center City, MN.; Hazelden. 1982.

Eckart, M., "Health Hazards associated with alcohol
consumption." Journal of the American Medical Assn.,
246(6) 1981, pp. 648-666.

Elmore, Paul Ross. "The Silent Self: an inquiry into the
self-conceptions of deaf adolescents." Doctoral
dissertation. University of MN.; 1978.

Erickson, M.H., in the Foreward to Change Principles of
Problem Formationand Problem Resolution, by Paul
Watzlawick, John Weakland & Richard Fisch. (N.Y.;
W.W. Norton & Co.; 1974) p.x

Evans, Wm. J. & Elliott, Holly. "Screening Criteria for the
Diagnosis of Schizophrenia in Deaf Patients" Archives
of General Psychiatry. Vol. 38(7) 1981. pp. 787-790.

Fact Is, The. Office for Substance Abuse Prevention.
Rockville, MD. July 1988.

Fairbanks Hospital Information Packet. June 20, 1988.

Farrugia, David L. "A Study of Deaf High School Students'
Vocational Interests and Attitudes" Ed.D.
Dissertation, Northern IL. Univ., 1981.

Ferreyra, Nancy "Technical Assistance in California" The
Seed. Spring 1992. p. 6.

Fine, Sam (producer) "Blitzed, Ripped and Wasted;" 20/20
Television Program. ABC News; forum transcript
#1320. May 7, 1993. pp. 3-10.

Ford, Jo Ann & Moore, Dennis "Substance Abuse Resources & Disability Issues: TRAINING MANUAL" Dayton, OH. U.S. Center for Substance Abuse Prevention Publ.; 1992.

Fortney, Olin "Recovery of a Deaf Man, the" The Seed Winter 1989. p. 2.

Fox, "The Effect of Alcoholism in Children," Paper distributed by the National Council on Alcoholism. New York, NY; 1976.

Freeman, R.D., Malkin, S.F., & Hastings, J. "Psychosocial Problems of Deaf Children and their Families: a comparative study," AAD. 120(4) Aug., 1975. pp. 391-405.

Friedman, F., Friedman, M., Leeds, N. & Sussman, A.; "Adjustment Problems of the Deaf." panel discussion. Wash. D.C.; Gallaudet University. n.d.

Fulton, Kay "Alcoholism & Drug Abuse Among the Deaf" Wash. D.C.; Gallaudet College Publ. 1990. pp. 365-386.

Furth, Hans G. "Linguistic Deficiency & Thinking: Research with Deaf Subjects, 1964-1969." Psychological Bulletin. (76) Jul. 1971. pp. 58-72.

Gallo, Patricia & A. Choban. "Relationship of competencies required by industry to training provided for secondary and post secondary hearing impaired students of business and office occupations." Doctoral dissertation. New Brunswick, N.J.; Rutgers Univ. 1982.

Gallaudet College/National Information Center on Deafness. Deafness: A Fact Sheet. Wash. D.C.; Gallaudet Univ. Press. 1984. p. 1.

Garretson, Mervin (ed) NAD "Viewpoints on Deafness" newsletter. n.d.

Giombetti, C. "Alcohol abuse counselor needs skills in many areas." Silent News (18) Sep. 1992.

Gitlow, Stanley E. "The Clinical Pharmacology & Drug Interaction of Ethanol" in Encyclopedic Handbook of Alcoholism. Pattison & Kaufman (eds) N.Y. Gardner Press, 1982.

"Gold Award: Mental Health Services for the Deaf." Hospital & Community Psychiatry. Vol. 29 (10) 1978. pp. 674-677.

Gold, Mark S. 800-Cocaine. N.Y.; Bantam Books. 1984.

Goldman, R. "Cultural Factos & Hearing" Except. Child 35(6) Feb. 69 pp. 489-90.

Goleman, Daniel. "Scientists Pinpoint Brain Irregularities in Drug Addicts." in N.Y. Times. Jun. 26, 1990. p. C-1.

Gonzalez, Teresa D. "The Impact of hearing impairment upon communication, apprehension & self-disclosure." Master's thesis. Denton, TX; N. TX State Univ. 1980.

Gorey, J. "Rational alcoholism services for hearing-impaired people." Journal of Rehabilitation of the Deaf. 12(4) 1979. pp. 6-8.

Grant-Mackie, D. "Deafness Linked to Behavior Problems of Children" Aukland. n.d.

Grant, T.N., Kramer & Nash "Working with Deaf Alcoholics in a Vocational Training Program," Journal of Rehabilitation of the Deaf, 15(4) 1982, pp. 14-20.

Grimmett, John O. "Barriers Against Recovery." Center City, MN.: Hazelden. 1972.

Guthmann, Debra, MA & Staff "National Information Catalog" Minn., MN; 1992.

Guthmann, Debra, MA "Saying no in college: How to Deal with Substance Abuse Among Deaf and Hard of Hearing Students" MN Chem. Depend. Program. 1990.

Guthmann, Debra MA "An Innovative Substance Abuse Program for Hearing Impaired Youth;" MN Chemical Dependency Program; n.d.

Guthmann, Debra The Minnesota Chemical Dependency Program for the Hearing Impaired. Minn., MN 1990.

Guthmann, D.; Swan, K. "Placement, Treatment, Transition & Ethical Issues when Serving Chemically Dependent Deaf and Hard-of-Hearing Clients. MN 1990.

H., Yale. "The Beginners' Meeting;" Center City, MN; Hazelden. 1984.

Hairston, Earnest & Smith, Linwood Black and Deaf in America: Are We that Different? Silver Spring, MD; T.J. Publishers, Inc.; 1983.

Hancock, David C. "Points for Parents Perplexed About Drugs" Center City, MN. Hazelden Publ. 1975.

Harrie, Adrienne, "Are Brains Genetic? The Intelligence Controversy." The New York Times Book Review. May 31, 1981. pp. 11-12.

Harris, Ann R. "The Development of appropriate work behaviors in deaf multiply handicapped adolescents." Doctoral dissertaiton. Austin, TX; Univ. of TX. 1982.

Harry, B. & Favazza, A. "Brief Reactive Psychosis in a Deaf Man" Am. J. Psychiat. 141(7) Jul. 84. pp. 898-9.

Harvey, B. & Favazza, A. "Brief Reactive Psychosis in a Deaf Man" Am. J. Psychiat. 141(7) Jul. 84. pp. 898-9.

Harvey, Michael A. Psychotherapy with Deaf and Hard-of-Hearing Persons: A Systemic Model. Hillsdale, N.J.; Lawrence Erlbaum Assoc. Publ.; 1989.

Harwitz, V. & Morrison, P. Silent News; Alcohol Services handout; n.d.

"Hearing Impairments in the U.S." Statistical Bulletin of the Metropolitan Life Insurance Company. (57) Feb., 1976. pp. 7-9.

Heath, Dwight, "Sociocultural Variants in Alcoholism," in Pattison & Kaufman (ed.s) <u>Encyclopedic Handbook of Alcoholism,</u> Gardner Press; N.Y., 1982.

Heran, William contact for the Belmont Center for Comprehensive Treatment's Deaf program. Philadelphia, PA. Belmont Center. n.d.

Heritage Residential Treatment Center. Data sheet & program description. Provo, UT. Residential Treatment for Deaf Adolescents; Jul., 1993.

Higgins, Paul C. "The Deaf community: Identity and interaction in a hearing world." Doctoral dissertation. Evanston, IL.; Northwestern Univ.; 1977.

Higgins, Paul C. <u>Outsiders in a Hearing World.</u> Beverly Hills, CA; Sage Publications. 1980.

Higgins, Paul C. & Nash, Jeffrey <u>Understanding Deafness Socially.</u> Springfield, IL. Charles C. Thomas, Publ.; n.d.

Hindman, M.H., & Widem, P. "The Multidisabled: Emerging Responses." <u>Alcohol, Health and Research World.</u> 5(1981) pp. 4-10.

Hilts, Philip J. "How the Brain is Stimulated by Marijuana is Discovered." in <u>N.Y. Times.</u> Jul. 21, 1990. p. 1.

Holewa, Lisa "Drug Dealers Said Learning Sign Language" <u>Silent News.</u> Jul. 1993. p. 10.

Hook, Pamela E. "Learning Disabilities in the Hearing Impaired" <u>Ear, Nose & Throat Journal,</u> Jul. 1958 (58) pp. 303-309.

Hotchkiss, David. <u>Demographic Aspects of Hearing Impairment: Questions & Answers.</u> 2nd edition. Wash. D.C.; Gallaudet Univ. 1989.

House, Stephen Miller "12 Step Translation for/by deaf" n.p.; n.d.

Hoyt, Michael, Siegelman, Ellen & Schlesinger, Hilde. "Special Issues Regarding Psychotherapy with Deaf."

American Journal of Psychiatry. 138(6) Jun. 1981. pp. 807-811.

"Interpreting Signs of Recovery" A Handbook to help facilitate Intervention & Recovery of Alcohol and other Drug-Related Problems. Tulare County Alcoholism Council. Visalia, CA. CA Dept. of Alcohol & Drug Programs. n.d.

Isaacs, M.; Buckley, G.; Martin, D. "Patterns of Drinking among the Deaf" Amer. J. Drug & alc. Abuse. 6(4)1979. pp. 463-476.

J.B., "AA and the Deaf Mute." The Grapevine. Dec. 1968. pp. 32-33.

Jackson, Dorothy G. & Engstrom. "The Quality of Life" Journal of Rehabilitation. Vol. 37(2) 1971. pp. 10-12.

Jacobs, Leo. "The Community of the Adult Deaf" A.A.D. Feb. '74 pp. 41-46.

"James Learning Method, The" Info leaflet. Santa Rosa, CA. n.d.

Jasper, Louis R. "Assessing the moral reasoning of hearing impaired adolescents." Doctoral dissertation. Columbia University Teachers College. 1981.

Jellinek, E.M. "The Disease Concept of Alcoholism" New Haven, CN.; Hillhouse Press. pp. 35-36.

Jeter, Irma K. "Reflexive & voluntary contraction of the middle ear muscles in normals and alcoholics." Doctoral dissertation; Univ. of MD.; 1975.

Johnson, Rosalinda "Tobey's Tales wins apple, gives deaf children a boost" in Tribune News, Apr. 26, 1991. Local News section.

Johnson, S. & Locke, R. "Student Drug Use in a School for the Deaf." Paper presented at the annual meeting of the National Conference on Drugs; Seattle, 1978.

Johnson, Vernon E. I'll Quit Tomorrow. San Francisco, CA.; Harper & Row. 1980.

Jones, D. A., Vettor, & Vetter, "Hearing Difficulty & Its Psychological Implications for the Elderly" J. Epidemiol. Commun. Health. 38 (1) Mar., 1984. pp. 75-8.

Jongkees, L.B.W. "Psychological Problems of the Deaf" Ann Otol Rhinol Laryngol. 92(1) Jan., 1983. pp. 8-13.

Jorgensen, D.G., & Russert, C. "An Outpatient Treatment Approach for Hearing-Impaired Alcoholics." A.A.D. 127(1) Jan. 1982. pp. 41-44.

Jourard, Sidney M. The Transparent Self: Self Disclosure & Well Being. N.Y., N.Y.; Van Nostrand Press. 1964.

Kannapell, Barbara "The Trust-Mistrust Syndrome" in Mental Health, Substance Abuse, and Deafness. Watson, D et al. (eds) Silver Spring, MD; American Deafness & Rehab. Assn., 1983. pp. 20-22.

Karchmer, Michael A. "Demographics & Deaf Adolescents" Wash. D.C.; Gallaudet Univ. Press. n.d. pp. 29-31.

Kavanaugh, Philip, MD Magnificent Addiction: Discovering Addiction as Gateway to Healing Lower Lake, CA., Aslan Publishing. 1992. pp. 128-131 & 224.

Kearns, G. "Hearing Impaired Alcoholics—An Underserved Community" Alcohol Health & Research World. Vol. 13(2) 1989. pp. 162-166.

Keystone: Residential Services for Deaf & Hard of Hearing Chemically Dependent Adult Men & Women. Program admission packet. Milwaukee, WI. 1992.

Kinney, Jean. & Leaton, Gwen Loosening the Grip: A handbook of alcohol information. St. Louis, MO.; The C.V. Mosby Co.; 1983.

Klass, Joe The Twelve Steps to Happiness Center City, MN.; Hazelden. 1982.

Klein, J.A. and A.C. Roberts; "A Residential Alcoholism Treatment Program for American Indians," Quarterly Journal for the Study of Alcohol, 34 (1973).

Klein, Mary A. & Avecedo, Pedro. "Self-help Groups for Deaf Adolescents: Problems of drug and alcohol abuse." paper presented at 2nd Nat.l Conf. on Habilitation & Rehabilitation of Deaf Adolescents, Afton, OK. Apr. 1986.

Knast, Jerome F. "Attitudes toward deafness and deaf persons of selected rehabilitation counselors." Doctoral dissertation. N.Y. Univ.; 1982.

Knott D. & Beard "Effects of Alcohol Ingestion on the Cardiovascular System" in Pattison & Kaufman (eds) Encyclopedic Handbook of Alcoholism N.Y., Gardner Press; pp. 332-343.

Krucoff, Carol. "Exercise: A Natural High." in Health, 4 (52) Dec. 27, 1988. p. 20.

Krupski, Ann M. Inside the Adolescent Alcoholic. Center City, MN.; Hazelden. 1992.

Kusche, Carol A., Greenberg, M. & Garfield, T. "Nonverbal Intelligence & Verbal Achievement in Deaf Adolescents: An Examination of Heredity & Environment" A.A.D. 128.

Kusche, Carol A., Greenberg, Mark T., Calderon, Rosemary, and Gustafson, Ruth. "Generalization Strategies from the PATHS Project for the Prevention of Substance Abuse Disorders." paper presented at 2nd Nat.l Conf. on Habilitation & Rehabilitation of Deaf Adolescents, Afton, OK. Apr. 1986.

LA Council on Deafness. "Sign Language & Lip Reading Classes" NID fact sheet. n.d.

LaFitte, Jose A. "Rehabilitation potential of urban hearing-impaired young adults." Doctoral dissertation; N.Y. Univ.; 1976.

Lambert, Michael J. "Conceptualizing and Selecting Measures of Treatment Outcome: Implications for Drug Abuse Outcome Studies." NIDA Research

Monograph Series: Psychotherapy and Counseling in the Treatment of Drug Abuse. #104. Rockville, MD. 1990. pp. 80-90.

Landers, Ann "Lowdown on Dope, the" Reader service of newspaper & Creators Syndicate. 1987.

Lane, Harlan. The Mask of Benevolence: Disabling the Deaf Community. N.Y.; Knopf Publ. 1992.

Lane, Harlan (ed). The Deaf Experience: Classics in Language and Education. Cambridge, Mass.; Harvard Univ. Press. 1984.

Lane, Harlan "Psychology of the Deaf: Dangerous Stereotypes?" DCARA News. May 1988. pp. 1-2.

Lane, Katherine E. "Substance abuse among the deaf population: an overview of current strategies, programs & barriers to recovery" vol. 22(4) Apr. 89. pp. 79-85.

Langholtz, Daniel, & Heller, Bruce "Deaf & Hearing Psychotherapists: differences in their delivery of clinical services to deaf clients" in Watson, D., Anderson, G., & Taff-Watson, M. (eds.) Integrating Human Resources, Technology & Systems in Deafness. silver Springs, MD; ADARA, n.d. pp. 34-45.

LeBuffe, Francis P. & LeBuffe, Leon A. "Psychiatric Aspects of Deafness" Symposium on Psychological Issues in Primary Care. Vol. 6, #2, Jun. 1979. pp. 295-309.

Lee, Essie E. Breaking the Connection How Young People Achieve Drug Free Lives. N.Y., Messner, 1988.

Legal Rights. The Guide for Deaf & Hard of Hearing People. Washington D.C.; National Center for Law & Deafness; Gallaudet University Press. 4th edition. 1992.

Levine, E.S. The Psychology of Deafness. N.Y.; Columbia Univ. Press, 1960.

Lisowski, Kathleen A. "A naturalistic study of the experience of living as a deaf person." Doctoral dissertation. Humanistic Psychology Institute. 1980.

Lowenthal, A., Anderson, P. "Network Development: Linking the disabled community to alcoholism and drug abuse programs" Alcohol, Health & Research World. Winter 1980. pp. 16-19.

Luetke-Stahlman, B., "Recruiting Black Teacher Trainees into Programs for the Hearing Impaired" AAD. (128) Oct., 1983. pp. 851-2.

Luey, Helen S. "Between Worlds; the problems of deafened adults" Social Work in Health Care. Vol. 5. 1980. pp. 253-265.

Luey, Helen Sloss, Elliott, H; & Glass, L. (ed.s) Mental Health Assessment of Deaf Clients: Special Conditions. San Francisco, CA; Univ. of CA. 1988.

Luszki, Walter A. "Hearing Loss & Intelligence Among Retardates" Amer. J. of Mental Deficiency. Vol. 70. Jul. 1965. pp. 93-101.

Luterman, Barry F. "Human Brainstem Auditory Evoked Responses During Alcohol Intoxication and Recovery." Doctoral dissertation. Columbia, MO. Univ. of MO. 1982.

M. Mary. "Choices" Center City, MN.; Hazelden. 1984.

Mahapatra, S.B. "Deafness and mental health: psychiatric and psychosomatic illness in the deaf" Acia Psychiatry Scandanavia 50(6) 1974. pp. 596-611.

Mahapatra, S.B. "Psychiatric and Psychosomatic Illness in the Deaf" Brit. Journal of Psychiatry. vol. 125. 11, 1974. pp. 450-451.

Maletta, G.J. "Alcoholism and the Aged," in Encyclopedic Handbook of Alcoholism. Pattison & Kaufman, (eds) N.Y.; Gardner Press, 1982.

Manors, The "Mental Health Hearing Impaired Program" Silent Bridges Program. Info. packet. Oct. 1992.

Markowitz, John & Nininger, J. "A Case Report of Mania & Congenital Deafness" <u>Am. J. Psychiat.</u> 171(7) Jul. 1984. pp. 894-5.

Maslow, Abraham H. <u>Towards a Psychology of Being.</u> 2nd ed. N.Y.; Van Nostrand Press. 1968.

Mathers, Carla (ed.) The Deafpride Advocate #7 <u>Deaf Pride:</u> newsletter n.p.; n.d.

Mathis, Steve L. (ed.) <u>International Directory of Services for the Deaf.</u> Wash. D.C.; Gallaudet College. 1980.

McBrien, F.E. "The social handicap of deafness" <u>J. of Laryngology & Otology.</u> Vol. 96. Jul. 1982. pp. 577-583.

McCartney, J. & Nadler, G., "How to Help your Patient Cope with Hearing Loss" <u>Geriatrics.</u> 34(3) Mar., 1979. pp. 69-71, 75 & 76.

McCrone, Wm. P. "Serving the Deaf Substance Abuser;" <u>J. of Psychoactive Drugs.</u> Vol. 14; Jul.-Sep., 1988. pp. 199-203.

McCrone, Wm.; Beach, R.; Zieziula, F. (ed.s) <u>Networking & Deafness.</u> Silver Spring, MD. ADRA Publ.; 1983.

McCrone, Wm. "Empowerment through Advocacy for Deaf People for Meaningfully Accessible Substance Abuse/Alcoholism Treatment" paper presented at conference: Jun 8-9, 1990.

McKay, Timothy A. "The Rorschach Concept Evaluation technique and the Assessment of Psychopathology in a Deaf Population." Doctoral dissertation. Fuller Theological Seminary. 1984.

McKeown, Benny Center: San Jose, info. sheet. CA. Oct. 1992.

McLaughlin, Joseph & Andrews, Jean "The Reading Habits of Deaf Adults in Baltimore" American Annals of the Deaf. Vol. 120(10) 1975. pp. 497-501.

McQuay, Sidney L. "Attitudes of community college faculty toward the deaf: a Guttman Facet theory analysis." Doctoral dissertation. Univ. of CT.; 1978.

Meadow, Katherine P. "Burnout in Professionals Working with Deaf Children" AAD. 126(1) Feb., 1981. pp. 13-22.

Meadow, K.P., and Trybus, R.J. "Behavorial and Emotional Problems of Deaf Children: An Overview" Hearing & Hearing Impairment. L.J. Bradford & W.G. Hardy (eds.) New York, NY. Grune & Stratton, 1979.

"Medical Side of the War on Drugs, The" Health in The Wash. Post; 27 Dec., 1988. p. 5.

Meddis, Sam V. "Disparities Suggest the Answer is Yes" USA Today; Jul. 23-25, 1993; pp. 1, 2 & 4.

Menninger Phoenix: St. Jos. Hosp.: Addiction Treatment Center: Info. leaflet. Apr. '93.

"Men Who Created Crack, the" U.S. News & World Report. Aug. 19, 1991. pp. 44-53.

"Mental Health, Substance Abuse & Deafness" proceedings 1st Nat.l Conference. Rochester, N.Y.; 1981. ADARA Monograph #7.

Metropolitan Life Insurance Co. "Hearing Impairment in the United States" Statistical Bulletin - Metropolitan Life" N.Y. Vol. 57 (2) 1976. p. 7-9.

Meyerson, Lee in Identity Crisis in Deafness. Schowe, B.M. Tempe, AZ. The Scholar's Press. 1979.

Mihall, John B., Smith, E., & Wilding, M. "Gallaudet's Student Development Approach to Substance Abuse Education and Identification/Treatment" paper presented at the 2nd Nat.l Conf. of the Habilitation &

Rehabilitation of Deaf Adolescents; Afton, Oklahoma. Apr. 28-May 2, 1986.

Miller, Betty G. "Empowerment:" Treatment approaches for the Deaf & Chemically Addicted." Counselor. 7(3) 1989. pp. 24-25.

Miller, Betty G. "Interpreters & The Recovering Process" Project: A Second Chance. Jul., 1991.

Miller, J.D. & Cisin, I.H. Highlights from the National Survey on Drug Abuse. Rockville, MD; NIDA 1980.

Minn. Chemical Dependency Program: Minn, MN. Access materials. 1992.

Modry, Jean, Sullivan, R.; Whitehouse, A. "National Directory" Substance Abuse Services & Related Resources for the Deaf/Hearing Impaired. ADARA Conference; Chicago, IL. May 21-24. 1991.

Mooney, A.J., Eisenberg A. & Eisenberg, H. The Recovery Book; N.Y.; Workman Publishing Co.' 1992.

Moore, Dennis & Ford, JoAnn "Prevention of substance abuse among the deaf" Paper presented at ADARA Conference; Chi. IL. May 21-24, 1991.

Moore, Dennis & Polsgrove L. "Disabilities, Developmental Handicaps & Substance Misuse: A Review" Social Pharmacology. 3(4) 1989. pp. 375-408.

Moore, Dennis, "Research in Substance Abuse & Disabilities" Conference presentation at the Annual Meeting of the National Prevention & Training Conference: People with Disabilities (3rd Annual Conf.) Apr. 4-7, 1990.

Moore, Dennis. "Substance Abuse assessment & Diagnosis in Medical Rehabilitation." in NeuroRehabilitation. 2 (1) 1992. p. 7-13.

Moore, Dennis "Substance Use Patterns of Persons with Hearing Impairments: A Regional Survey." paper presented at conference. Denver, CO July, 1992.

Moore, Matthew S. & Levitan, Linda. For Hearing People
    Only. Rochester, N.Y.; Deaf Life Press. 1992.
Moores, Donald F. Educating the Deaf: Psychology,
    Principles & Practices. Boston, Mass.; Houghton
    Mifflin Co.' 1978.
Moores, Donald F. & Oden, Chester W. "Emotional Needs
    of Black Deaf Children;" American Annals of the Deaf;
    vol. 122, Jun, 1977. pp. 313-317.
Moser, Nancy Center on Deafness at the University of CA,
    San Francisco, quoted in "Handicapped Persons:
    Many barriers to be overcome in treating addiction in
    the deaf." in Reference Guide to Addiction Counseling,
    n.d., n.a.; p. 4.
Mulford, H.A. "The epidemiology of alcoholism & its
    implications: in Pattison & Kaufman (eds)
    Encyclopedic Handbook of Alcoholism. N.Y. Gardner
    Press, '82.
Mulvaney, D. "Not Quite Deaf, Not Quite Hearing," The
    Glad News, Fall, 1988, p. 18.
Murphy, Grace B. Your Deafness Is Not You, N.Y.; Harper
    & Bros; 1954.
Murray, R.M. & James R. Stabenau, "Genetic Factors in
    Alcoholism Predisposition," in Pattison & Kaufman,
    (eds.) Encyclopedic Handbook on Alcoholism, 1982. p.
    142.
Naiman, Doris, Schein, Jerome, & Stewart, Larry. "New
    Vistas for Emotionally Disturbed Deaf Children."
    A.A.D. Vol. 118 (8) 1973. pp. 480-487.
Nakken, Jane. "Straight Back Home: To the young person
    leaving treatment." Center City, MN.; Hazelden.
    1984.
National Clearinghouse for Alcohol Information. NIAAA.
    Information & Feature Service #1. 1971 & NCADI,
    1988.

National Information Center on Deafness "Barriers Deaf
People Face" Washington, D.C. Gallaudet University;
n.d.

National Institute on Drug Abuse handout: staff
information sheet. n.d.

"Never Too Early, Never Too Late: a booklet for parents &
others concerned about drug and alcohol use
problems" Center City, MN; Hazelden, 1983.

New Bridge Foundation Info. packet. Berkeley, CA. Dec.
'92.

New York Society for the Deaf: Substance Abuse Info.
Letter. N.Y. Oct. 1992.

N.I.C.D. "Communicating with Deaf People" Wash., D.C.;
Gallaudet Univ.; n.d.

N.I.C.D. "Programs & Resources for Deaf Alcoholics &
Substance Abusers" Wash. D.C.; Gallaudet Univ.;
July, 1992.

N.I.C.D. "What Are TDDs?"; Wash. D.C.; Gallaudet Univ.
Press. n.d.

Norris, Chuck. "The Kick Drugs Out of America
Foundation" Houston & Galveston, TX; & Wash. D.C.,
1991.

O'Neill, Catherine. "Slang and Reality." in Health, 4 (52)
Dec. 27, 1988. p. 21.

Onken, Lisa S. & Blaine, Jack (Ed.s) Psychotherapy and
Counseling in the Treatment of Drug Abuse.
Rockville, MD; National Institute on Drug Abuse's
Research Monograph Series. #104. 1990. 134 p.

Olsen, Gary W. (Ed.) Kaleidoscope of Deaf america. Wash.
D.C. The National Assoc. of the Deaf & Gallaudet
Univ. Alumni Assoc.; n.d.

Opperman, John Joseph. "A follow-up study of selected
former clients of a program of comprehensive services

for the adult deaf." Doctoral dissertation. Case
Western Reserve Univ.; 1979.

Owens, Diane Johnson. "The Relationship of frequency and
types of activity to life satisfaction in elderly deaf
people." Doctoral dissertation. N.Y. Univ.; 1981.

Owner, S.Z., & Ulissi, S.M. "Conflict Resolution Training
Program: Problem Solving Strategies for Hearing-
Impaired Students with Behavior Problems."
American Annals of the Deaf. 126 (6) Sep. 1981. pp.
619-626.

Pacific Research & Training Alliance. Fact/Access sheet.
Oakland, CA. 1992.

Padden, Carol & Humphries, Tom. Deaf in America:
Voices from a Culture. Cambridge, Mass.; Harvard
Univ. Press. 1988.

Palmer, J. Ursula. "A Comparison of the opinions of deaf &
hearing professionals regarding the research needs in
the field of deafness." Doctoral dissertation. East
Texas State Univ.; 1989.

Panara, Robert & Panara, John. Great Deaf Americans.
Silver Spring, MD.; T.J. Publishers, Inc.; 1983.

Park East Mental Health Center "Community Mental
Health Services for the Deaf" n.d.

Patterson, C.H. Theories of Counseling & Psychotherapy.
4th Ed.; N.Y. Harper & Row 1986.

Pattison, E. Mansell & Kaufman, Edward. (eds).
Encyclopedic Handbook of Alcoholism. N.Y.; Gardner
Press. 1982.

Payette, Bruce A. "Community Based Grantwriting
Strategies for Substance Abuse Prevention with Deaf
and Hard of Hearing Youth." pp. 109-112. n.p.; n.d.

Pearson, Barbara F. "Personality characteristics of the
college educated congenital deaf adult as revealed by

the Rorschack psychodiagnostic test." Doctoral
dissertation. Fordham Univ.; 1975.

Pholer, Patricia, counselor Pittsburg, PA, quoted in staff
written article in The Addiction Letter, a resource
exchange for professionals on preventing & treating
alcoholism and drug abuse. Vol. 5 (8) Aug. 1989. p. 1.

Piastro, Dianne; "Ending the Silent Isolation of Deafness"
The Press Telegram 12 Mar., 1991. p. C3.

Pickens, Roy W. "Children of Alcoholics." Center City, MN;
Hazelden. 1984.

Pitts, John H. "An analysis of predictors of success and
failure in rehabilitation of hearing impaired caseload
clients in the Dallas, Texas area." Doctoral
Dissertation. E. TX. State Univ. 1979.

"Police are learning the signs" staff The Modesto Bee. July
25, 1993. p. B-8.

Polpathapee, S. & Tuchinda, P. & Chipawong. "Sensorineural Hearing Loss in a Heroin Addict." Journal of
the Medical Association of Thailand. 67 (1) Jan. '84;
pp. 57-60.

Powell, Laura. "Deaf Advocates Call Substance Abuse
Programs" Silent News. Jul., 1992.

Powers, J. & Powers, E., "Hearing problems of elderly
persons: social consequences and prevalence."
American Speech and Hearing Association, 20(2) Feb.
1978 pp. 79-83.

"Program, the" San Mateo Alcohol & Drug Program. leaflet.
n.d.

Public Law 101-336, 42 U.S. Code (U.S.C.) 12101 et seq. 28
C.F.R.; #35.160 (b) 1989.

Pyke, Jennifer & Littmann, Sebastian. "A Psychiatric clinic
for the Deaf." Canadian Journal of Psychiatry. 27 (5)
1982. pp. 384-389.

Raco, Thomas G. "Analysis of employment opportunities in technical occupations within art, photography and printing for students at the National Technical Institute for the Deaf." Doctoral dissertation. Buffalo, N.Y.; Univ. of N.Y. at Buffalo. 1981.

Rainer, John D. & Altshuler, Ken. Z.; "A Psychiatric Program for the Deaf: Experiences & Implications." American Journal of Psychiatry. 127(11) May 1971. pp. 1527-32.

Randal, Judith. & Hines, Wm. "New Power for Divided Minority" Washington Post "Health" Mar. 29, 1988.

Reivich, R.S. & Rothrock. I.A. "Behavior Problems of Deaf Children & Adolescents: A Factor-Analytic Study" J. of Speech & hearing Research 15(1) Mar., 1972. pp. 93-104.

"Relapse Prevention Guide" The MN Chem. Dependency Program for the Hearing Impaired; Fairview Deaconess Chem. Depend. Program. Minn., MN. 1992.

Rendon, Marie E. "Deaf Culture & Alcohol/Substance Abuse" J. Subs. Abuse Treatment, anticipated publ. date: Feb. 7, '92.

Resource Center on Substance Abuse Prevention & Disability. "Information Package." Wash., D.C. 1991.

Rice, Matilda "Alcohol Use and Abuse in Children," in Pattison & Kaufman (eds) Encyclopedic Handbook of Alcoholism N.Y.; Gardner Press, 1982.

Ries, Peter W. "Hearing Ability of Persons by Sociodemographic & Health Characteristics" Vital Health Statistics. (140) Aug. 1982. pp. 1-60, at p. 2.

Risser, D. "Program Helps Deaf Students Hone Living Skills" Los Angeles Times: Expressions. Aug. 27, 1987. pp. 1, 3.

Riverside Medical Center; brochure. MN. Minnesota Chemical Dependency Program for the Deaf. 1991.

Robinson, Luther D. "A Program for Deaf Mental Patients" Hospital & Community Psychiatry. Vol. 24(1) 1973. pp. 40-42.

Renn, Ron, (unit manager-contact) Moose Lake Regional Treatment Center. Info. '92.

Rosen, Jeanette K. "Psychological & Social Aspects of the Evaluation of Acquired Hearing Impairment" Audiology. 18: 1979. pp. 238-252.

Rosenthal, M. quoted in Essie Lee's Breaking the Connection: How Young People Achieve Drug Free Lives. N.Y. Julian Messner, 1988.

Ross, Alan O. Psychological Disorders of Children: A Behavioral Approach to Theory, Research & Therapy. 2nd Ed. N.Y.; McGraw-Hill, 1980.

Ross Hospital information packet for Ross Hospital Inpatient psychiatric services; 1992.

Ross, Tamara "A Psychiatric Unit for Deaf" Nursing Mirror. #145 Nov. 1977 pp. 20.

Rousey, Clyde L. "Psychological Reactions to Hearing Loss" J.S.H.D.; Vol. 36 (8) 1971. pp. 82-89.

Rovner, Sandy. "Treating the Whole Family" in Health, 4 (52) Dec. 27, 1988. p. 16.

Rowan, Roanne. "Chemical Abuse and Dependency." A Resource Guide prepared by Hearing Impaired Health & Wellness Services; Dept. of Psychiatry, St. Paul-Ramsey Med. Center. St. Paul, MN. 1988.

Rowan, Roanne. "Chemical Abuse & Dependency: An Information Book for the Hearing Impaired" Prepared by the Hearing Impaired Health & Wellness Services; Dept. of Psychiatry, St. Paul-Ramsey Medical Center; St. Paul, MN. 1988.

Rowland, Carolyn R, "Strengths & Weaknesses of Deaf Workers as Evaluated by Employers & Supervisors,"

Master of Arts Thesis, CA State Univ.; Long Beach,
CA. 1979.

SAISD information flier. Rochester, N.Y.; Substance &
Alcohol Intervention Services for the Deaf. 1992.

Salamy, Albert. "The effects of alcohol upon sensory evoked
and spontaneous cerebral responses. Doctoral
dissertation. Okla. City, OK.; Univ. of OK. 1972.

Salerno, Maria. "Interpersonal anxiety as a function of
hearing handicap in the elderly." Doctoral
dissertation. Wash. D.C.; The Catholic Univ. of
America. 1981.

San Mateo County Alc. & Drug Program: Human Service
Agency. Directory. 1992.

Sarlin, M. Bruce "The Use of Dreams in Psychotherapy with
the Deaf" J. Am. Acad. Psychoanal. (1) Jan., 1984. pp.
75-88.

Satir, Virginia Conjoint Family Therapy Palo Alto, CA.
Science & Behavior Books; 1967.

Scanlan, John "Is There a Need for Mental Health &
Substance Abuse Services to Deaf People?" in Mental
Health, Substance Abuse & Deafness. Watson,
Steitler, Peterson, & Fulton (eds) Silver Spring, MD.
ADRA, 1983. pp. 7-9.

Schein, Jerome & Delk, Marcus. The Deaf Population of
the United States. Silver Spring, MD.; National
Association of the Deaf. 1974.

Schein, Jerome. "Hearing Impairments and Deafness" in
Stollow, Walter (ed) Handbook of Severe Disability: a
text for rehabilitation. Washington, D.C.; U.S. Dept.
of Education, Rehabilitation Services Publ.; 1981. pp.
395-407.

Schein, Jerome & Naiman, D. (eds) The Use of Group
Techniques with Deaf Persons, workshop lecture

presented in N.Y. by PASHI & N.Y. University's
Deafness Research & Training Center. Mar. 19, 1971.

Schein, Jerome D. (ed) Model State Plan for Vocational
Rehabilitation of Deaf Clients: 2nd revision. N.Y.
Univ., Deafness Research & Training Center. 1980.

Schiff, Naomi & Ventry, Ira "Communication Problems in
Hearing Children of Deaf Parents." J.S.H.D. vol. 41
(8) 1976. pp. 348-358.

Schlesinger, Hilde & Meadow, K. "A Conceptual Model for a
Program of Community Psychiatry for a Deaf
Population." Community Mental Health Journal. Vol.
8 (1) 1972. pp. 47-59.

Schlesinger, H. & Meadow, K. "Development of Maturity in
Deaf Children" Exceptional Child 38 (6) Feb., 1972. pp.
461-7.

Schlossberg, Harvey. "The autokinetic phenomenon:
alcohol and autitory modification." N.Y.; Yeshiva
Univ.; 1971.

Schowe, B.M. Identity Crisis in Deafness. Tempe, AZ.; The
Scholar's Press. 1979.

Schroedel, John G. "Variables related to the attainment of
occupational status among deaf adults." Doctoral
dissertation. N.Y. University. 1976.

Schuchman, John S. Hollywood Speaks: Deafness and the
Film Entertainment Industry. Urbana, IL.; Univ. of
Illinois Press. 1988.

Scoggins, B.B. "The Feasibility Study on a need for A State
Commission on Deafness and Hearing Impairment in
the State of California" M.A. Thesis; CA State at
Northridge. Aug. 1988.

S E Council on Alcohol & Drug Problems. "Proposal to
provide residential drug-free & outpatient drug free to
hearing-impaired persons of Los Angeles County;"
Sections C & D; July 7, 1988.

Seffinger, Daniel J. "Deviance: A study in the perpetuation of stigmatization using persons with a hearing impairment." Doctoral dissertation. L.A., CA.; CA School of Professional Psychology. 1973.

Seidman, Betty L. "Effects of Group Therapy on the Deaf." Doctoral dissertation. San Diego, CA.; U.S. International Univ.; 1979.

Seligson, Jose L. M.D. "Problems of Psychiatric care of the Deaf-Blind Population" Int. J. Psychiat Med.' 13(1) 1983-84. pp. 85-92.

Seppala, Teresa A. A Primer on the Prevention of Chemical Use Problems. Center City, MN.; Hazelden. 1977.

Seward, K. (contact) Phoenix Treatment Center: Psych services for deaf info. sheet. '92.

Shapiro, Rodney & Harris, Robert. "Family Therapy in Treatment of the Deaf: A Case Report." Family Process. 15 (1) Mar. 1976. pp. 83-96.

Signs of Recovery, Inc.; newsletter of Deaf-to-Deaf Alcoholism Recovery Support services. Santa Monica, CA; V: (213) 829-1196.

Silent Sobriety Foundation packet #11. "Some Sobering Facts." Nov. 20, 1985.

Sims, Donald G.; Gottermeier, L. & Walter, G. "Factors Contributing to the Development of Intelligible Speech Among Prelingually Deaf Persons." AAD. #125; May 1980. pp. 374-381.

Siwek, Jay. "A Drug Using Spouse" Health, 4 (52) Dec. 27, 1988. p. 17.

Skovronsky, O., Boleloucky, Z., & Bastecky, J. "Anxiety and other neurotic Symptoms in Patients Suffering from acoustic and vestibular Disorders" Agressologie. 22. C. 1981. pp. 25-26. Prague.

Skyer, Solange C. "Psycho-Social Aspects of Deafness Course as a Counseling Tool for the Hearing Impaired;" A.A.D. Journal; June, 1982. pp. 349-355.

Smart, R.G. & Gray, "Multiple predictors of dropout from alcoholism treatment;" Archives of General Psychiatry, 35 (1978) pp. 363-367.

Solomon, David & Sparadeo, Frank. "Effects of Substance Use on Persons with Traumatic Brain Injury" NeuroRehabilitation. 2 (1) 1992. pp. 16-26.

Southeast Council on Alcoholism & Drug Problems, Inc. Treatment Proposal. 1989.

Spitzer, R.J. & Klein, D.F. (Ed.s) Evaluation of Psychological Therapies. Baltimore, MD. The Johns Hopkins University Press; 1976. pp. 16-17.

Squires, Sally. "A Psychology of Addiction." in Health, 4 (52) Dec. 27, 1988. p. 10.

Squires, Sally. "Role of the Schools." in Health, 4 (52) Dec. 27, 1988. p. 18.

St. Vincent's Hospital NY Psych Dept Alc. Outpatient Treatment Program; Info. 1989.

Stephens, Maria & Walker, Frankie. "Increasing Self-Esteem, Decreasing Drug Abuse: A Positive Approach to a Negative Situation" Positive Day Program Louisiana School for the Deaf. 1992.

Stepp, Laura S. "Deaf Generation Leaps 'Wall:' Hearing World breached by New Work Force." The Washington Post. Mar. 21, 1988. pp. 1, 19.

Sternberg, Martin L. "Group Counseling with the Non-Communicating Deaf." in The Use of Group Techniques with Deaf Persons. N.Y.; DRTC. n.d. p. 33.

Stevens, John M. "Some Psychological Problems of Acquired Deafness" Brit. J. Psychiat. 140(1) May, 1982. pp. 453-6.

Stewart, Larry G. "Hearing Impaired Substance Abusers" Paper disseminated by Gallaudet University, Wash, D.C. re: STAMP Program. n.d.

Stewart, Larry G. "Hearing Impaired/Developmentally Disabled Persons in the U.S.: Definitions, Causes, Effects, & Prevalence Estimates." AAD. 4(6) 1978.

Stone, R. "America is Getting Older and Deafer," in Deaf Life, 1 (7) Rochester, N.Y.; Jan. 1989. pp. 9-13 at P. 10.

Sugawara, Sandra "Signs of Success for Deaf Entrepreneur." The Washington Post; Mar. 20, 1989. pp. 1 & 34.

Sussman, Allen E. & Stewart, Larry G. Counseling with Deaf People. New York Univ.; Deafness Research & Training Center. 1971.

Sussman, Allen E. "An investigation into the relationship between self-concepts of deaf adults and their perceived attitudes toward deafness." Doctoral dissertation. N.Y. Univ.; 1973.

Swan, Kristen "Dual Disorders in Chemical Dependency Treatment" Steps to Recovery MN Chem. Dep. Prog. Publ. Issue VI. Aug. 1992. pp. 1-2.

Taft, Brenda "Employability of Black Deaf Persons in Wash. D.C.: National Implications American Annals of the Deaf. Aug. 1983. 453-457.

"Teaching the Deaf" n.a.; n.p.; n.d.

Thayer, Stephen "Lend Me Your Ears: Racial & Sexual Factors in Helping the Deaf" J. Pers. Soc. Psychol. 28(1) Oct., 1973. pp. 8-11.

Thomas, Alan J. "Social & Psychological Implications of Acquired Deafness for Adults of Employment Age." Brit. J. Audiol. 14(3) Aug. '80. pp. 76-85.

Thomas, Paula D., Hunt, Wm. C., Garry, Philip, Hood, R., Goodwin, J.M., & Goodwin, J.S. "Hearing Acuity in a

Healthy Elderly Population: Effects on Emotional, Cognitive, and Social Status" J. Gerontol. 38(3) May, 1983. pp. 321-5.

Thomas, Steve. Interpreting Signs of Recovery. Visalia, CA. State of CA Dept. of Alc. & Drug Programs; Tulare County Alc. Council, Inc. 1988. p. 3.

Thompson, Larry. "How Drugs Attack the Brain." Health, 4 (52) Dec. 27, 1988. p. 12.

"Tobey's Tales" Info. brochure. Substance Abuse Recovery Programs. Nov., 1991.

Trafford, Abigal. "Beyond Medicine." Health, 4 (52) Dec. 27, 1988. p. 22.

Treaster, Jos. B. "Cocaine Users Adding Heroin to their Menus" N.Y. Times 21 Jul., '90. p. 1.

Trotter, Jim. "The Fatal Pursuit of Happiness" in West of the San Jose Mercury. San Jose, CA. 28 Feb., 1993. pp. 18-20.

Twerski, Abraham, J., "Self-Discovery in Recovery." Center City, MN.; Hazelden, 1984.

"Unique Video Wins Prestigious National Award" Silent News. Dec. 1991.

UC Center on deafness "Meeting the Challenge: of the Deaf" n.p.; n.d.

US Dept. of Education What Works: Schools Without Drugs Wash. D.C.; U.S. Dept. of Education. 1986.

US Dept. of Health & Human Services Office "Substance abuse prevention assistance"

VA Division for Deaf & Hard of Hearing "Alcoholism & Deafness;" n.d.

VanCleve, John V. & Crouch, Barry. A Place of Their Own: Creating the Deaf Community in America. Wash. D.C.; Gallaudet Univ. Press; 1989.

Van de Vusse, David "Verbal learning in alcoholics: semantic vs. acoustic encoding processes." Doctoral dissertation. Detroit, MI.; Wayne State Univ.; 1978.

Ventry, (letter to Editor) "The Case for Psychogenic Deafness" n.p.; n.d.

Vernon, McCay "The Decade of the Eighties: Significant Trends and Developments for Hearing Impaired Individuals" Rehabilitation Literature, Vol. 42, Jan.-Feb. 1981. pp. 2-7.

Vernon, McCay "Potential, Achievement, and Rehabilitation in the Deaf Population" in Readings on Deafness; (ed.) Douglas Watson; Deafness Research & Training Center; N.Y. University School of Education; 1973; pp. 91-105.

Vernon, McCay. The Psychology of the Deaf. N.Y.; Longman Publ. Co. n.d.

Vernon, McCay "Sociological & Psychological Factors Associated with Hearing Loss." JSHR. Vol. 12. Sep. 1969. pp. 541-550.

VIP Peers "Promoting Education, Encouragement, Resources and Support" Rochester, N.Y.; Substance and Alcohol Intervention Services for the Deaf; 1992.

Wagner, Robin S. Sarah T. Portrait of an alcoholic. N.Y., Ballantine Books; 1975.

Walker, Bobby & Kelly, Phil. "Professional Education: The Elderly, a Guide for Counselors;" Center City, MN.; HJazelden, 1981.

Walker, Elaine. "After 20 years of addiction, Deaf man finds sobriety, helps others" Silent News. Mar., 1993, p. 17.

Waller, P.A., "Alcohol and Highway Safety," in Pattison & Kaufman (eds) Encyclopedic Handbook of Alcoholism; N.Y., Gardner Press, 1982. p. 395.

Waltzer, Deborah R. "A Sobering Tale" Focus. National
    Council on Alcoholism & the N.Y. State Div. of
    Alcoholism, et al pp. 17-22.
Ward, Leslie "Big Bucks in 'Abuse' Clinics" Los Angeles
    Herald Examiner; Nov. 17, 1985. pp. A 1 & 10.
Ward, Leslie "The Fashionable Way to Kick the Habit" Los
    Angeles Herald Examiner. Nov. 18, 1985. pp C 1 & 4.
Washton, Arnold M. & Boundy, Donna Willpower's Not
    Enough: Understanding & Recovering from
    Addictions of Every Kind. N.Y.; Harper & Row. 1989.
Watson, Douglas Ph.D. (Ed) Readings on Deafness. N.Y.;
    Deafness Research & Training Center; N.Y. Univ.
    School of Education. 1973.
Watson, Douglas, Anderson, G., et al. "Adjustment Services
    for Hearing Impaired Persons: Research and
    Practice;" Fayetteville, AR; Univ. of AR; 1983.
Watson, Douglas, "Substance Abuse Services for Deaf
    Clients: A Question of Accessibility," in Mental
    Health, Substance Abuse & Deafness. Watson, D.
    Steitler, K., Peterson, P. & Fulton, Wm. (ed.s) Silver
    Spring, MD; Amer. Deafness & Rehab. Assn. 1983. pp.
    13-16.
Watts, Thomas D. & Wright, Roosevelt (ed.s) Alcoholism in
    Minority Populations. Springfield, IL.; Charles C.
    Thomas, Publ.; 1989.
Watzlawick, P., Weakland, J. & Fisch, R. Change. N.Y.;
    W.W. Norton & Co., Inc. '74.
Watzlawick, P. & Beavin, J. & Jackson, D. Pragmatics of
    Human Communication: a study of interactional
    patterns,m pathologies, and paradoxes. N.Y.; W.W.
    Norton & Co., Inc.; 1967.
Webster, Noah New World Dictionary of the American
    Language: College Edition. Cleveland, OH; The
    World Publ. Co. 1964.

Wegscheider, Sharon. Another Chance: Hope & Health for the Alcoholic Family. Palo Alto, CA.; Science & Behavior Books, Inc.; 1981.

Weinberger, Morris. "Labeling the physically disabled: the hearing impaired." Doctoral dissertation. Purdue Univ.; 1978.

Weingartner, H., Faillace, & Markley; "Verbal retention in alcoholics" in Quarterly J. Studies on alcohol, 1971, (32) 293-303.

Weinstein, Barbara E. "Hearing impairment and social isolation in the elderly." Doctoral dissertation. Columbia Univ.; 1980.

Westermeyer, "Alcoholism and Services for Ethnic Populations," in Pattison & Kaufman (eds) Encyclopedic Handbook of Alcoholism; N.Y., Gardner Press, 1982.

Wetlaufer, S. "Teen age drug use: Personality traits can predict abusers" The Daily Breeze. Mar., 5, 1986.

Whalen, Thomas E. "A Report of a project to prepare a manual of procedures for serving deaf defendants, victims and witnesses." Doctoral dissertation. N.Y. Univ.; 1981.

Wheeler, D., DeWolfe, A. & Rausch, M. "Audiometric Configurations in Patients Being Treated for Alcoholism." Drug and Alcohol Dependence; 5; 1980. pp. 63-68.

Whitehouse, A., Sherman, R. & Kozlowski, K. "Needs of Deaf Substance Abusers in Illinois." American J of Drug & Alcohol Abuse. 17 (1) 1991. pp. 103-113.

Williams, Peyton Jr. "Admission Policies & Practices of State-Operated Residential School for the Deaf." Exceptional Children. (50)Apr., 1984. pp. 550-551.

Wilsnack, Sharon "Alcohol Abuse and Alcoholism in Women," in Pattison & Kaufman, Encyclopedic Handbook on Alcoholism N.Y. Gardner Press, 1982.

Wilson, Catherine & Benedict, Beth "Stop Teenage Abuse of Marijuana Program" Wash., D.C. Gallaudet College Press. n.d.

Woititz, Janet G. Adult Children of Alcoholics. 10th printing; Hollywood, FL.; Health Communications, Inc. Publ.; 1983.

Wolk, Steve & Schildroth, A. "A Longitudinal Study of Deaf Students' Use of an Associational Strategy on a Reading Comprehension Test." J. Research in Reading; (2) aug., 1985. pp. 82-93.

Woodward, J. Signs of Drug Use. Silver Springs, MD; T.J. Publ.; 1980.

Wright, Charles L. "Follow-up study of the graduates from CA School for the Deaf at Riverside, 1972-1976." Master's thesis. Long Beach, CA. CA State Univ.; 1979.

Wright, Wayne K. "A Study of self-concept of hearing-impaired students as compared to the self-concept of normal-hearing students." Doctoral diss. Andrews Univ. 1981.

Wynne, R. quoted in staff written article, "The Medical Side of the War on Drugs." in Health weekly supplement of The Washington Post. Dec. 27, 1988. p. 5.

Yale, H. The Beginner's Meetings AA handout; Center City, MN; Hazelden Press, 1984.

Yoder, Barbara The Recovery Resource Book N.Y.; Simon & Schuster, Inc. 1990.

Youniss, James. "Intelligence Implication of & for Deafness." Advanced Experimental Medicine & Biology. Vol. 30; 1972. pp. 151-159.

Zieziula, Frank R. (ed) "Assessment of Hearing-Impaired People" Wash. D.C.; Gallaudet College Press. 1983.

Zinberg, N. "Report of the Liason Task Panel on Psychoactive Drug Use/Misuse" in The Yearbook of Substance Use & Abuse. Brill & Winick (ed.s) Vol. II. N.Y. Human Sciences Press. 1980.

Zivkovic, Momcilo. "Influence of Deafness on the structure of personality" Perceptual Motor Skills. 33(3) Dec., 1971. pp. 863-6.

Zuckerman, William Bernard. "Deaf, blind, and non-handicapped adults' attitudes toward each other as related to authoritarianism, alienation, and ego strength." Doctoral Dissertation. N.Y. Univ.; 1981.

APPENDIX A: RESOURCES

Here are a number of basal resources, service providing agencies and resource materials. Each of these entities, in turn, provides access information, sometimes including contact names, for various subsidiary materials and resources in that category.

ADARA's "National Directory" of Substance Abuse Services and Related Resources for the Deaf/Hearing Impaired. Edited by Jean Modry, B.S., Robin Sullivan, M.A. C.R.C. Adelaide Whitehouse, M.S. Lists contacts for approximately 100 programs and/or AA meetings available to the deaf.

Addiction Intervention with the Disabled; *Project Aid*; % Alexander Boros; Department of Sociology; Kent State University; Kent, Ohio 44242.

Addictions Program for the Hearing Impaired Person; The James Learning Method; 3755 Porter Creek Rd., Santa Rosa, CA 95404.

Alcohol & Drug Services Directory; 225 West 37th Ave.; San Mateo, CA 94403.

Alcoholics Anonymous; Grand Central Station; New York, NY 10163.

Benny McKeown Center: 1281 Fleming Ave.; San Jose, CA 95127. Recovery program based on 12-step programs, and drop-in day care facility.

American Deafness and Rehabilitation Association; 814 Thayer Ave. Silver Spring, MD 20910.

CALADDS: California Alcohol, Drug & Disability Study and other publications: Linda Cherry; 3224 Round Hill Dr.; Hayward, CA 94542.

California Department of Alcohol & Drug Programs Publications; "A Directory of Community Services in California." 1700 K. St.; Sacramento, CA 95814.

California State Office of Deaf Access; Department of Social Services, 744 P. St., MS 5-510. Sacramento, CA 95814.

Canadian Hearing society; 271 Spadina Rd.; Toronto, Ontario M5 R 2V3.

CEDAR: Center for Empowerment of Deaf Alcoholics in Recovery: 3041 University Ave.; San Diego, CA 92104.

CHID: The Combined Health Information Database; managed by the U.S. Government, accessible via the NIDCD Clearinghouse subfile "DC Subfile." National Institute of Health.

Children of Alcoholics Foundation, Inc.; P.O. Box 4185; Grand Central Station; New York, NY 10163-4185.

Counseling & Communications Center for the Hearing Impaired: 7335 Van Nuys Blvd.; Van Nuys, CA 91405.

Deaf Communication Foundation, 2801 Daubenbiss #5; Soquel, CA 95703.

Deaf Services Program, The, Albert Witzke Medical Center; 3411 Bank St.; Baltimore, MD 21224.

Deafness Research Foundation: 9 East 38th St.; New York, NY 10016-0003.

Deafpride Inc. Project Access; 1350 Potomac Ave. S.E.; Washington, DC 20003.

Gallaudet Outreach Services; KDES, PAS6. 800 Florida Ave. NE; Washington, DC 20002-3695.

Hazelden (Press): Pleasant Valley Rd.; P.O. Box 176; Center City, MN 55012-0176.

IADD (Institute on Alcohol, Drugs, and Disability) P.O. Box 7044; San Mateo, Ca 94403.

Minesota Chemical Dependency Program for the Hearing Impaired: Riverside Medical Center; 2450 Riverside Ave.; Minneapolis, MN 55454.

National Association of the Deaf: 814 Thayer Ave.; Silver Spring, MD 20910.

National Center for Youth with Disabilities; University of Minnesota; Box 721 UMHC, Haravard St. at East River Rd.; Minneapolis, MN 55455.

National Clearinghouse for Alcohol & Drug Information (from the Office for Substance Abuse Prevention): P.O. Box 2345; Rockville, MD 20852.

National Federation of Parents for Drug-Free Youth (NFP): 8730 Georgia Ave.; Suite 200, Silver Spring, MD 20910.

National Information Catalogue; The Minnesota Chemical Dependency Program for the Hearing Impaired at Riverside Medical Center; Minneapolis, MN 55454.

National Information Center on Deafness; Gallaudet University; 800 Florida Ave., NE, Washington, D.C. 20002-3695.

National Institute on Deafness Clearinghouse: P.O. Box 37777; Washington, D.C. 20013-37777.

National Institute on Deafness & Other Communication Disorders; NIH; Building 31, Room 1B-62; Bethesda, Maryland 20892.

National Organization on Disability; 910 16th St. NW; Suite 600; Washington, DC 20006.

National Prevention Network; 444 North Capitol St. NW; Suite 520; Washington, DC 20001. An organization of alcohol & drug abuse prevention directors subsidiary to the National Association of State Alcohol & Drug Abuse Directors (NASADAD).

NORCAL Center on Deafness, 2345 Hallmark Dr.; Suite 4, Sacramento, CA 95828.

Office for Substance Abuse Prevention; National Clearinghouse for Alcohol & Drug Information; P.O. Box 2345; Rockville, MD 20847-2345.

Parents' Resource Institute for Drug Education, Inc. (PRIDE) Woodruff Bldg., Suite 1002, 100 Edgewood Ave., Atlanta, GA 30303.

Rehabilitation Institute of Chicago: 448 E. Ontario St.; Suite 650; Chicago, IL 60611.

Resource Center on Substance Abuse Prevention and Disability: 1331 F Street NW; Suite 800; Washington, DC 20004.

SAISD: Substance and Alcohol Intervention Services for the Deaf. Volunteers in Prevention; Rochester Institute of Technology, P.O. Box 9887; Rochester, NY 14623-0887.

SARDI (Substance Abuse Resources and Disability Issues) School of Medicine; Wright State University. Dayton, OH 45435.

Services for the Hearing Impaired: 201-115 Second Ave. N.; Saskatoon, Saskatchewan S7K 1B2.

SIGN: Seeking Independent Growth Now: P.O. Box 1021; Aurora, CO 80040.

Southern California Alcohol and Drug Programs, Inc. 11500 Paramount Blvd., Downey, CA 90241 (AWAKENINGS Program)

Substance Abuse Information for the Disabled: 1331 F St. NW; Suite 800; Washington, DC 20004.

Union County Council on Alcoholism, Inc.: 300 N. Avenue East; Westfield, N.J. 07090.

University of California Center on Deafness; Deaf Services Network-North: 3333 California Street, Suite 10; San Francisco, CA 94143-1208.

U.S. Department of Health & Human Services; National Institute of Health; Washington, DC 20004.

Valley Women's Center, Inc. Family Recovery Center: 20969 Ventura Blvd., #18-19; Woodland Hills, Ca 91364.

Western Institute for the Deaf: 2125 West 7th Ave.; Vancouver, BC V6K1X9.

World Federation of the Deaf: P.O. Box 65; SF-00401 Helsinki, Finland.

APPENDIX B

This section consists of poems which have
special meaning for the author.

THE SCENE THAT WAS MINE

by Gerry Anonymous

Dope is like a jealous lover, it comes in all kinds of dress,
   bottles, pills, needles, cigarettes.   It knows no rivals.
Work, family, hobbies are not allowed on this trip.
Dope demands all your time and all your money,
   all your thoughts and eventually, your body.
Nothing else ever comes first.   Not even God.

Dope destroys your will power and self-respect; it cripples
   you completely.
In return for your slavish devotion, it will turn you into a
   conniving liar,
      a thief, a self-involved bore, a simpering idiot, and a
         worthless bum.
Whatever junk you are on will choke the life out of you.

It will kill everything in you that is useful, decent and
   independent.
After it has twisted your brains, if you are lucky, it will kill
   you.
Otherwise you may linger for years as a mindless zombie.
Dope has only one deadly enemy. It is the word NO.
No starts out haltingly; it is shy and painful to say.

But the more you say it, the more it is respected, and finally
   accepted.

No is the only cure for the curse that is ruining your life.
What is dope?
It is the expensive private road to a permanent home with
   the living dead.
It is the trip the peddlers try to talk you into taking.
It puts them on easy street and you in hell.
The day I learned the word "No," I got off a 10-year merry-
   go-round.
Thank God I did, or I would not be here to tell you how my
   trip was,
And how lucky I am to have found my way back.

KING HEROIN DESTROYETH MY SOUL

author unknown

King Heroin is my shepherd; I
shall always want. He maketh me
to lie down in the gutters.
He leadeth me beside the troubled
waters. He destroyeth my soul.
He leadeth me in the paths of
wickedness.
Yea, I shall walk through the
valley of poverty and will fear no
evil, for thou, Heroin, art with me.
Thy Needle and Capsule comfort
me. Thou strippest the table
of groceries in the presence of my
family. Thou robbest my head of
reason.
My cup of sorrow runneth
over. Surely heroin addiction shall
stalk me all the days of my life
and I will dwell in the House of the
Damned forever.

MY NAME IS COCAINE

author unknown

My name is cocaine -- call me coke for short.
I entered this country without a passport.
Ever since then, I've made lots of scum rich.
Some have been murdered and found in a ditch.

I'm more valued than diamonds, more treasured
    than gold.
Use me just once and you, too, will be sold.
I'll make a schoolboy forget his books.
I'll make a beauty-queen forget her looks.

I'll take a renowned speaker and make him a bore.
I'll take your mother and make her a whore.
I'll make a school-teacher forget how to teach.
I'll make a preacher not want to preach.

I'll take all your rent money and you'll be evicted.
I'll murder your babies or they'll be born addicted.
I'll make you rob, and steal and kill.
When you're under my power, you have no will.

Remember, my friend, my name is "Big C,"
If you try me one time you may never be free.
I've destroyed actors, politicians and many a hero.
I've decreased bank accounts from millions to zero.

I make shooting and stabbing a common affair.
Once I take charge, you won't have a prayer.
Now that you know me, what will you do?
You'll have to decide, it's all up to you.

The day you agree to sit in my saddle,
The decision is one that no one can straddle.
Listen to me, and please listen well,
When you ride with cocaine, you are headed for
    hell.

MISS HEROIN

by an anonymous addict

So now, little man, you've grown tired of grass,
LSD, goofballs, cocaine and hash;
And someone pretending to be a true friend
said, "I'll introduce you to Miss Heroin."
Well, honey, before you start fooling with me,
just let me inform you of how it will be.

For I will seduce you and make you my slave,
I've sent men much stronger than you to their graves.
You think you could never become a disgrace
and end up addicted to poppy seed waste.
So you'll start inhaling me one afternoon,
You'll take me into your arms very soon.

And once I have entered deep down in your veins,
the craving will nearly drive you insane.
You'll need lots of money (as you have been told),
for, darling, I am much more expensive than gold.
You'll swindle your mother, and, just for a buck,
you'll turn into something vile and corrupt.

You'll mug and you'll steal for my narcotic charm,
and feel contentment when I'm in your arm.
The day you realize the monster you've grown,
you'll solemnly promise to leave me alone.
If you think you've got that mystical knack,
then, sweetie, just try getting me off your back.

The vomit, the cramps, your guts tied in a knot,
the jangling nerves screaming for just one more shot.
The hot chills and cold sweats, the withdrawal pains
can only be saved by my little white grains.
There's no other way, and there's no need to look,
for deep down inside, you'll know you are hooked.

You'll desperately run to the pusher, and then
you'll welcome me back on your arm again.
And when you return (just as I foretold),
I know that you'll give me your body and soul.
You'll give up your morals, your conscience, your
                heart,
and you will be mine until DEATH DO US PART.

BLESSINGS IN DISGUISE

by Isabel G. Lala

As You travel along life's road
And something makes you feel blessed
You will find it comes from inside
You just wanted this more than the rest

But as you go along a little farther
And troubles come your way
Don't worry about tomorrow
You can bet it will be a better day

For troubles are just blessings
Disguised as they may be
Just as the dawn follows the darkness
So it works this way for you and me

For everything you lose
You gain a little more
For everything you give away
You're just adding up your score

Each time God took a step
On that road to Calvary
He wasn't thinking of the pain or sorrow
Just His reward - His gift to us of eternity

So if each of us would ponder then
About God's gifts from above
I think that we would all realize
Troubles are really blessings in disguise

Author's mother died of substance abuse

THE JOURNEY TRAIN

by Frank James John Lala, Jr.

People from all walks of life
Have something in common -- Birth, and Death.
Birth is independent of us.
Death is dependent on how we live our lives.

We are often the decisive factor
In our fate or destiny.
We are all on Journey Train,
From Birth to Death.

The destination of Journey Train
To the ultimate and inevitable -- Death,
Is distinct for everyone of us,
Much like the snowflakes.

Desecrating ourselves with the scourge of
Substance abuse is like a slow suicide
That affects our well-being and quality of life.
It is jumping off the Journey Train while it is in motion.

Our unique characters and personality traits
Vanish into thin air with the ethereal spectre of death
The moment we jump off, and preclude
Any decent second chance we might have at life.

The only rational thing for us to do
To save ourselves from this sinister curse
Is to seek help by attending A.A. or N.A. programs,
Which have saved many from the impending doom of death.

A Credo for Deaf Americans

by Frank James John Lala, Jr.

We don't choose to be the common silent minority.
    It is our right to be the uncommon and noble silent
    minority.

If we can, we seek opportunity, not security.

We don't wish to be "kept" citizens, humbled and dulled by
    having the state look after us.

We want to take the calculated risk . . . to dream and to
    build, to fail and to succeed.

We want to abolish being stereotyping, and to remove the
    prevalent public mentality of prejudice.

We will not tolerate any biased perceptions, criticisms or
    censures of our beloved American Sign Language.

We will not accept abuse of our Deaf identity by oppressors,
    nor our rights to self-determination.

We refuse to barter incentive for a dole.

We prefer the challenge of life to a guaranteed existence;
    the thrill of fulfillment to the stale calm of Utopia.

We will not trade freedom for beneficence, nor our dignity
    for a handout.

We will never cower before any master or paternalistic
   attitudes, nor bend to any threat of discrimination.

It is the heritage of our Deaf Culture to stand erect, proud
   and unafraid; to think and act for ourselves; to enjoy
   the benefits of our creations, and to face the hearing
   world boldly and say, "This we have achieved."

All of this is what it means to be Deaf Americans.

APPENDIX C

PROGRAMS FOR DEAF ALCOHOLICS AND SUBSTANCE ABUSERS

<u>ALASKA</u>

Clitheroe Center, 227 Spenard Road, Anchorage, AL 99503
(907)276-2892 Voice; (907)279-0822 TDD

<u>ARIZONA</u>

Calvary Rehabilitation, 329 N. 3rd Avenue, Phoenix, AZ
85003   (602)254-7092 Voice; (602)253-3254 TDD

Menninger-Phoenix Counseling Services, 300 West
Claredon, Phoenix, AZ 85013
(602)280-1020 Voice; (602)280-1002 TDD

Community Outreach Program for the Deaf, 268 West
Adam Street, Tucson, AZ 85705   (602)792-1906 Voice/TDD

<u>CALIFORNIA</u>

New Bridge Foundation, 1820 Scenic Avenue, Berkeley, CA
94709   (510)548-7270 Voice; (510)548-7274 TDD

Awakenings Program for Deaf and Hard of Hearing
Persons, 11500 Paramount Blvd., Downey, CA 90241
(310)923-0969 Voice; (310)923-3929 TDD

Valley Advocacy & Communication Center, 5070 N. 6th,
Suite 169, Fresno, CA 93710   (209)225-3323 Voice/TDD

Antelope Valley Council on Alcohol/Drug Dependency, 1543-F E. Palmdale Blvd., Palmdale, CA 93550 (805)274-1062 Voice; (805)274-0086 TDD

Center for Empowerment of Deaf Alcoholics in Recovery, 3041 University Avenue, San Diego, CA 92104 (619)293-3820 Voice; (619)293-3746 TDD

University of California Center on Deafness, Deaf Services Network - North, 3333 California Street, Suite 10, San Francisco, CA 94143
(415)476-4980 Voice; (415)476-7600 TDD

Benny McKeown Center, Alcohol and Drug Recovery Home, 1281 Fleming Avenue, San Jose, CA 95127
(408)259-1983 Voice/TDD

Horizon Community Center, 1403 164th Avenue, San Leandro, CA 94578
(510)278-8654 Voice; (510)278-5676 TDD

County of Orange Alcohol Programs, Health Care Agency, 1200 N. Main, Suite 826, Santa Ana, CA 92701
(714)568-4834 Voice; (714)896-7512 TDD

Signs of Recovery/CLARE Foundation, 1871 9th Street, Santa Monica, CA 90405
(310)450-4184 Voice; (310)450-4164 TDD

The James Learning Method, 3755 Porter Creek Road, Santa Rosa, CA 95404   (707)545-7707 Voice/TDD

Tulare County Alcoholism Council, Inc., 120 W. School Street, Visalia, CA 93291 (209)625-4100 Voice

COLORADO

McMaster Center for Drug and Alcohol, 301 S. Union, Colorado Springs, CO 80910
(719)578-3150 Voice; (719)578-3181 TDD

Boulder County Health Department, Substance Abuse Program, 3450 Broadway, Boulder, CO 80304
(303)441-1275 Voice; (303)441-1281 TTY

Pikes Peak Mental Health Center, 175 Parkside Drive, Colorado Springs, CO 80910
(719)389-4900 Voice; (719)471-8256 TDD

Tejon Clinic, El Paso County Health Department, 710 So. Tejon, Colorado Springs, CO 80903
(719)578-3150; Voice; (719)578-3183 TDD

Human Services, Inc., Hearing Impaired Programs, 4280 Hale Parkway, Denver, CO 80220
(303)321-4906 Voice; (303)321-5609 TDD

Washington House, 7373 Birch Street, Commerce City, CO 80022 (303)289-3391 Voice/TDD

Colorado West Recovery Center, 711 Grand Avenue, Glennwood Springs, CO 81601 (303)945-8439 Voice

Island Grove Regional Treatment Center, Inc., P.O. Box 5100, 421 N. 15th Street, Greeley, CO 80632
(303)356-6664 Voice/TDD; (303)352-3784 Voice/TDD

Pueblo Treatment Services, Inc., 1301 W. 17th Street, Pueblo, CO 81003   (719)564-3758 Voice

Arapahoe House, 8801 Lipan, Thornton, CO 80221
(303)657-3737 Voice/TDD

CONNECTICUT

Shirley Frank Foundation, 659 George Street, New Haven,
CT 06511-5392 (203)787-2771 Voice

Connecticut Commission on the Deaf and Hearing Impaired
Counseling Services, 141 No. Main Street, West Hartford,
CT 06107 (203)566-7414 Voice/TDD

DISTRICT OF COLUMBIA

Deafpride, Inc., Project Second Chance, 1350 Potomac
Avenue, SE, Washington,DC 20003
(202)675-6700 Voice/TDD

FLORIDA

United Hearing & Deaf Services, Inc., 4850 W. Oakland
Park Boulevard, Suite 207, Lauderdale Lakes, FL 33313
(305)731-7203 Voice/TDD

National Mental Health Institute on Deafness, P.O. Box
365, Safety Harbor, FL 34695 (813)726-7345 Voice;
(800)752-7345 Voice; (800)242-0232 TDD

Silent Bridges at the Manors, 1527 Riverside Drive, Tarpon
Springs, FL34689
(813)937-4211 Voice/TDD; (800)277-6266 Voice/TDD

GEORGIA

Georgia Council for the Hearing Impaired, Inc., Kensington Office Park, 4151 Memorial Drive, Suite 103-B, Decatur, GA 30032 (404)292-5312 Voice/TDD

HAWAII

Students Staying Straight, 1325 Lower Main Street, Suite #205 D, Wailuku, Hawaii 96793
(808)242-9544 Voice

IDAHO

Alcoholism Treatment Unit, Hospital North Drive, P.O. Box 672, Orofino, Idaho 83544
(208)476-4513 Voice; (208)476-4511, Ext. 278 TDD

ILLINOIS

Lighthouse, Chestnut Health Systems, 1003 Martin Luther King Drive, bloomington, IL 61701
(309)827-6026 Voice/TDD

Central East Alcohol and Drug Council, 635 Division Street, Charleston, IL 61920
(217)348-8101 Voice

Wells Center, 1300 Lincoln, Jacksonville, IL 62650
(217)243-1871 Voice: (217)243-0470 TDD

Franklin-Williamson Human Services, Inc., Garavalia Building, 1307 West Main, P.O. Box 365, Marion, IL 62959 (618)993-8629 TDD; (618)997-5336 Voice; (618)932-2188 Voice

Center on Deafness, 3444 Dundee Road, Northbrook, IL 60062   (708)559-0110 Voice; (708)559-9493 TDD

Addiction Recovery Program for People Who Are Deaf, 108 N. Sangamon, Chicago, IL 60607 (312)243-7696 Voice; (312)243-7698 TDD

Triangle Center, 120 No. 11th Street, Springfield, IL 62703 (217)544-9858 Voice; (217)544-8751 TDD

INDIANA

Tri-County-Deaf Services, 9011 N. Meridian, Suite 112, Indianapolis, IN 46260 (317)574-1256 Voice; (317)574-1240 TDD

Institute for Addiction and Behavioral Treatment, The Methodist Hospitals, 8409 Virginia Street, Merrillville, IN 46410 (219)738-5545 Voice/TDD

KANSAS

Johnson County Substance Abuse Services, Inc., 6221 Richards Drive, Shawnee, KS 66216 (913)268-7125 Voice; (913)268-7134 TDD

KENTUCKY

Jefferson Alcohol and Drug Abuse Center, 600 South
Preston Street, Louisville, KY 40202
(502)583-3951 Voice/TDD

Adanta Clinical Services, 101 Hardin Lane, Somerset, KY
42501   (606)679-7348 Voice; (606679-4782 TDD

LOUISIANA

Baton Rouge Area Substance Abuse Clinic, 3615
Government Street, Building A, Baton Rouge, LA 70806
(504)922-0050 Voice

Division of Alcohol and Drug Abuse, 521 Legion Avenue,
Houma, LA 70364   (504)857-3612 Voice

MAINE

Caron Street House, 26 Caron Street, Portland, Maine,
04103   (207)797-8046 Voice/TDD

MARYLAND

Family Services Foundation, Inc., 4806 Seton Drive,
Baltimore, MD 21215
(301)764-0663 Voice; (301)764-0664 TDD

Psychiatric Institute of Montgomery County, 14901
Broschart Road, Rockville, MD 20850
(301)251-4545 Voice

MASSACHUSETTS

The Prevention Center, 95 Berkeley Street, Boston, MA 02116   (617)451-0049 Voice/TDD

Womanplace, Women's Alcoholism Program, 11 Russell Street, Cambridge, MA 02140   (617)661-5855 Voice/TDD

Project for the Deaf at Stephen Miller House, P.O. Box CC, Falmouth, MA 02151   (508)540-5052 Voice/TDD

MICHIGAN

Harbor Light Center, 3580 South Custer, Monroe, MI 48161 (313)242-5050 Voice

Northville Regional Psychiatric Hospital, Center for Deaf Treatment Services, 41001 West Seven Mile, Northville, MI 48167   (313)349-1800 ext. 2173 Voice; (313)349-1865 TDD

Medical Resource Center, 21700 Greenfield, Suite 226, Oak Park, MI 48237   (313)967-4312 Voice; (313)967-4322 TDD

MINNESOTA

Minnesota Chemical Dependency Program for Deaf & Hard of Hearing, Fairview-Riverside Medical Center, 2450 Riverside Avenue, Minneapolis, MN 55454 (800)282-3323 Voice/TDD; (612)672-4402 Voice; (612)672-4114 TDD

Hearing Impaired Health and Wellness Program, St. Paul-Ramsey Medical Center, 640 Jackson Street, St. Paul, MN 55101-2595 (612)221-2719 Voice; (612)221-3761 TDD

MISSOURI

Kansas City Community Center, 1534 Campbell, Kansas City, MO 64108 (816)421-6670 Voice; (816)421-4701 TDD

NEBRASKA

Lincoln General Hospital, Independence Center, 1650 Lake Street, Lincoln, NE 68502 (402)473-5268 Voice/TDD

NEVADA

Community Counseling Center, 1006 East Sahara Avenue, Las Vegas, NV 89104 (702)369-8700 Voice/TDD

NEW HAMPSHIRE

Southeastern New Hampshire Alcohol and Drug Treatment Services, Box 978, Dover, NH 03820 (800)451-1715 Voice

NEW JERSEY

Burlington Comprehensive Counseling, Inc., 75 Washington Street, Mt. Holly, NJ 08060
(609)267-3610 Voice; (609)267-9284 TDD

Palisades Counseling Center Deaf Program, 7101 Kennedy Boulevard, North Bergen, NJ 07047
(201)854-0500 Voice; (201)854-4457 TDD

Access Regional Resource Center, 660 Broadway, Paterson, NJ 07026
(201)977-6660 Voice/TDD; (201)977-6690 Voice/TDD

Community Mental Health Center at Piscataway, University of Medicine & Dentistry of New Jersey, 667 Hoes Lane, P.O. Box 1392, Piscataway, NJ 08855-1392
(908)463-4929 Voice/TDD

Signs of Sobriety, Inc., 986 South Broadway Street, Trenton, NJ 08611
(609)392-4477 Voice; (609)392-6561 TDD; (800)332-7677 TDD

Reality House, 1 Alpha Avenue, Suite 43, Voorhees, NJ 08043   (609)428-5688 Voice; (609)428-8373 TDD

National Council on Alcoholism and Drug Dependence of Union County, Inc., 300 North Avenue, East, Westfield, NJ 07090 (908)233-8892 Voice/TDD

NEW YORK

Greater Buffalo Council on Alcoholism and Substance Abuse, 220 Delaware Avenue, Suite 509, Buffalo, NY 14202
(716)852-1781 Voice/TDD

New York Society for the Deaf, Substance Abuse Program, 817 Broadway, 7th Floor, New York, NY 10003 (212)777-3900 Voice/TDD

St. Vincent's Hospital and Medical Center of New York, Program for Services to Deaf Patients, 203 West 12th Street, 6th Floor, New York, NY 10011 (212)790-8802 Voice; (212) 790-8265 TDD

John L. Norris Clinic, Alcoholism Treatment Center, 1600 South Avenue, Rochester, NY 14620 (716)461-0410 Voice; (716)461-4253 TDD

Substance and Alcohol Intervention Services for the Deaf (S.A.I.S.D.), Rochester Institute of Technology, Hale-Andrews Student Life Center, P.O. Box 9887, Rochester, NY 14623 (716)475-4978 Voice/TDD

Crouse Irving Memorial Hospital, Chemical Dependency Treatment Services, 410 South Crouse Avenue, Syracuse, NY 13210 (315)470-7381

NORTH CAROLINA

Walter B. Jones Alcohol and Drug Abuse Treatment Center, Route 1, Box 20-A, Greenville, NC 27834 (919)830-3426 Voice

NORTH DAKOTA

South Central Human Service Center, P.O. Box 2055, 520 3rd Street NW, Jamestown, ND 58402 (701)252-2641 Voice/TDD

OHIO

Alcoholism Council of the Cincinnati Area, N.C.A.D.D., 118 William Howard Taft Road, Cincinnati, OH 45219 (513)281-7880 Voice/TDD

Center for Comprehensive Alcoholism Treatment, 830 Ezzard Charles Drive, Cincinnati, OH 45214 (513)381-6672 Voice; (513)281-7880 TDD

Genesis Hearing Impaired Program, 3233 Euclid Avenue, Cleveland, OH 44115   (216)431-4722 Voice/TDD

Deaf Hope, 1500 West Third Avenue, Suite 224, Columbus, OH 43212   (614)488-4773 Voice/TDD

Harding Hospital, 445 E. Granville Road, Worthington, OH 43085   (614)885-5381 Voice

OKLAHOMA

Department of Mental Health and Substance Abuse Services, P.O. Box 53277, Oklahoma City, OK 73125 (405)271-8653 Voice; (405)271-7474 TDD

Opportunities, Inc., 120 West First, P.O. Box 249, Watonga, OK 73772   (405)623-2545 Voice/TDD

OREGON

Bridgeway to Recovery, P.O. Box 17818 Salem, OR 97305 (503)363-2021 Voice/TDD

PENNSYLVANIA

Belmont Center for Comprehensive Treatment, 4200
Monument Road, Philadelphia, PA 19131 Inpatient
(215)581-9144 Voice; (215)581-3764 TDD Outpatient
(215)581-3873 Voice; (215)581-5477 TDD

Deaf/Hearing Impaired Chemical Dependency Program,
Pittsburgh Hearing, Speech, and Deaf Services, 1945 Fifth
Avenue, Pittsburgh, PA 15219   (412)281-1375 Voice/TDD

RHODE ISLAND

Northern Rhode Island Community Mental Health Center,
P.O. Box 1700, Woonsocket, RI 02895
(401)766-3330 Voice; (401)762-1577 TDD

SOUTH CAROLINA

Patrick B. Harris Psychiatric Hospital, P.O. Box 2907,
Anderson, SC 29622
(803)231-2710 Voice/TDD

South Carolina Commission on alcohol and Drug Abuse,
3700 Forest Drive, Columbia, SC 29204
(803)734-9540 Voice/TDD

Spartanburg Alcohol & Drug Abuse Commission, P.O. Box
1251, 131 N. Spring Street, Spartanburg, SC 29304
(803)582-7588 Voice/TDD

SOUTH DAKOTA

Communication Service for the Deaf, 3520 Gateway Lane, Sioux Falls, SD 57106   (605)339-6718 Voice/TDD

TENNESSEE

Hearing Impaired Therapy Line Program, St. Joseph Hospital, 220 Overton Street, Memphis, TN 38105 (800)888-6470 Voice/TDD

Deaf & Hard-of-Hearing Services, 2612 Westwood Drive, Nashville, TN 37204   (615)269-0029 Voice/TDD

TEXAS

St. David's Pavilion, 1025 E. 32nd, P.O. Box 4280, Austin, TX 78705   (512)867-5800 Voice; (512)472-1160 TDD

Goodrich Center for the Deaf, Chemical Dependency Program, 2500 Lipscomb Street, Fort Worth, TX 76110 (817)926-5305 Voice; (817)926-4101 TDD

Nightingale Rehabilitation, Inc., 5802 Holly, Houston, TX 77074   (713)981-1543 Voice/TDD

Vocational Guidance Service, Inc., Alternative Hearing Impaired Program, 3100 Richmond Avenue, Suite 301, Houston, TX 77098 (713)520-6308 Voice; (713)520-6309 TDD

Charter Hospital, Charter Hearing Impaired Program Service, 1550 First Colony Blvd., Sugarland, TX 77479 (713)908-4000 Voice/TDD

APPENDIX D

HEALTH AND DRUG
EDUCATION SERIES

The Health and Drug Education Series
are reprinted with permission of
Bruce Algra's
HEALTH AND DRUG EDUCATION SERIES,
3125 19th Street, Suite 305, Bakersfield, CA 93301;
(805)399-2897 © The Algra Corporation 1992.

THE HARMFUL EFFECTS OF
ALCOHOL

BRAIN & CENTRAL NERVOUS SYSTEM
IMPAIRED BEHAVIOR, JUDGEMENT, MEMORY, CONCENTRATION, AND COORDINATION
- Drinker experiences mild euphoria and loss of inhibition as alcohol impairs regions of the brain controlling behavior and emotion. Alcohol impairs judgement, memory, concentration, and coordination; as well as inducing extreme mood swings and emotional outbursts.

BRAIN DAMAGE & AFFECT
- Alcohol acts as a sedative on the Central Nervous System, depressing the nerve cells in brain, dulling, altering, and damaging their ability to respond. Large doses cause sleep, anesthesia, respiratory failure, coma, and death.

BRAIN DISORDERS & ADDICTION
- Long term drinking may result in permanent brain damage, serious mental disorders, and addiction to alcohol.

LUNGS
- High amounts of alcohol may cause breathing to stop; then death.
- Lowered resistance to infection.

LIVER
- Chronic heavy drinking may cause alcoholic hepatitis (inflammation and destruction of liver cells) and then cirrhosis (irreversible lesions, scarring, and destruction of liver cells). Impairs the liver's ability to remove yellow pigment and skin appears yellow (Jaundice).
- Liver damage causes fluid to build in extremities (Edema).
- Decreases production of blood-clotting factors; may cause uncontrolled bleeding.
- Liver accumulates fat which can cause liver failure, coma, and death.

REPRODUCTIVE SYSTEM
MALES & FEMALES
- Sexual functioning can be impaired and deteriorate, resulting in impotence and infertility, sometimes irreversible. Females also have high risk of developing breast cancer.

PREGNANCY & UNBORN BABIES
- Drinking during pregnancy significantly increases chance of delivering a baby with Fetal Alcohol Syndrome; small head, possible brain damage, abnormal facial features, poor muscle tone, speech and sleep disorders, and retarded growth and development.

OTHER AFFECTS ON CENTRAL NERVOUS SYSTEM
- Impaired visual ability
- Unclear hearing
- Dulled smell and taste
- Loss of pain perception
- Altered sense of time and space
- Impaired fine motor skills
- Slows reactions
- Impaired sexual performance

EYES
Distorted vision and ability to adjust to lights. Pinpoint pupils and red eyes.

EARS
Diminishes ability to distinguish between sounds and perceive their direction.

MOUTH
Slurred speech. Dulls taste and smell, reducing desire to eat.

THROAT
Irritation and damage of lining of esophagus, induces severe vomiting, hemorrhaging, pain, and difficulty swallowing. Cancer.

HEART
- Weakens the heart muscle and ability to pump (Cardiomyopathy).
- Heart enlargement, abnormal heart signs, and irregular heart beat.
- Increases blood pressure, risk of heart attack, and strokes.
- Inhibits production of white and red blood cells.

MUSCLES
Muscles become weaker and atrophy, pain, spasms, and tenderness.

STOMACH
Irritation of stomach lining, peptic ulcers, inflammation, bleeding lesions, and cancer.

PANCREAS
Significant risk of pancreatis, a chronic inflammation of pancreas.

INTESTINES
Irritation of the lining of the intestinal tract and colon. Chronic drinking may result in inflammation, ulcers, and cancer of intestines and colon. Nausea, diarrhea, vomiting, sweating, and loss of appetite are common. Alcohol impairs small intestine's ability to process nutrients and vitamins.

BONES
Alcohol interferes with body's ability to absorb calcium resulting in bones being weak, soft, brittle, and thinner (Osteoporosis).

Bruce Algra's HEALTH AND DRUG EDUCATION SERIES 3125 19th Street • Suite 305 • Bakersfield, CA 93301 • (805) 399-2897 ®The Algra Corporation 1992

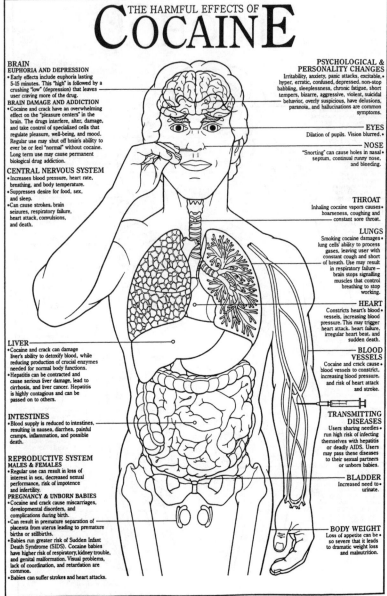

THE HARMFUL EFFECTS OF COCAINE

BRAIN
EUPHORIA AND DEPRESSION
• Early effects include euphoria lasting 5-15 minutes. This "high" is followed by a crushing "low" (depression) that leaves user craving more of the drug.
BRAIN DAMAGE AND ADDICTION
• Cocaine and crack have an overwhelming effect on the "pleasure centers" in the brain. The drugs interfere, alter, damage, and take control of specialized cells that regulate pleasure, well-being, and mood. Regular use may shut off brain's ability to ever be or feel "normal" without cocaine. Long term use may cause permanent biological drug addiction.

CENTRAL NERVOUS SYSTEM
• Increases blood pressure, heart rate, breathing, and body temperature.
• Suppresses desire for food, sex, and sleep.
• Can cause strokes, brain seizures, respiratory failure, heart attack, convulsions, and death.

LIVER
• Cocaine and crack can damage liver's ability to detoxify blood, while reducing production of crucial enzymes needed for normal body functions.
• Hepatitis can be contracted and cause serious liver damage, lead to cirrhosis, and liver cancer. Hepatitis is highly contagious and can be passed on to others.

INTESTINES
• Blood supply is reduced to intestines, resulting in nausea, diarrhea, painful cramps, inflammation, and possible death.

REPRODUCTIVE SYSTEM
MALES & FEMALES
• Regular use can result in loss of interest in sex, decreased sexual performance, risk of impotence and infertility.
PREGNANCY & UNBORN BABIES
• Cocaine and crack cause miscarriages, developmental disorders, and complications during birth.
• Can result in premature separation of placenta from uterus leading to premature births or stillbirths.
• Babies run greater risk of Sudden Infant Death Syndrome (SIDS). Cocaine babies have higher risk of respiratory, kidney trouble, and genital malformation. Visual problems, lack of coordination, and retardation are common.
• Babies can suffer strokes and heart attacks.

PSYCHOLOGICAL & PERSONALITY CHANGES
Irritability, anxiety, panic attacks, excitable, hyper, erratic, confused, depressed, non-stop babbling, sleeplessness, chronic fatigue, short tempers, bizarre, aggressive, violent, suicidal behavior, overly suspicious, have delusions, paranoia, and hallucinations are common symptoms.

EYES
Dilation of pupils. Vision blurred. •

NOSE
"Snorting" can cause holes in nasal septum, continual runny nose, and bleeding.

THROAT
Inhaling cocaine vapors causes • hoarseness, coughing and constant sore throat.

LUNGS
Smoking cocaine damages • lung cells' ability to process gases, leaving user with constant cough and short of breath. Use may result in respiratory failure — brain stops signaling muscles that control breathing to stop working.

HEART
Constricts heart's blood • vessels, increasing blood pressure. This may trigger heart attack, heart failure, irregular heart beat, and sudden death.

BLOOD VESSELS
Cocaine and crack cause • blood vessels to constrict, increasing blood pressure, and risk of heart attack and stroke.

TRANSMITTING DISEASES
Users sharing needles • run high risk of infecting themselves with hepatitis or deadly AIDS. Users may pass these diseases to their sexual partners or unborn babies.

BLADDER
Increased need to • urinate.

BODY WEIGHT
Loss of appetite can be • so severe that it leads to dramatic weight loss and malnutrition.

Bruce Alzen's HEALTH AND DRUG EDUCATION SERIES 3225 19th Street • Suite 305 • Bakersfield, CA 93308 • (805) 398-2007 ©The Algen Corporation 1992

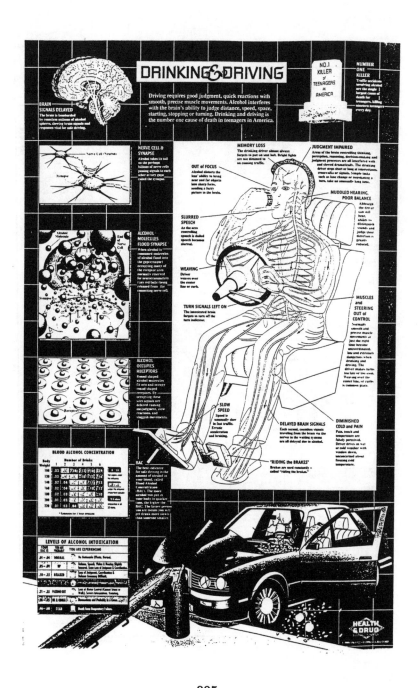

HARMFUL EFFECTS OF ALCOHOL & DRUGS ON THE
FETUS & INFANT

ALCOHOL

- Drinking alcohol during pregnancy significantly increases risk of having a baby born with Fetal Alcohol Syndrome (FAS). A pregnant mother must realize that if she drinks, then so does her baby!
- FAS babies are abnormally small at birth and have small heads.
- FAS babies' brains are smaller and frequently have behavioral and learning problems associated with mental retardation.
- FAS babies are hyperactive, jittery and lack coordination.
- FAS babies are often born with noticeable to severe abnormal facial features.

FETAL ALCOHOL SYNDROME

HEAD
- Small head size through-out life.

NOSE
- Broad and flat.
- Upturned nostrils.

LIPS
- Narrow upper lip.

CHIN
- Small chin.

BRAIN
- Brain damage.
- Mental retardation.
- Below average growth and maturation.
- Hyperactive.

EYES
- Short eye folds.
- Droopy eye lids.
- Small, widely spaced eyes.

EARS
- Large, poorly malformed ears.

OTHER ABNORMALITIES
- Stunting of growth.
- Liver damage.
- Heart and kidney damage.
- Alcoholic withdrawal, tremors, and seizures.

SMOKING

Smoking during pregnancy:
- Increases risk of miscarriage.
- Increases premature labor and birth.
- Causes constriction and damage to the blood vessels of the umbilical cord, decreasing the flow of blood, oxygen, and nutrients vital to the developing fetus.
- Almost always causes low-birth weight babies.
- May cause baby to be born with a small head and brain, impairs growth, intellect, and emotional development.

SMOKING REDUCES FLOW OF OXYGEN & NUTRIENTS TO FETUS

Reduces blood, oxygen, and nutrients to fetus.

Smoking damages blood vessels.

LOW-BIRTH WEIGHT BABY BORN THREE WEEKS PREMATURE

MARIJUANA

Mothers who smoke marijuana during pregnancy:
- Damage blood levels of the umbilical cord, and reduce their ability to transport and supply oxygen and nutrients to the developing fetus.
- Increase risk of low-birth weight baby.
- Increase risk of miscarriage.
- Increase risk of baby being born with a small head and brain, poor growth, irritability, birth defects and deformities.

COCAINE

Cocaine use during pregnancy increases risk of:
- Fetal death.
- Premature labor and delivery.
- Miscarriage.
- Sudden Infant Death Syndrome (SIDS). Babies die in their sleep without warning.
- Blood/pressure changes, caused by cocaine use.
- Respiratory failure, kidney trouble, visual problems, lack of coordination and retardation.

BLOOD VESSEL BURSTING IN BRAIN

Increases in blood pressure may cause blood vessels in the fetal brain to burst, resulting in permanent physical and mental damage.

HOW DRUGS TRAVEL FROM THE MOTHER TO FETUS AND INFANT

PATHWAY OF DRUGS THROUGH THE MOTHER TO THE FETUS

1. Drug enters body through the mouth. (Drugs also enter the body through intravenous injection and by smiffing or snorting chemicals through the nose.)
2. Drug enters the stomach.
3. Drug enters the intestine.
4. Drug is absorbed through the intestine and enters the mother's bloodstream.
5. Drug passes through the placenta and is carried through the umbilical cord to fetus.
6. Drug enters blood circulation of fetus and is pumped throughout the infant.

ALCOHOL, DRUGS, AND HARMFUL SUBSTANCES TAKEN BY THE PREGNANT MOTHER THAT TRAVEL THROUGH THE BLOODSTREAM TO THE FETUS
(Alcohol • Nicotine • Marijuana • Cocaine • LSD • PCP • Heroine • Medications • Sleeping Pills • Sedatives • Aspirins • Foods containing caffeine such as Coffee, Tea, Colas, and Chocolate)

Drug molecules

Blood vessels of the mother

Placenta

The fetus shares almost everything the mother takes into her body, whether eaten, smoked, injected, sniffed, or swallowed. Drugs and harmful substances such as alcohol, nicotine, marijuana, cocaine, LSD, PCP, heroine, medications, aspirins, and foods containing caffeine, are all transferred from the mother's bloodstream to the blood circulation of the fetus—and therefore must be avoided! These chemicals easily pass through the placenta and are transported through the large blood vessel of the umbilical cord to the fetus, with the two smaller arteries carrying deoxygenated blood, containing waste products, back to the placenta. During the entire pregnancy, especially the first few months, the developing fetus is extremely fragile, vulnerable, and has great difficulty in ridding itself of harmful chemicals remaining unprocessed in the bloodstream or circulating in the amniotic fluid. Exposure to these substances greatly increases the risk of miscarriage, early infant death, low-birth weight, SIDS, stillbirth, premature birth, brain damage, mental retardation, growth impairment, birth defects and deformities, addiction and withdrawal.

Umbilical cord

Artery

Vein

Fetus

Drug molecules being transported throughout the blood circulation system of the fetus.

Drug molecules circulating in the amniotic fluid.

Uterus

DRUGS BEING TRANSFERRED TO THE INFANT DURING BREASTFEEDING

Alcohol, drugs, and harmful substances taken by the mother are transferred to her infant while breast feeding. These microscopic chemicals pass through milk glands and ducts in the breast when the infant is feeding. The chemicals are then absorbed and pumped throughout the infant.

Milk glands and ducts

Drug molecules

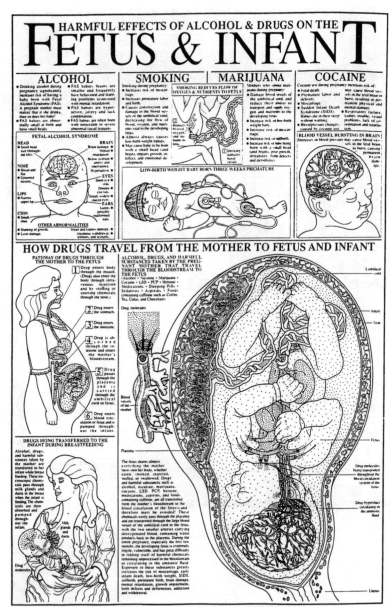

Bruce Algra's HEALTH AND DRUG EDUCATION SERIES • 3123 19th Street • Suite 305 • Bakersfield, CA 93301 • 1-800-336-4322 • © The Algra Corporation 1995

336

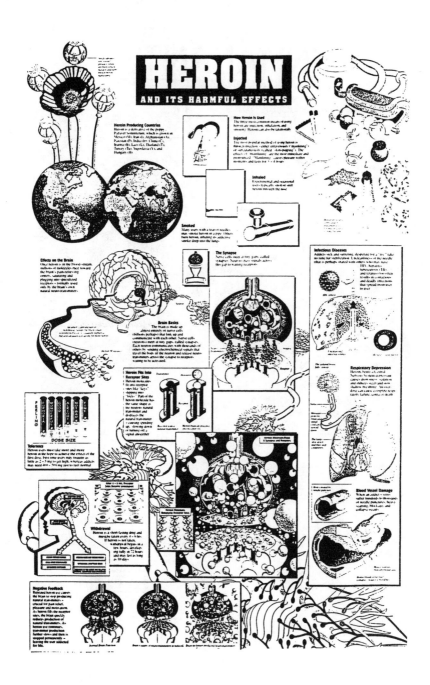

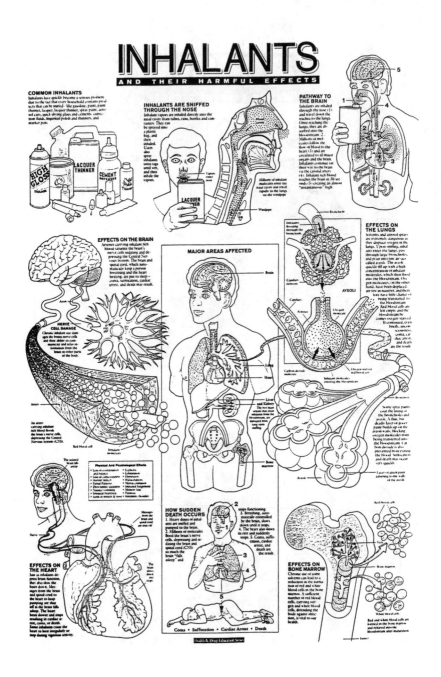

338

MARIJUANA

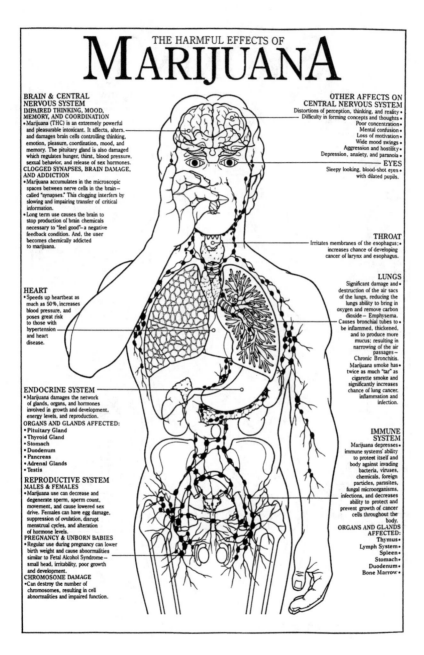

BRAIN & CENTRAL NERVOUS SYSTEM
IMPAIRED THINKING, MOOD, MEMORY, AND COORDINATION
• Marijuana (THC) is an extremely powerful and pleasurable intoxicant. It affects, alters, and damages brain cells controlling thinking, emotion, pleasure, coordination, mood, and memory. The pituitary gland is also damaged which regulates hunger, thirst, blood pressure, sexual behavior, and release of sex hormones.
CLOGGED SYNAPSES, BRAIN DAMAGE, AND ADDICTION
• Marijuana accumulates in the microscopic spaces between nerve cells in the brain – called "synapses." This clogging interfers by slowing and impairing transfer of critical information.
• Long term use causes the brain to stop production of brain chemicals necessary to "feel good"– a negative feedback condition. And, the user becomes chemically addicted to marijuana.

HEART
• Speeds up heartbeat as much as 50%, increases blood pressure, and poses great risk to those with hypertension and heart disease.

ENDOCRINE SYSTEM
• Marijuana damages the network of glands, organs, and hormones involved in growth and development, energy levels, and reproduction.
ORGANS AND GLANDS AFFECTED:
• Pituitary Gland
• Thyroid Gland
• Stomach
• Duodenum
• Pancreas
• Adrenal Glands
• Testis

REPRODUCTIVE SYSTEM
MALES & FEMALES
• Marijuana use can decrease and degenerate sperm, sperm count, movement, and cause lowered sex drive. Females can have egg damage, suppression of ovulation, disrupt menstrual cycles, and alteration of hormone levels.
PREGNANCY & UNBORN BABIES
• Regular use during pregnancy can lower birth weight and cause abnormalities similar to Fetal Alcohol Syndrome – small head, irritability, poor growth and development.
CHROMOSOME DAMAGE
•Can destroy the number of chromosomes, resulting in cell abnormalities and impaired function.

OTHER AFFECTS ON CENTRAL NERVOUS SYSTEM
Distortions of perception, thinking, and reality •
Difficulty in forming concepts and thoughts •
Poor concentration •
Mental confusion •
Loss of motivation •
Wide mood swings •
Aggression and hostility •
Depression, anxiety, and paranoia •

EYES
Sleepy looking, blood-shot eyes •
with dilated pupils.

THROAT
Irritates membranes of the esophagus; •
increases chance of developing cancer of larynx and esophagus.

LUNGS
Significant damage and •
destruction of the air sacs of the lungs, reducing the lungs ability to bring in oxygen and remove carbon dioxide – Emphysema.
Causes bronchial tubes to •
be inflammed, thickened, and to produce more mucus; resulting in narrowing of the air passages –
Chronic Bronchitis.
Marijuana smoke has •
twice as much "tar" as cigarette smoke and significantly increases chance of lung cancer, inflammation and infection.

IMMUNE SYSTEM
Marijuana depresses •
immune systems' ability to protect itself and body against invading bacteria, viruses, chemicals, foreign particles, parasites, fungal microorganisms, infections, and decreases ability to protect and prevent growth of cancer cells throughout the body.
ORGANS AND GLANDS AFFECTED:
Thymus •
Lymph System •
Spleen •
Stomach •
Duodenum •
Bone Marrow •

THE HARMFUL EFFECTS OF SMOKING

BRAIN
PLEASURE AND THEN SEDATION
- Nicotine, the highly addictive chemical in cigarettes and tobacco, stimulates the "pleasure centers" in the brain - creating pleasure and alertness. Nicotine initially stimulates the brain, then acts as a tranquilizer and sedative.

BRAIN ALTERATION, WITHDRAWAL, AND ADDICTION
- Nicotine directly affects, alters, and takes control of specialized receptor cells in the brain responsible for regulating well-being, mood, and memory. The drug remains active 20-40 minutes, then withdrawal symptoms begin. Mood changes, person becomes irritable, anxious, and discomfort becomes more severe - stimulating intense cravings for more nicotine. Regular and long term use lead to addiction.

THROAT
- Cancer of larynx and esophagus, irritates membranes of the throat.

HEART
- Nicotine raises heart rate, increases blood pressure, and constricts blood vessels.
- Carbon monoxide (deadly gas produced from cigarette smoke) decreases delivery of oxygen to the heart, increasing risk of heart attack and strokes.
- Causes weakening of the heart muscle's ability to pump blood, leading to death.
- Causes aortic aneurysms (blood-filled sac in aorta) and pulmonary heart disease.

LIVER
- Cirrhosis of the liver.

ADRENAL GLANDS
- Stimulates adrenaline production, speeding up the heart and increasing blood pressure.

VERTEBRAE
- Increased risk of vertebral cancer.

REPRODUCTIVE SYSTEM
MALES & FEMALES
- Reduces sex drive and increases risk of impotence in males. In females, increased chance of cervical cancer, less fertile, and brings on menopause earlier.

PREGNANCY & UNBORN BABIES
- Smoking increases chance of miscarriage, pregnancy complications, bleeding, and premature delivery.
- Smoking during pregnancy may cause impairment of baby's growth, intellect, and emotional development.

CENTRAL NERVOUS SYSTEM
- Nicotine stimulates adrenaline production
- Heart rate goes up 15-20 beats per minute
- Increases blood pressure
- Constricts blood vessels
- Reduces sex drive
- Inhibits urine formation
- Depresses hunger
- Reduces anxiety and pain
- Irritates mouth and throat
- Major cause of heart attack, lung diseases, strokes, and death

MOUTH
Dulls taste buds, irritates membranes of mouth, bleeding and receding gums, gum disease, foul breath, and numbness. Staining teeth, tooth decay and loss of teeth. Cancer of mouth.

LUNGS
Causes progressive limitation of air flow in and out of lungs–Chronic Obstructive Lung Disease. Damages and destroys tiny air sacs of the lung reducing lungs' ability to bring in oxygen and remove carbon dioxide –Emphysema.
Causes bronchial tubes to be inflamed, thickened, and mucus increases; resulting in narrowing of air passages –Chronic Bronchitis.
Tar and other particles settle in bronchial tubes causing lung cancer. Tar and smoke destroy tiny cells that clean, protect, and remove foreign particles from lungs.

STOMACH AND DUODENUM
Stomach and duodenal ulcers develop, creating burning pain.

KIDNEYS
Reduces kidneys' ability to process fluids and waste, inhibiting formation of urine. Cancer.

BLOOD VESSELS
Nicotine causes blood vessels to constrict, increasing blood pressure, and risk of heart attack.

BLADDER
Cancer of bladder.

BONES
Increases risk of early onset of Osteoporosis (weakening, softening and thinning of the bone).

Bruce Algra's HEALTH AND DRUG EDUCATION SERIES 3125 19th Street • Suite 305 • Bakersfield, CA 93301 • (805) 399-2897 ©The Algra Corporation 1992

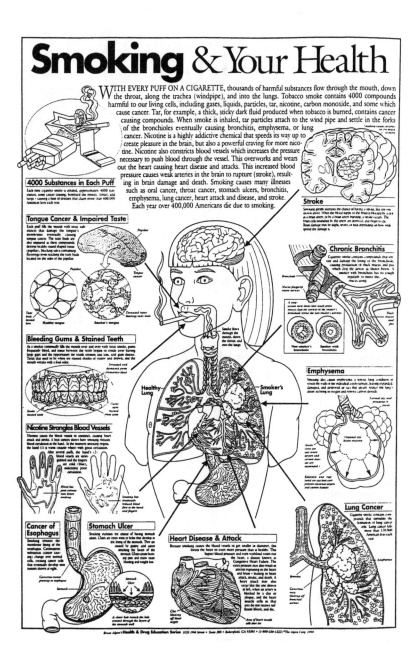

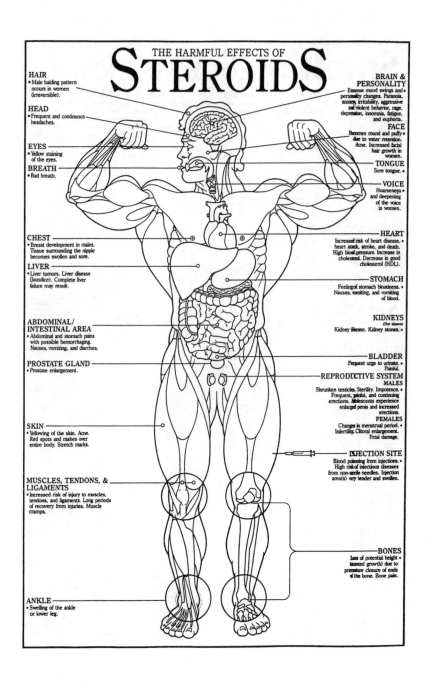

THE HARMFUL EFFECTS OF
STEROIDS

HAIR
• Male balding pattern occurs in women (irreversible).

HEAD
• Frequent and continuous headaches.

EYES
• Yellow staining of the eyes.

BREATH
• Bad breath.

CHEST
• Breast development in males. Tissue surrounding the nipple becomes swollen and sore.

LIVER
• Liver tumors. Liver disease (Jaundice). Complete liver failure may result.

ABDOMINAL/ INTESTINAL AREA
• Abdominal and stomach pains with possible hemorrhaging. Nausea, vomiting, and diarrhea.

PROSTATE GLAND
• Prostate enlargement.

SKIN
• Yellowing of the skin. Acne. Red spots and rashes over entire body. Stretch marks.

MUSCLES, TENDONS, & LIGAMENTS
• Increased risk of injury to muscles, tendons, and ligaments. Long periods of recovery from injuries. Muscle cramps.

ANKLE
• Swelling of the ankle or lower leg.

BRAIN & PERSONALITY
Extreme mood swings and • personality changes. Paranoia, anxiety, irritability, aggressive and violent behavior, rage, depression, insomnia, fatigue, and euphoria.

FACE
Becomes round and puffy • due to water retention. Acne. Increased facial hair growth in women.

TONGUE
Sore tongue. •

VOICE
Hoarseness • and deepening of the voice in women.

HEART
Increased risk of heart disease, • heart attack, stroke, and death. High blood pressure. Increase in cholesterol. Decrease in good cholesterol (HDL).

STOMACH
Feeling of stomach bloatiness. • Nausea, vomiting, and vomiting of blood.

KIDNEYS
(Not shown)
Kidney disease. Kidney stones. •

BLADDER
Frequent urge to urinate. • Painful.

REPRODUCTIVE SYSTEM
MALES
Shrunken testicles. Sterility. Impotence. • Frequent, painful, and continuing erections. Adolescents experience enlarged penis and increased erections.
FEMALES
Changes in menstrual period. • Infertility. Clitoral enlargement. Fetal damage.

INJECTION SITE
Blood poisoning from injections. • High risk of infectious diseases from non-sterile needles. Injection area(s) very tender and swollen.

BONES
loss of potential height • (stunted growth) due to premature closure of ends of the bone. Bone pain.

342

APPENDIX E

TWELVE STEPS
&
TWELVE TRADITIONS

The Twelve Steps, both the standard version and the ASL version, are reprinted with permission of Alcoholics Anonymous World Services, Inc. Permission to reprint this material does not mean that A.A. has reviewed or approved the contents of this publication, nor that A.A. agrees with the views expressed herein. A.A. is a program of recovery from alcoholism only–use of the Twelve Steps in connection with programs and activities which are patterned after A.A., but which addresses other problems, or in any other non-A.A. context, does not imply otherwise.

STANDARD VERSION [ENGLISH]

—THE TWELVE STEPS—	—THE TWELVE TRADITIONS—
1. We admitted we were powerless over alcohol—that our lives had become unmanageable.	1. Our common welfare should come first; personal recovery depends upon AA unity.
2. Came to believe that a power greater than ourselves could restore us to sanity.	2. For our group purpose there is but one ultimate authority—a loving God as he may express Himself in our group conscience. Our leaders are but trusted servants; they do not govern.
3. Made a decision to turn our will and lives over to the care of God as we understood him.	3. The only requirement for AA membership is a desire to stop drinking.
4. Made a searching and fearless moral inventory of ourselves.	4. Each group should be autonomous except in matters affecting other groups or AA as a whole.
5. Admitted to God, to ourselves, and to another human being the exact nature of our wrongs.	5. Each group has but one primary purpose—to carry its message to the alcoholic who still suffers.
6. Were entirely ready to have God remove all these defects of character.	6. An AA group ought never endorse, finance, or lend the AA name to any related facility or outside enterprise, lest problems of money, property, and prestige divert us from our primary purpose.
7. Humbly asked Him to remove our shortcomings.	7. Every AA group ought to be fully self-supporting, declining outside contributions.
8. Made a list of all persons we had harmed, and became willing to make amends to them all.	8. Alcoholics Anonymous should remain forever nonprofessional, but our service centers may employ special workers.
9. Made direct amends to such people wherever possible, except when to do so would injure them or others.	9. AA, as such, ought never be organized; but we may create service boards or committees directly responsible to those they serve.
10. Continued to take personal inventory and when we were wrong promptly admitted it.	10. Alcoholics Anonymous has no opinion on outside issues; hence the AA name ought never be drawn into public controversy.
11. Sought through prayer and meditation to improve our conscious contact with God as we understood him, praying only for knowledge of His will for us and the power to carry that out.	11. Our public relations policy is based on attraction rather than promotion; we need always maintain personal anonymity at the level of press, radio and films.
12. Having had a spiritual awakening as the result of these steps, we tried to carry this message to alcoholics, and to practice these principles in all our affairs.	12. Anonymity is the spiritual foundation of all our Traditions, ever reminding us to place principles before personalities.

ASL VERSION

One translation of the Twelve Steps for signing purposes, developed by several hearing impaired A.A. members and interpreters. ("GOD" can mean anything, anybody or group of things, people.)

—THE TWELVE STEPS—	—THE TWELVE TRADITIONS—
1. Admit alcohol more strong than us. We can't help ourselves.	1. Taking care ourselves should come first, recovery individual depends on A.A. unity.
2. Believe "GOD," which is stronger than alcohol and us, can make our minds well again.	2. For our group purpose—there (is) only one (final) authority—(loving) God (as) He maybe express himself (in) our group conscience. Our leader trusted servants; they not govern.
3. We decided to allow "GOD" to help our minds and lives. We pick "GOD"; to believe.	3. Only requirement for A.A. membership: Desire (to) stop drinking.
4. We made list of things, good and bad, about ourselves. Not afraid, ashamed to make list.	4. Each group should be independent except for something affecting other groups or A.A. as whole.
5. Tell "GOD" and friends about list of good and bad about ourselves.	5. Each group has (but) one important purpose— Carry its message (to) alcoholics who still suffers.
6. Ready to allow "GOD" to help our bad habits.	6. Any A.A. group should never receive payment, rule money or lend A.A.'s name (to) any related facility or outside business (enterprise). Why? Problems—money, property, pride (prestige) separated us from our primary (important) purpose.
7. Humbly ask "GOD" to help change our bad habits to good habits.	7. Every A.A. group should be fully self-supporting, declining outside contributions.
8. Make a list of people we caused trouble, hurt. Become ready to tell them we are sorry.	8. A.A. should remain forever Non-professional, but our service centers can hire special workers.
9. Tell people we are sorry, never do it again. Make sure not to hurt those people or any other person.	9. A.A. (itself) should never be organized; but maybe we create service boards or committees directly responsible (to) those they serve.
10. Keep on, continue looking at our good, bad ways, habits. Change bad ones.	10. A.A. has no opinion on outside issues; so name A.A. should never be involved into public controversy.
11. We pray to "GOD" to help us talk with and understand His way and follow His way.	11. Our public relation (PR) policy based on attraction rather than promotion; we need always to maintain personal anonymity—(level of) press, radio, films.
12. Spirit becomes better, improved because we follow these 12 Steps. We try to tell other alcoholics about the 12 Steps. We want to follow the 12 Steps everyday	12. Anonymity (is) spiritual foundation (of) all our traditions, (ever) reminding us show principles first, 2nd—personalties (names).

The Twelve Steps, both the standard version and the ASL version, are reprinted with permission of Alcoholics Anonymous World Services, Inc. Permission to reprint this material does not mean that A.A.as reviewed or approved the contents of this publication, nor that A.A. agrees with the views expressed herein. A.A. is a program of recovery from alcoholism only—use of the Twelve Steps in connection with programs and activities which are patterned after A.A., but which addresses other problems, or in any other non-A.A. context, does not imply otherwise.

APPENDIX F

THE GENOCIDE OF DEAF CULTURE

Published in LAMENT
November 1997

The United States law against genocide says that, "genocide is the destruction of an ethnic group," and that an ethnic group is "a set of individuals whose identity is distinctive in terms of common cultural traditions or heritage." Deaf people are "a set of individuals whose identity is distinctive in terms of common cultural traditions or heritage." Cochlear implants are an attempt to eliminate the trait of Deafness. Eliminating the trait of Deafness will destroy "a set of individuals whose identity is distinctive in terms of common cultural traditions or heritage." (That "set" of individuals will no longer exist. Or, restated, those individuals will no longer exist as a "set".) Therefore, cochlear implants are genocide. Some may say that I am being extreme when I point out that cochlear implants in Deaf children meet the legal definition of genocide. However, my response is appropriate when compared to the truly extreme action of cochlear implants in Deaf children. If cochlear implants do succeed in eliminating Deaf Culture, then a fascinating culture and an exquisitely beautiful language will be destroyed. And that will be a tragedy.

HOW COCHLEAR IMPLANTS IN DEAF CHILDREN, MAINSTREAMING, ORALISM, AND TOTAL COMMUNICATION MEET THE LEGAL DEFINITION OF GENOCIDE

The U.S. law against genocide—excerpted:

> Basic offense: Whoever, whether in time of peace or in time of war .... and with the specific intent to destroy, in whole or in substantial part, a national, ethnic, racial, or religious group as such: causes serious bodily injury to members of that group OR causes the permanent impairment of the mental faculties of members of

346

the group through drugs, torture, or similar techniques OR subjects the group to conditions of life that are intended to cause the physical destruction of the group in whole or in part OR transfers by force children of the group to another group or attempts to do so guilty of the crime of genocide.

The term 'ethnic group' means a set of individuals whose identity as such is distinctive in terms of common cultural traditions or heritage. The term 'racial group' means a set of individuals whose identity as such is distinctive in terms of physical characteristics or biological descent. The term 'substantial part' means a part of a group of such numerical significance that the destruction or loss of that part would cause the destruction of the group as a viable entity within the nation of which such group is a part.

HOW THE LAW RELATES TO THE GENOCIDE BEING PERPETRATED AGAINST DEAF CULTURE

"causes serious bodily injury to members of that group." [Cochlear implant surgery is bodily injury. This bodily injury can be exacerbated by nerve damage, the side effects of anesthesia or an accident by the surgeon.]

"causes the permanent impairment of the mental faculties of members of the group through drugs, torture, or similar techniques." [Children develop with a permanent impairment of the mental faculties if they are not given complete access to a full, natural language. The only full, natural language to which Deaf children have complete access is ASL. This means that using oral English ('oralism') or 'total communication' to teach Deaf children is a form of genocide.]

"subjects the group to conditions of life that are intended to cause the physical destruction of the group in whole or in part," [Cochlear implants and mainstreaming clearly are attempts to cause the physical destruction of Deaf Culture in whole or in part.]

"transfers by force children of the group to another group;" [This is the very definition of mainstreaming.]

"the term 'ethnic group' means a set of individuals whose identity as such is distinctive in terms of common cultural traditions or heritage." [The term 'ethnic group' accurately describes the members of Deaf Culture because Deaf Culture is distinctive in terms of common cultural traditions and heritage.]

"the term 'racial group' means a set of individuals whose identity as such is distinctive in terms of physical characteristics or biological descent," [This definition of 'racial group' does include the members of Deaf Culture because deafness is a 'physical characteristic.' And the trait of deafness sometimes is inherited.]

"the term 'substantial part' means a part of a group of such numerical significance that the destruction or loss of that part would cause the destruction of the group as a viable entity within the nation of which such group is a part." [When cochlear implant technology is improved, it very easily will cause the destruction of Deaf Culture as a viable entity.]

CULTURAL INFORMATION

For over a century, American men defined women as mentally and emotionally incompetent to own anything, vote in elections, or hold political office. The Africans defined themselves as cultural minorities. The Europeans defined the Africans as sub-human, and enslaved and murdered them. The Native Americans defined themselves as cultural minorities. The Europeans defined the Native Americans as sub-human and perpetrated genocide against them. The Jews defined themselves as a cultural minority. The Nazis defined the Jews as sub-human and perpetrated genocide against them.

What we learn from this is that we must accept and respect how a group defines itself. Deaf people define themselves as a cultural minority. Hearing people define them as handicapped and perpetrate genocide against their culture, with cochlear implants in Deaf children, mainstreaming, oralism, and "total communication."

GENOCIDE WITHOUT KILLING

According to the legal definition, genocide is the *destruction of a group* by subjecting the group to conditions of life that are intended to cause the physical destruction of the group in whole or in part; or imposing measures intended to prevent births within the group; or transferring by force children of the group to another group. In other words, it is not necessary to kill anyone in order to commit genocide. Genocide is NOT the killing of people, genocide is the 'destruction of a group' or, in other words, the killing of a culture. Killing the members of a culture is only one way to kill a culture—there are others.

THE GENOCIDE OF DEAF CULTURE is reprinted with the permission of Brice Alden, 3066 Geronimo Avenue, Simi Valley, CA 93063. Alair@aol.com

ATTITUDES TOWARD DEAFNESS

TOLERANCE AND UNDERSTANDING

by Charmaine Letourneau

This paper represents an overall view of the core Deaf Community toward the attitudes of the hearing on deafness.

It is indeed a rare occasion when a deaf person is asked to discuss anything related to deafness. Such information is usually sought from well-intentioned hearing people who think they know best. I appreciate being given this opportunity to present the "deaf point of view."

WHAT IS DEAFNESS?

Communication difficulties are caused more by deafness than any other handicap. All other disabled groups such as the blind, amputees, those confined to wheelchairs, the mentally retarded, can hear. Therefore, deafness is more a communication disability than a physical disability.

Yet so called "normal" people tend to put all disabled groups under one umbrella and try to solve each problem the same way.

WHAT IS THE DEAF COMMUNITY?

We members of the Deaf Community consider our deafness a unifying aspect of our cultural heritage. We liken ourselves more to an ethnic group than to a disabled group. We share a unique language, ASL (American Sign Language), just as any other cultural group. We also share similar experiences of everyday problems encountered in a hearing world and attitudes of the hearing toward the deaf.

350

Since childhood, members of deaf communities have experienced repeated frustrations in trying to make ourselves understood; embarrassment due to frequent misunderstandings; and loneliness as a result of being left out by family, neighbourhood acquaintances, and others. Such past and present experiences help to strengthen a deaf person's identification with the deaf world.

The hearing often appear to reject the deaf as human beings and reject the language of the deaf, ASL. These rejections have contributed significantly to the creation of a tightly-knit Deaf Community.

UNDERSTANDING OF DEAFNESS

Knowledge of deafness is generally sought through the perspectives of the hearing, not the deaf. If the hearing want to know about deafness, they tend to go to audiologists, speech therapists, doctors and others who are hearing and who give freely of their opinions which are generally based on their own assumptions.

Surely, there can be no explanation for this other than that hearing people believe that deaf people are unable to think and to know what it is like to be deaf. The hearing tend to assume that—thinking cannot develop without language. Language, in turn, cannot develop without speech. Speech cannot develop without hearing. Therefore, those who cannot hear cannot think.

Negative evaluations of deafness as a mental disability are very difficult to eradicate. This kind of thinking has been around for thousands of years. Therefore, the assumptions and opinions of those who hear have had a devastating impact on the lives of deaf people.

ATTITUDES OF THE HEARING TOWARD THE DEAF

As mentioned above, membership in deaf communities is solidified by shared experiences, language and identification with the deaf. I would like to elaborate on the negative perspectives of the hearing toward the deaf:

EMPLOYMENT: The deaf are often unemployed, underemployed, underpaid, and passed over for promotion because of communication problems.

SIGN LANGUAGE: Signing often attracts stares and ridicule from the hearing. Even though research done by various linguists shows that ASL is a legitimate language with its own complex structural and grammatical rules, many hearing people refuse to recognize it as a language. They prefer to classify it as a poor approximation of English, or an abbreviation of English.

SPEECH: The deaf are often forced to develop speech and speechreading skills in order to be normalized. It is like forcing the blind to see and the crippled to walk. Without speech skills, the deaf are viewed as slightly less than human.

AUDITORY TRAINING: Deaf children and their parents are constantly advised of the absolute necessity of purchasing the almighty hearing aid. It is a known fact that speech therapists have told some deaf children that they would be much more clever if they wore hearing aids and had good speech. The Deaf Community has known for many years that this is all hogwash, and that, try as we might, developing intelligible speech is nigh unto impossible—an exercise in futility resulting in deep feelings of inadequacy.

JOKES: In newspapers, in novels, on radio and television, there are jokes which lend a negative connotation to deafness.

MEDIA: Deaf people are often portrayed as terrible, stupid, dumb, dangerous, violent and hateful.

HEARING PARENTS: Some parents are embarrassed to have deaf children and do not want others to know that their children are deaf. These parents give their children the impression that signing should be suppressed in public, thus inhibiting their language development. They try to normalize their children by forcing them to go to public schools.

Many deaf children are socially impaired because all through their growing years, they are given to believe that there is something wrong with being deaf and that they should try their best to emulate hearing children. In adulthood, these deaf people often gravitate toward the Deaf Community where repairs can begin to be done to their damaged self-images.

It doesn't matter how hard we try to educate parents about deafness, it is very hard for them to accept the benefit of our experiences and all the research pointing to social impairment due to pressure imposed by the hearing in general for normalization. It is very difficult for them to stand back and.watch their children being ridiculed and pitied.

HEARING PEOPLE: There is a segment of society which treats deaf people as if we were "animals" who can neither read nor write. (I have had lots of experience with this attitude in spite of my university education.)

MODERN TECHNOLOGY: It is of no use to us. Even television, the cinema and telephone have their limitations. Sure, we do have decoders which enable us to watch captioned TV programs, but not all programs are captioned and not all the captioning is accurate. We do have telecommunication devices which enable us to use the telephone, but again, we can call only a very limited number of people—mainly other deaf people. The devices are expensive for unemployed and underpaid deaf people who form the majority of the Deaf Community. It is very difficult to get financial aid to purchase such devices.

However, it's no problem at all to get hearing aids which the majority of the deaf do not need and do not find useful, but which hearing people recommend we have.

THE GOVERNMENT: When the Deaf Community asks for something they know they need, the government invariably asks for proof of need and for numbers of potential consumers. (We are not numbers. We are human beings with very real needs.) When hearing people ask the government for something they believe the deaf need, we are more often than not misrepresented, but the government takes action. Here are some examples of provisions made for us against our wishes and often to our detriment:

- mainstream education
- auditory equipment
- cochlear implants
- driving privilege restrictions
- repression of our native language
- seeing-eye dogs

Deaf people are often discussed as objects requiring maintenance, parts, replacements, etc.

While many hearing people make it their life's work to normalize and mainstream the deaf to prepare us for a society which doesn't accept us anyway, the Deaf Community provides a refuge from the curiosity, ridicule and awkward communication which the deaf face among the hearing. The Deaf Community provides a sense of wholeness and belonging not found in the hearing world. Within the Deaf Community, there is understanding of common frustrations and recognition of successes as well. Only within the Deaf Community can a deaf individual experience a feeling of normalcy and self-worth.

We would like to see more respect shown for our culture, our language, our deafness. Toward this end, we make the following points.

1.   We would like to be directly involved in all decision making processes that affect any aspect of our lives. We can no longer tolerate "token" participation.

2.   As a general rule, none of the decision makers in the government has enough knowledge of our empathy for the deaf to be in a position to meet the needs of the deaf. In other words, the degree of insensitivity toward deafness is very high mainly due to ignorance rather than malice. We would like to request that an advisory group be established by and for the government to give better insight into the problems of being deaf and that this group be composed largely of deaf individuals.

3.   Discourage and remove notations from any materials that suggest or imply that the deaf function at a level below that of other people, i.e. "deaf and dumb" or "deaf mute."

4.   Interference and recommendations from outsiders as to what method of communication is best for the deaf must cease. This means that speech, speechreading and aural training must not constitute the "be all and end all" of communication while the preferred and practical language of the deaf, ASL, is suppressed.

5.   The language of the deaf, ASL, must be legalized and recognized as a legitimate language just like any other language, i.e. French, German, etc.

6.   We do not want government representatives to act on requests or demands of parents or other individuals whose knowledge of deafness is at best superficial. We are asking that input from such people not be considered as necessarily best for deaf people including deaf children. We ask that such one-sided and often misguided input be referred to the Deaf Community for consideration.

ATTITUDES TOWARD DEAFNESS Tolerance and Understanding—is reprinted with the permission of the author, Charmaine Letourneau, Past President of the Canadian Cultural Society of the Deaf.

APPENDIX H

Is There Room in the DSM
for
Consideration of Deaf People?

ABSTRACT

The need for accurate and precise diagnosis and comprehensive understanding of underlying causes of psychological and psychiatric disorders is unchallenged fact. Revisions of the American Psychiatric Association's Diagnostic and Statistical Manual acknowledge this need. Recent changes in the DSM have recognized factors of culture as relevant for assessment, thus including specific information relevant to the Deaf culture, Deaf language and Deaf values would be helpful for users of the DSM to understand Deaf clients.

The purpose of this study was to survey relevant writings on the general topic of psychological needs of Deaf people, and specifically to survey how Deaf people view those needs.

A number of recent articles were previewed and out of these, four were selected for review on the general topic of how Deaf people perceive their own psychiatric and psychological needs. These articles all offer informed opinion and refer to research studies previously performed. Authors Edward Dolnick, Roger J. Carver and Mark J. Myers were selected for inclusion.

From these different points of view, highly overlapping conclusions were drawn, suggesting widespread agreement on the thesis that Deaf people, as a minority culture, should contribute summary information regarding Deaf culture, Deaf language and Deaf values to people in the helping professions, for their use in serving Deaf clients. This would bring greater understanding of Deaf people to care providers, and would help the larger society include Deaf people in important planning. Culturally deaf people, as per these authors, would consistently urge inclusion of relevant information about Deaf people in the next revision of the DSM.

Is There Room in the DSM
for Consideration of Deaf People?

Mental illness is a serious issue–or group of issues. Since humankind first realized that psychiatric disturbances were to be treated humanely, consideration of what falls under the rubric of mental illness has been seen as germane to societal benefaction. From time to time, diagnostic criteria, treatment rationale and explanation of etiology have changed in the profession, as witness the several revisions of the Diagnostic and Statistical Manual of the American Psychiatric Association. Some change can be seen as the gradually evolving consciousness of concerned people. Writers of the DSM IV say, "Most readers use it (the DSM IV) as a reference and expect it to be detailed and authoritative."[1]

Revisions are intended to reflect advances in knowledge regarding differential diagnosis and criteria associated with variations in age, gender and culture. Revisions show a desire to be accurate among people in the helping professions. An increasing sensitivity to cultural values and sub-strains of societal norms has lately broadened the view of a number of behaviors and mental phenomena which formerly were given less specific but more pejorative labeling.[2]

Deaf people would like to benefit from this increasing sensitivity to cultural variance. Deaf people have long felt misunderstood and have lacked adequate access to appropriate psychiatric and psychological services.[3] At the same time Deaf people frequently believed they have had a surfeit of paternalistic control which purported to serve their needs but which actually left many Deaf people feeling somehow cheated and under-served by the psychology and psychiatry fields.[4]

Deaf people have the same psychological and psychiatric range of behaviors and concerns as do hearing people, and they deserve to have their psychological and psychiatric needs addressed accurately and precisely, without irrelevancies clouding the issue. Professor McCay Vernon, of Western Maryland College, says, "one must note that society usually responds inappropriately to the needs of deaf people and to the reality of deafness. Such response is the cause for a significant amount of the psychopathology seen in deaf people. Furthermore, certain normal coping responses by deaf persons are misconstrued as abnormal by the general public."[5]

Numerous researchers and clinicians have studied mental health needs of Deaf people for several decades now, and the bulk of these studies reveal an overlap tending toward consensus regarding basic needs which Deaf people bring to a psychiatric relationship or situation. These basics include several primary elements, but: being understood consistently supersedes other psychotherapy concerns.[6]

As long as the communication needs of Deaf people are not perceived and met, psychological treatment must necessarily be less than maximally effective. Because of poor communication, many Deaf people in the past have been misdiagnosed as mentally retarded or otherwise judged, however subtly, as "inferior." Public attitudes toward Deaf people are even now not consistently enlightened.[7]

In the recent past, a spate of position papers and informed opinion, including that wrought by clinical experience, have noted the need for clarity in the statement of psychological and psychiatric variables which are relevant for Deaf people, which should be included in the DSM IV. Since the DSM is the primary tool for diagnostic and treatment consultation, and professional service workers of a number of social and psychological fields look to the DSM as a final authority, inclusion of specific concerns of the culturally Deaf would have far reaching applications and could prevent untold frustrations of misdiagnosis.

Addressing this matter, sometimes circuitously, sometimes directly, a number of writers have commented on the treatment Deaf people receive in a hearing culture. Ed Dolnick explains how Deaf people represent a new ethnic group, not a disability group, in a seminal article, "Deafness as Culture" (Sep. 1993). Roger Carver has written "It takes a village to raise a deaf child" (Sep-Oct 1997). And he has also written, "Attitudes Toward the Deaf: a historical overview." (Sep-Oct 1995), both of which make a case for letting Deaf people's viewpoints be considered as primary in matters concerning them. Kris Chapman has written "Psychiatric disability and Deafness" (June, 1994). These few articles represent the crux of the viewpoint which Deaf culture currently espouses in regard to its treatment from the hearing world, particularly psychiatric workers.

This paper will examine these writers' theses and discuss the implications of their views. It is hoped that cogent argument and clear example will lead Deaf educators, leaders of Deaf industry, social service agency personnel, organizations for Deaf people and other people concerned about Deaf issues to add their voice in a plea for the A.P.A. to add guidelines regarding diagnosis, assessment and treatment of psychotherapy for culturally Deaf people. Salient information regarding Deaf culture, history, language and values should be offered by the Deaf community for inclusion in A.P.A.'s DSM IV.

Edward Dolnick says that Deaf people see their condition primarily as a cultural identity. They are tired of being seen as people who need to be "fixed," and believe that they are members of a culture which is distinctive and rewarding. Viewing the Deaf simply as a linguistic minority speaking ASL, rather than the language of the nation wherein they reside, rejects the view of deafness as disabling, per se. This view does not deny that there are some Deaf people who need the assistance of mental health services, but denies the notion that a Deaf person is automatically a candidate for remediation.

Dolnick carefully guides readers through an array of insights the culturally Deaf have found to be intertwined–difficulties of communication with hearing people, the naturalness for Deaf people of visual sign language, especially ASL, the problems associated with viewing deafness as a problem-filled condition, explanations of the outrage of the Deaf community over the televised promotion of cochlear implants, the case against mainstreaming in education, the probable superiority of residential schools for Deaf children, and a plea for partnership between hearing people who care and Deaf people toward improved quality of life for Deaf people.[8]

Dolnick's article, offered in a general interest lay publication, did not cite reams of statistics or relate the path of research to which it alluded. It did not survey literature on the topic. The article offered a view of Deafness as normal for Deaf people, not pathological, and buttressed that viewpoint with examples, primarily in the field of education. The author did state that his view is not universally held among Deaf people. Still, the preponderance of statements and impassioned quotations can be seen to promote the majority view, upon which Dolnick reported.

A different aspect of the topic of the need for consideration for Deaf people comes from Kris Chapman. Chapman strongly espouses psychiatric and psychological facilities which serve Deaf people to be staffed by mental health professionals who are also Deaf"[9]

Chapman notes that Deafness is frequently misdiagnosed as an intellectual disability, and that, at times, psychiatric illness is not discerned and at other times, a mental illness label is foisted upon a client, when no psychiatric disorder actually exists.[10]

Chapman posits that professionals in social services, especially mental health workers should have: a) a sound basis of clinical knowledge of psychology, psychiatry and psychotherapy; b) an understanding of the psychological implications of the various different types of deafness and their etiology; c) an understanding of the assorted developmental contributing factors and a fairly comprehensive overview of issues germane to the communication process; and d) an understanding of audiology.

Many staff people in helping professions routinely underestimate the communication and accessibility problems Deaf people experience in trying to avail themselves of a given program or agency's offerings. Some research has stated that over 70% of people identified as DDD are capable of using some sign language, although approximately 90% of staff working with these clients do not understand sign language.[11]

Carver's two short articles approach the same topic from slightly different aspects. In the 1997 article, Carter related several stories about people who were raising deaf children as a part of a community effort, and offered insights regarding their experiences. Then he offers opinion regarding how rearing a Deaf child should be accomplished within a group. He notes, "For too many years countless thousands of Deaf persons have been disabled by professional intervention. Well-meaning but uninformed professionals prescribed to families how they should raise and train their deaf children, often getting involved themselves and controlling the agenda."[12]

Carver concludes that such intervention hasn't in the past, and indeed cannot, in the future succeed, since it exacerbates the situation of lack of cohesiveness in the family. Carver notes that the best way for hearing parents to "help" a Deaf child is by learning sign language and communicating with their child. Carver alludes to a German movie, *Beyond silence,* which graphically portrayed the plight of hearing and Deaf family members trying to communicate.[13]

Carver's "Attitudes toward the Deaf: a historical overview" cites early recorded references to Deaf people and how they were treated. To people familiar with the history of the Deaf, these references are familiar, with examples from Greek, Roman and ancient Hebrew cultures. Carver believes that historical precedent in the treatment of Deaf people has a profound effect today, revealed in attitudes of hearing people toward Deaf people. Carver says our multi-cultural society is beginning to appreciate diversity and to respect minority groups and their rights, but he concludes that only through hearing people's acceptance of Deaf people's perceptions about their lives can the larger society heal the breach between the two groups.[14]

Carver's last article alludes to a running timeline of treatment of the Deaf by hearing people, but does not analyze any of the cited instances. No statement is made regarding how representative the chosen allusions are, but they are presumed to be typical.

These articles are, in this writer's opinion, representative of the voice of people of Deaf culture regarding how Deaf people wish to be regarded and evidence of the view that Deaf people frequently are patronized, ignored, under-served or are delivered less than complete satisfaction regarding their psychological and psychiatric needs. Inclusion of specifics of Deaf culture information to people in the helping professions, i.e. via a supplemental section to the DSM IV, would improve the lot of Deaf people and would foster improved relationships between Deaf and hearing people.

Endnotes:

1   Allen Frances, Michael B. First and Harold Alan Pincus "DSM-IV: its value and limitations" The Harvard Mental Health Letter, June 1995, pp. 4-6.

2   American Psychiatric Association. diagnostic & Statistical Manual: IV, A.P.A., 1994, Washington, D.C.; and Jack Gorman The New Psychiatry, 1996. St. Martin's Press, N.Y., N.Y., pp. 157-160.

3   McCay, Vernon, & Jean F. Andrews. The Psychology of Deafness, 1990 Longman Press; N.Y.

4   Marie E. Rendon "Deaf culture and alcohol/substance abuse" J. Substance Abuse Treatment, Feb. '92; Kristen Swan "Dual disorders in chemical dependency treatment" Steps to Recovery, Aug., 1992, pp. 1-2; Deborah R. Waltzer "A sobering tale: drug and alcohol abuse and recovery in the deaf community" Focus, Winter, Spring 1992, pp. 16-22, and Dennis Moore "Substance use patterns with hearing impairments: a regional survey" paper presented at The Next Step conference in Denver, CO, July 5-8, 1992, pp. 1-6.

5   Vernon, M. 1990. (ibid), p. 161.

6   Vernon, M. 1990 (ibid); Jack Gorman The New Psychiatry, 1996, ibid. pp. 36-37; Bettijane Levine, "A Crucial Connection" Life & Style section, L.A. Times: Dec. 9, 1994; and Christine Giombetti "Alcohol abuse counselor needs skills in many areas" Silent News, Sep. 1992, p. 18.

7   Edward Dolnick. "Deafness as Culture" The Atlantic, Sep., 1993. p. 37.

8   Dolnick, E. (1993) ibid. pp. 37-51.

9   Kris Chapman, "Psychiatric disability and Deafness" New Paradigm, June, 1994.

10 Chapman, (1994) ibid.

11 Mark Myers, "Rehabilitation and Community services: for individuals who are Deaf-Developmentally Disabled" who

Speaks for the Deaf: a Deaf American Monograph, N.A.D., Silver Spring, MD, Vol. #47, 1997.

12   Roger Carver "It takes a village to raise a Deaf child" Deaf Children's Society newsletter, Sep-Oct. 1997.

13   Roger Carver, (1997) ibid.

14   Roger J. Carver "Attitudes toward the Deaf: a historical overview" DCS newsletter, Sep-Oct., 1995.

Bibliography

American Psychiatric Association. <u>Diagnostic and Statistical Manual of Mental Disorders: 4th edition,</u> A.P.A., Washington D.C., 1994, pp. xxiv, xxv, 185, and 843-844.

Carver, Roger J., M.Ed., "Attitudes towards the deaf: a historical overview" <u>Deaf Children's Society Newsletter,</u> Sep-Oct. 1995.

Carver, Roger J., M. Ed., "It takes a village to raise a deaf child" <u>Deaf Children's Society Newsletter,</u> Sep-Oct., 1997.

Chapman, Chris "Psychiatric disability and Deafness" <u>New Paradigm,</u> June 1994.

Dolnick, Edward "Deafness as Culture" <u>The Atlantic,</u> Sep., 1993, pp. 37-53.

Frances, Allen, First, Michael B. & Pincus, H.A. "DSM-IV: Its value and limitations" <u>The Harvard Mental Health Letter,</u> June 1995, pp. 4-6.

Gorman, Jack M., MD, <u>The New Psychiatry,</u> St. Martin's Press, N.Y., N.Y. 1996.

Levine, Bettijane, "A Crucial Connection" Life & Style section <u>L.A. Times,</u> Dec. 9, 1994, p. E1.

Moore, Dennis "Substance use patterns with hearing impairments: a regional survey" paper presented at

The Next Step conference in Denver, CO, July 5-8, 1992, pp. 1-6.

Myers, Mark J. "Rehabilitation and community services: for individuals who are Deaf-developmentally disabled" Who Speaks for the Deaf Community: a Deaf American Monograph, N.A.D., Silver Spring, MD., Vol. 47, 1997. pp. 21-23.

Rendon, Marie E. "Deaf culture and alcohol/substance abuse" J. Substance Abuse Treatment, Feb. '92.

Sattler, Michael "Deaf Culture and ASL" via Internet Web page, n/d.

Swan, Kristen "Dual disorders in chemical dependency treatment" Steps to Recovery, Aug. 1992, pp. 1-2.

Vernon, McCay, Andrews, Jean F. The Psychology of Deafness, Longman Press, N.Y., 1990.

Waltzer, Deborah R. "A sobering tale: drug and alcohol abuse and recovery in the deaf community: focus, Winter, Spring 1992, pp. 16-22.

Wixton, Chris "Two Views of Deafness;" n.d.

AUTOBIOGRAPHY

From an Abyss of Addiction, a Deaf Adult Child Survives

Becoming a victim of alcohol or drugs is a terrible fate for any individual and a loss for society. The losses are compounded when the victim is already handicapped with a hearing impairment, and when treatment is difficult to find.

Perhaps one should first examine Helen Keller's definition of deafness:

> "The problems of deafness are deeper and more complex, if not more important, than those of blindness. Deafness is a much worse misfortune. For it means the loss of the most vital stimulus–the sound of the voice that brings language, sets thoughts astir, and keeps us in the intellectual company of man."

As a deaf adult child of an addicted family, I was born to middle class parents in Los Angeles, California. My *hearing* parents, Frank, Sr., and Isabel made their living as a salesman and IBM key punch operator, respectively. I was a healthy *hearing* child. The first five years of my life was blessed with two wonderful, loving and devoted parents. They provided everything a child would need.

Unfortunately, at the young age of five I began to lose my hearing due to an antibiotic drug (Streptomycin) intended to combat tonsillitis infection. My parents were heartbroken at the prospect of profound deafness and concerned as to how it would impact my life. They continued to shower me with their affection and love. To evaluate my hearing and speech status, I was sent to John

Tracy Clinic. Thereafter, I attended a number of schools before being placed in a private military academy, which, of course, was a regular *hearing* academy.

At first things ran smooth. One day an older boy (officer) was in our dormitory for inspection. We all stood at attention in front of our beds. I was about eight years old and was extremely concerned that I might not be able to hear him calling my name if he had anything to say to me about the drawers or closet. I knew if he stood in front of me, I would be able to read his lips and respond verbally without any problem. However, he called my name from behind and I did not respond. I looked for clues from others who stood by their beds to see if there was any indication that my name was being called. There was none. Finally the officer tapped me on my shoulder. I looked him straight in the face as he asked me if I heard him call my name. I told him no. He reported this to the principal and I was called into his office. I was asked if I had a hearing problem. I replied that I did not hear well. The principal requested a hearing test and found that I had a hearing impairment indicating that I had a 60db level of hearing. Consequently, my parents were informed of this and it was suggested that I attend a special school for hearing impaired children. I attended Mary E. Bennett School and eventually was placed at California School for the Deaf in Riverside ("CSDR") around the young impressionable age of nine.

Afterward and while undergoing this major change in my young life, my parents divorced. CSDR was only temporary for a year as my parents planned that I would attend another private military school the next year. A culture shock doesn't even come close to describing the ordeal of attending CSDR school as an oralist with a student body of deaf children who used sign language to converse. I was unable to communicate with them except for primitive gestures.

As I look back though, the first ten years of my life seemed wonderful. Every Christmas I awoke finding our living room filled with hundreds of balloons. Presents were piled high under the tree. I recall one special Christmas morning I found an adorable German Shepherd puppy just for me!

Even during my first year at CSDR, twice a week dad sent many packages of goodies and toys. They were for all of my classmates or for all thirty-two boys in the dormitory! Today I ponder whether he was just spoiling me or felt bad about the divorce or maybe guilty that I was placed in a boarding school. I suspect all three might be a correct assessment and motive.

At the end of the first year at CSDR and during that summer, tragically, dad passed away suddenly. He died of a heart attack alone on the corner of Hollywood and Vine. Simultaneously, mom was in the hospital with an acute ear infection when the heartbreaking news hit me about dad. And as a strange twist of fate she lost her hearing too (five years after me). How ironic this seemed because there was absolutely no deafness in our family history other than mother's twin sister, Aunt Mary, who had a similar ear infection and became deaf also as a result. Both sisters were twenty-eight and in their prime of life. Naturally, they met this hardship with great distress. First, they lost their jobs that almost immediately forced us into poverty. They loved music and could no longer appreciate the beautiful sounds. Communication with the world–friends and family, became hopeless and doomed. For us, subsistence diminished to a feeling of total abandonment and our outlook became bleak, desolate and joyless. At the formidable young age of ten, I was compelled to grow up very fast or did I? Physically I became a young man but psychologically the consequences were many.

The private school was no longer an option and I returned to CSDR, reluctantly. I felt betrayed by broken promises. All the boys questioned me about the goodies and toys. I was angry at dad for placing me in such an embarrassing situation. I struggled with the reality he left me. Scrambling with all of these horrendous hurdles and roadblocks, I changed from an outgoing, friendly person to a withdrawn and frightened young boy. I was so ill-at-ease that I retreated.

Isolation and confusion consumed me together with hostility and anger that had not yet surfaced.

Just like her sister Mary, I sadly watched mother become an alcoholic. They also abused prescription drugs. Gone were the Christmas trees, the presents or even someone to talk with on Christmas morning. The life I once knew became a dismal shadow that seemed a fantasy. Probably in search of love, approval and wanting a normal life, I began to shoulder many of the responsibilities. Later, I realized these burdens were out of necessity. I collected empty soda bottles from the seedy streets of Los Angeles and exchanged them for cash deposits at the markets. Potato or corn chips and pretzels satisfied my hunger pains. If I was lucky and fortunate for the day's collection of bottles, then I treated myself to a slice of pizza or a cold, plastic-wrapped sandwich from a liquor store. Once a kind man at Ralph's Supermarket apparently recognized that I was a hungry kid and instructed me to go around back and loaded me up with edible vegetables and fruits that were about to be tossed.

While at Mac Arthur Park in Los Angeles, I watched an elderly man tend to his video game machine business. Every Wednesday afternoon at the boat house, he collected his money from the slots, cleaned the glass of each machine and repaired them if necessary. One day, he inadvertently left a large ring of keys still inserted in one of the slots. I took them. When he came in the next week, he didn't have an extra set so I walked up to him and told him that he left them. He was astonished and immediately checked to see if anything was stolen from the slots. He realized that I couldn't hear, but still offered me a job at the boat house. He paid me cash and fed me at the boat house cafe! I will never forget his kindness and compassionate spirit. Because CSDR was closed, existence during the summer months was extremely harsh and that particular summer he literally kept me going until school resumed.

During the summers and some holidays, there were many times that I didn't eat for two days. Sometimes, I bought a package of macaroni or spaghetti–but I ate it without any sauce or even butter. It wasn't too tasty for a eleven year old kid, but it filled me up nonetheless. Once back at CSDR, the environment became normal, healthy and placid. The teachers cared about our learning and the counselors advised and protected us. I had some friends, and the surroundings and atmosphere were peaceful and unobtrusive. It was a place where I could sleep undisturbed for eight hours a night while enjoying hot meals three times a day. It was heaven–the only real home I had–and marvelously so, not infested with cockroaches and bed bugs!

I am convinced anger was an integral part of my emotions while I suffered and sustained the anguish of what substance abuse did to my life and family. I swore that as long as I lived I would not drink any alcohol, use drugs or smoke. Somehow in this terrifying and grim existence, I wanted to help others with their substance abuse. maybe once I graduated from school I would pursue this dream I had promised myself. Too young then to realize, the negative life I led as a young boy became my positive strength as a young adult. Much later I read philosopher Nietzsche who said something to this effect–

> When you experience suffering, you have two choices: either you are going to surrender, accept defeat and perish in the process; or you will overcome it and become a stronger person for it and survive.

Another incident occurred during one of those summers around 3 o'clock in the morning. Outside the rear door of our duplex was a fenced house where all the windows were boarded and the furnishings were covered with white sheets. A large conspicuous sign informed one "DO NOT TRESPASS." Obviously, the grass was not maintained standing tall at three feet. Weird and spooky, it looked like a haunted house. A man lurching at the rear entrance broke down the door and startled mom. She screamed and he fled the scene. Quickly she ordered me to get a butcher knife from the kitchen for protection. My heart trembled with fear questioning what chance I had as an eleven year old child to fend off this wild maniac, burglar or much worse a rapist attacking mom. I could only see, not *hear*. I stood tall trying to suck up courage to fight off the intruder. I glanced over at mother. She was passed out from the booze. Again I peeked at the doorway, the man was gone. Yet nothing but threatening darkness loomed beyond. I was so scared. We didn't have a phone and certainly back then a telecommunication device for deaf people ("TDD") wasn't in operation. I grabbed both our cats in my arms, and locked myself in the other bedroom and turned the light on. Half crazy with fear, I held on tightly to the cats all night. They were my ears. If they heard anything, I'd know someone was lurking around the house. Eventually, I fell asleep. The next morning I slowly unlocked the door to see if mom was okay. Thankfully, she was fine and remained asleep on the couch. This was another pitiful but typical childhood experience that affected me adversely.

I recall at sixteen while encountering another holiday break, I came home to our apartment and found it destroyed. The apartment manager informed me that it was my mother's lit cigarette that set the fire. He threw us out. Secretly, I knew she was probably drunk and passed out. She was hospitalized with burns from the accident. For three days I walked Hollywood Boulevard where it was safe because of the many all night tourists, until I caught the CSDR school bus on Sunday in downtown L.A.

The sad aftermath is that I attended the funerals of my entire family (mother, aunts, uncles and grandparents). They all died from substance abuse of one form or another. Mary was in a coma when mom died of an overdose of sleeping pills. One week later, she passed away without ever regaining consciousness–never knowing that mother had already died. What was so strange about them is that in life they shared everything together and even in death. They are buried beside one another.

As I questioned and examined earlier in this article, I grew up quickly in order to survive. Inwardly, I certainly did not understand nor comprehend the significance of consequence of how as a deaf adult child I suffered from severe psychological problems. I experienced and witnessed alcoholism and drug abuse at a very young age. I did not understand the concept of the disease as it related to alcohol or drug addiction until I was eighteen. By then I had watched mom go through four hours of agony when I refused to give her a bottle of vodka. She screamed, pleaded, and cried. She broke out with body shakes, cold sweats, withdrawal symptoms, binges, blackouts etc. She was pregnant and I refused to give her any liquor because I was concerned about her unborn child. I wanted to nourish her and the baby with food and attempted to bargain with her to eat first. Naturally, I was very naive and ignorant as to the outcome by my refusal to give her a bottle. She was completely at my mercy and she looked like she was dying before my eyes. I was so apprehensive that I finally surrendered. By this time she could not even hold the vodka bottle or open it for that matter. She acted like a total stranger. This was not the mother I knew all my life. At that moment, I realized and understood what the Big AA book was talking about.

My half brother Daniel was born with Fetal Alcohol Syndrome and since his birth is a ward of the State of California. My half sister who is four years older than Daniel has a learning disability due to mom's alcoholism. Fortunately, as the first child, I was spared from having any physical or health problems because mother did not drink.

A recent study was reported in the distinguished New England Journal of Medicine and according to this article, women become drunk faster than men because their stomach is less able to neutralize alcohol. An enzyme in the stomach breaks down most of the alcohol before it reaches the bloodstream. However, women have less of this enzyme than men and about thirty percent pure alcohol enters a woman's bloodstream. Researchers report this could explain why women feel the effects of liquor quicker than men do and it may explain why women are more susceptible than men to liver damage. Moreover, this also may explain why it took only ten years of heavy drinking for mother to reach the "chronic" late stage instead of what generally takes others thirty years to reach.

From a long and weary journey of heartbreak, confusion, and despair, I survived. Death surrounded my family and later, my friends from the plague of substance abuse. I knew they all died in vain, unless I learned something from their tribulation.

We are <u>not</u> in the hands of an inevitable fate or destiny–

Fate and destiny <u>is in our hands</u> to shape, mold and frame by the foresight and vision we dare to see for ourselves.

I was pushed into an uncharted territory when I grew up and stared death in the face when it took all of my family members by the time I was twenty-one. I refused to become a victim or a statistic from substance abuse. As a young man in conflict to overcome many psychological problems, the healing began once I learned how to *forgive* my parents for divorcing; my father for dying much too soon; and my beloved mother, Isabel, who drank her life away because she didn't know how to cope with life's substantial obstacles thrust at her. I fared much better than my parents' misfortunes and the entire family's afflictions. I certainly paid a heart-rendering price but to state it simply, *I made a choice and fought back.*

I remained in school and continued my education. I become one of the four co-founders of a recovery program for the Deaf and Hard-of-Hearing Alcohol and Drug Abusers in Southern California. I wrote my doctoral dissertation about the deaf substance abuser with my advisors on the dissertation committee, Dr. Harlan Lane and Dr. Betty G. Miller. Recently, I authored a lengthy article on deaf substance abuse, which was published October 1995 in the

National Association of the Deaf's Deaf American Monograph. I have authored many periodicals regarding my stance *against* substance abuse.

Sharing these childhood experiences growing up in a broken, impoverished and alcoholic home only touches the diminutive corners of my life and its adverse effects on me. We all recognize one cannot totally comprehend someone's life unless they have walked in their shoes. As I counsel today, it is impossible for anyone who dares to tell me that I do not understand the implications of alcoholism or drug abuse because I don't drink or use illegal drugs. They are in for a rude awakening and argumentive challenge!

Hearing adult children of alcoholics have difficulty experiencing a healthy and normal life. They have low self esteem, feelings of isolation, confusion, anger, fear, guilt, high level of anxiety with interpersonal relationships etc. As my intimate epic reveals children who are deaf already experience many of those same characteristics without having addicted families. If they grow up with addicted families, their dilemma is much more severe. Most of them have communication barriers with their families due to their deafness and the family's inability to communicate in sign language. Many deaf and hard-of-hearing people have communication, isolation and poor self esteem problems along with society's stigma and discrimination. If they are also deaf adult children of addicted families, their problems are compounded.

Recovering persons from A.A., N.A., A.C.O.A., etc. experience similar diseases from or result of alcoholism and/or chemical dependencies. We all go through our own 12 STEP program. *I am a recovering Adult Child of Alcoholics just like any recovering A.A. or N.A. member.*

An interesting note is that some famous adult children of alcoholics are: President Bill Clinton, his brother Roger, former President Ronald Reagan, Traci Lords, Dr. Claudia Black, Rodney King, actors Chuck Norris and Desi Arnaz, Jr., actresses Suzanne Somers and Angie Dickinson, and many, many more—all of whom do not have a hearing loss.

Today, I recommend and urge various universities/ colleges that have deaf programs to implement a certification program for deaf students in the areas of alcohol and drug abuse counseling, since there exists a shortage of deaf counselors to meet the needs of chemically dependent deaf people. Such certification programs could be subsets of general education programs, special education coursework, communication studies, deaf studies or they could be offered under the auspices of the psychology department. Gallaudet University should take the initiative by offering a certification program in alcohol and drug abuse counseling and further, to accept credits as part of the student's degree requirements as *an incentive* to encourage deaf students to enroll.

In the area of therapy, I continue to encourage and pursue the demand of more insightful caring counselors, intake personnel, therapists and other professionals. We need public support both monetarily and in less tangible areas such as morale. Overall commitment on the part of everyone involved in the therapeutic process is greatly needed on both giving and receiving ends, to enable people to bring their best to the process of eliminating *the deaf community* from the impediment of alcoholism and substance addiction.

The deaf experience is still discussed with opinions generally leading away from the assumption that deafness constitutes a disability which merits ameliorative action on the part of everyone from family to social service agencies toward the aspect that deafness need not be deemed a *defect* and that *deaf people* can be recognized as any other language-minority people.

In my opinion, the scourge of addiction or the underlying propensity to abuse substances is a disability. This can ultimately be overcome so that all deaf people shall have a greater probability of living well-adjusted lives.

I've had an interesting life full of death, drugs and alcohol. I've buried both parents and feel I come from an overload of addictive experiences to help others, deaf or not. This is a social problem that needs to be resolved through government programs, public awareness and education. Our deaf citizens have many problems to overcome and it's way too easy for them to go inward, I know, I was there. But through strength in conviction, I overcame any need for drugs or alcohol. I am helping others follow my way, *the way to a healthy, normal, self-sustaining life.*

EPILOGUE

Subsequent to the survey of literature included in the body of this work, additional writings have been published in areas relevant to deafness and substance abuse. These published writings add to the bulk of current thought focused on these topics, and may provide understanding of trends in opinion. This survey of literature has examined the special needs and characteristics of deaf people, information regarding alcoholism and drug abuse, existing programs or treatment plans designed to help deaf alcoholics and addicts and information regarding what changes might be required within the delivery of services to allow deaf people better access to treatment programs.

This epilogue shall attempt to summarize salient writings in the field which have appeared since the previous survey of literature of this book. Since the scope of these writings is broad, covering such diverse areas as social ramifications of deafness, further testimonials of recovering addicts and progress of empowerment groups, an attempt will be made to group these writings under general subject areas for reviewing purposes.

The deaf experience is still very much being discussed, with opinion generally tending away from the assumption that deafness constitutes a disability which merits ameliorative action on the part of everyone from family to social service agencies, toward the view that deafness need not be viewed as a defect and Deaf people can be viewed as any other language-minority people. Contributing a wealth of detail, both experiential and reported, is Higgins and

Nash's book, *Understanding Deafness Socially.*[1] These editors compiled a group of essays by current writers about deafness, centered around sociological principles. Higgins, et. al. challenges the assumption that deafness is de facto evidence of imperfection,[2] faulting old research for presumed inherent biases, and offering a lucid interpretation of his view.[3]

Jerome Schein, within Higgins & Nash's work, explores the philosophical stance that deafness' meaning is at least partially culturally determined and need not connote inadequacy to function.[4] He offers a simple definition of deafness as "the inability to hear and understand speech through the ear alone."[5] Since one major criticism of past research on deafness has been the neglect of researchers to state precisely how they were using the term deafness, allowing at least a suspicion of non-equivalency or shifting meaning to diminish the importance of their findings, the implementation of a standard of definition could mark a step forward in deafness research.

Several other writers have also recently offered definitions of other terms relevant to this work, in consideration for a standardized usage.[6] The National Council on Alcoholism & Drug Dependence Newsletter restates the 1980 NCADD and American Society of Addiction Medicine definition of alcoholism, saying that it is

---

[1] Paul C. Higgins, Ph.D. & Jeffrey E. Nash, Ph.D.
"Understanding Deafness Socially;" Charles Thomas Publ.'
Springfield, IL. n.d.

[2] Paul C. Higgins, Ph.D. Ibid; introduction.

[3] Ibid. p. ix. "An important part of that hearing world is (Sic) the man assumptions that people make."

[4] Jerome D. Schein, Ibid. p. 3.

[5] Ibid. p. 5.

[6] Ibid. p. 5 & Harlan Lane in NAD monograph.

a primary, chronic disease with genetic, psychosocial and environmental factors influencing its development and manifestations. It further offers a useful framework for consideration,

> Like other diseases, alcoholism is an interaction between the host (the person who gets the disease) and his/her genetic and biological makeup, the agent (alcohol and other mood-altering chemicals), and the environment.[7]

Higgins & Nash include a chapter by Gaylene Becker discussing the influence of peer groups on deaf children. This, too, reviews previous writings, and offers reasoned opinion regarding mainstreaming vs. separatism. e.g. "Integration into society is difficult for any individual who has been removed to a closed environment that teachers (sic) about the outside world without offering experience of it directly."[8] Other essayists in this book discuss other sociological ramifications of deafness, which overall, provides additional weight to forces aiming at consensus in the study of deafness and how it affects people socially.

Addressing similar concepts, Joseph P. Shapiro's *No Pity,* discusses aspects of life affected by more recent civil rights efforts for people with disabilities. In keeping with his title, Shapiro states that people who are classified as disabled do not want pity, they want respect, just as does everyone else.[9] Despite many recent changes in the world of people with disabilities, many problems, he states, such as continuing prejudicial treatment, society's low

---

[7] NCADD Newsletter, Torrance, Ca. Vol. 7, #2, Fall 1992. p. 4.

[8] Gaylene Becker, in Higgins & Nash, Ibid. pp. 62-63.

[9] Joseph P. Shapiro, "No Pity," Times Books, NY.; 1993.

expectations, an antiquated welfare system and other such frustrations still plague disabled people in their attempts to be independent.[10] These thoughts are consistent with findings reported earlier in this work. Their repetition underlies their importance and the need for society to resolve problems which are still receiving inadequate attention and response. Proposals of alternatives or solutions to these problems noted is also still needed.

Shapiro quotes Rosalyn Rosen, Gallaudet College's Dean of Continuing Education as support for the perception of deaf people that they have been conditioned to believe that "hearing is better." He cites the analogy of previous activists, that being deaf may be seen as being similar to being Black or Jewish in the way the larger society perceives the minority person. His parallel listing of historical occurrences, quoted from Yeh fliers, asserts the validity of the analogy:

> In 1886, a Jew became president of Yeshiva University. In 1926, a Black person became president of Howard University. AND in 1988, the Gallaudet University presidency belongs to a DEAF person.[11]

Shapiro, as have other reflective people, considers the mainstreaming vs. separatism issue, listing various pros and cons. He questions the wisdom of mass long-term use of residential schools for the deaf, asserting that they promote institutionalism. He notes that this is harmful both to deaf people and to the larger society, which is, in the absence of deaf people in their culture, left without their

---

10 Ibid. p. 4.
11 Ibid. pp. 76-77.

gifts and by default may fall prey to assumptions and stereotypes rather than first-hand evidence regarding deaf people.[12]

Shapiro cites numerous moving anecdotes and examples of people with disabilities whose quality of life was adversely affected by societal reaction to their handicaps, and offers hope, often via technology (e.g. the computer), of improved lifestyles and increased independence of people coping with disability. He closes with a view of how the disabilities rights movement is changing Western society, citing hope from surveys of public attitudes toward people with disabilities, and even newspaper articles regrading such things as whether deaf people constitute additional fire hazards in public buildings.

Speaking primarily to the needs of the Hispanic deaf, Gilbert Delgado has edited a compilation of topical essays. These discuss issues relevant to opportunities and challenges of people who are both of the Hispanic minority in a Caucasian society, and who also suffer some hearing impairment. He provides an historical timeline of legal mandates attempting to meet the needs of this population, pointing out that new adjustments are urgently needed in fields such as special education in the United States.[13]

Response to felt needs is inherently reactive, rather than proactive, we know, but simple projections of statistical trends, such as the rapidly increasing Hispanic population in the US, and the probable hearing impairments statistically represented, call for preemptive and proactive measures, or at the very least, less tardy responses. Delgado suggests that various sociological,

---

[12] Ibid. pp. 158-159.

[13] Gilbert L. Delgado, ed. "The Hispanic Deaf," Gallaudet College Press; Wash., DC.; n.d., but pre 1985. pp. 1-2.

economic and technological factors have re-created ethnic population clusters and mixes which produce new segregation, resulting in communities of "similar" people, e.g. a culture consisting mostly of people who are deaf. He suggests that several combined factors of this trend may be seen as causative in shaping behaviors of "clustered" people, and so could be regarded as suitable intervention and connection points for desired change.[14]

Especially relevant regarding the problems of bilingual and special education, Joan Erickson, in Delgado's work, profiles several currently espoused models for implementing bilingual programs, according to the regional cultural expectations regarding either multicultural heritage maintenance or mainstream cultural assimilation, detailing certain differences in these models and the ramifications of these.[15] She notes advantages and disadvantages in both viewpoints and attempts to focus our attention increasingly on unmet needs in the education field.

The massive data-gathering and detail-reporting shown in Delgado's work allows it to be useful for future studies as a benchmark for comparison of topical thought. The inclusion of numerous studies using quantifiable measures, such as the Sociocultural Scales (which attempts to measure a given minority family's distance from Anglo-American, middle-class society as well as that family's distance from its own ethnic group's mores), enables this work to offer relevant critiques of present attempts to provide equal educational, medical and other social service opportunities to all US citizens.

Researchers Alan Lerman and Carmina Vila, in Delgado's book also report on a survey of the needs of

---

[14] Ibid. pp. 29-33.

[15] Joan G. Erickson in Delgado's "The Hispanic Deaf." pp. 5-10.

Hispanic-origin children with hearing-impairment, which was conducted in the New York City area through both schools for the deaf and in classes for people with language impairment (Lerman & Cortez, 1977). They reported that, probably due to linguistic and cultural barriers, Hispanic families did not use existing school and community services, and that the individuals participating in the study were only minimally involved in the effort designed especially to help them. This finding parallels other studies this researcher has reviewed which indicate that enticing the target population to use services designed and/or provided for them remains a problem. They suggest that the simple offer to extend services to the families of these individuals might enhance the probability that the participants of the various programs would participate whole-heartedly, rather than reluctantly and with apathy.[16] Similar studies, reported in the bulk of this work, have suggested the same or similar approaches for improvement in meeting the needs of cultural-minority populations of other deaf people, who rely significantly upon the validation and approval of their peer groups. In building a skeleton of attributes which good treatment programs should possess, it has been noted that incentives to appeal to the target population are needed beyond merely making the program available.

The U.S. Department of Justice funded the Americans With Disabilities Act Communication Accommodations Project to publish several small pamphlets. One of these answers questions most commonly asked regarding mandated aids for people with hearing disabilities in public places, such as doctors' offices, hospitals and private nursing homes. Such needs as a skilled interpreter, TDDs,

---

[16] Alan Lerman and Carmina Vila, in Delgado's "The Hispanic Deaf." pp. 173-175.

permanent flashing visual alarm systems, permanent visual doorbells and other aids are also listed and explained. These auxiliary services and products, intended primarily for clientele and their families who cannot hear, are to be offered free of cost to participants.[17]

Providing a clear voice of a strong alternative view, Harlan Lane, in a NAD monograph, slices to the heart of one aspect of current opinion about deafness, stating that while it may be possible to view a middle aged or older person, who loses hearing after years of being able to hear, as greatly disabled, it is presumptuous and erroneous to view people who have never heard sound as disabled. These people, who primarily comprise the Deaf culture, have potential to live rich, full lives and do not experience a sense of deprivation, he states. he faults the helping professions, specifically, for self-servicing aggrandizement of their offerings and for actions which contribute to keeping deaf people in dependent, one-down, patronized positions in society.[18]

He draws a fine point on various relevant controversies, e.g. mainstreaming vs. separatism, in his discourse, stating incisively that money at stake constitutes a major factor in the disparate views i.e. Entire professions, (audiologists, speech pathologists, special education teachers, psychologists, hearing aid fitters, implant physicians, etc.) depend on deafness being viewed within a medical model, with prescriptive regimen and detailed parameters of authority and of interdisciplinary cooperation. Tax funds

---

[17] National Center for Law & Deafness, as part of the ADA Communication Accommodations Project. "ADA Questions and Answers for Health Care Providers." A U.S. Dept. of Justice Production, published at Gallaudet College Press, Wash., D.C. n.d. but post 1991.

[18] Harlan Lane NAD monograph; Vol. 43, 1993. p. 78.

are the primary stake, and proponents of given viewpoints who are able to convince us they are most expert on the subject of deafness are the ones who divide available funds along lines according to their perceptions and to maintain their positions.[19]

Dr. Lane also points out that if deafness were to cease being viewed as a disability, generally, deaf people would not draw regular taxpayer-funded checks simply because they are deaf, but neither would deaf people be so easily discriminated against in employment, housing and other areas in which deaf people have reported that financial equality and opportunity have formerly been denied them.[20] Being on SSI, with no incentive to work, too much free time and no visible hope of changing their lives toward the ideal they are presented via public media constitute, in this writer's opinion, an intertwined group of obstacles to the attainment of independence and self-esteem for deaf people. It is hoped that national health care reform, such as proposed by the Clinton administration, will address these synergistic factors limiting deaf people's quality of life at present.

In the same NAD monograph, Thomas Holcomb of Ohlone college writes of the need of a positive self-image for deaf people. He cites negative influences such as parental denial or fears which can sometimes be expressed as overprotective attitudes toward their deaf children, for impending the construction of widespread self-esteem among deaf people.[21] Holcomb also broaches the difficult topic of mainstreaming vs. separatism for deaf young

---

[19] Ibid. p. 78.

[20] Ibid. p. 79.

[21] Thomas K. Holcomb, "The Construction of Deaf Identity" NAD Monograph; Vol. 43, 1993. p. 42.

people, citing concerns regarding both viewpoints. He notes that deaf children whose hearing parents have tried primarily to integrate them into the larger society may develop a feeling of estrangement within their family as adolescence approaches, and show intense "hunger" for interactions with deaf people.[22] Because such experiences may be common among deaf adolescents raised in hearing homes, the need for strong, positive role-models of adult deaf people can be clearly seen.

Individual proponents of viewpoints of the deaf experience and needs of deaf people may seem, from the materials reviewed, to be converging around the purpose of depathologizing and re-humanizing deafness. This view leads away from viewing deafness as a disability and encourages deaf people to believe in their ability to live independent, full lives. Both Allen Sussman and Ann Makipaa, in recent writings, are critical of the medical-model view of deaf people, stating that such a perception is necessarily distorted and atypical.[23] They, and other concerned writers about deafness, continue trying to influence how deaf people are perceived by the larger society. Integrated vs. separatist modalities of deaf life are also briefly reviewed, with benefits and drawbacks of both option coming to attention.[24]

Although this researcher appreciates that deafness should be depathologized, the methods and paths of progress need to be carefully monitored to avoid mental cul-de-sacs. We may also distinguish more precisely between

---

[22] Ibid. p. 43.

[23] Allen E. Sussman, Ph.D. "Characteristics of a well-adjusted Deaf Person;" Deaf Life Plus; July, 1991, p. 13, and Ann Makipaa, "Medical Profession Needs a New Approach to Deafness;" WFD News, Vol. #2, July, 1993. pp. 16-17.

[24] Ibid: Ann Makipaa; p. 17.

various social ramifications of deafness and of other sociological effects of modern living which affect many people, regardless of their cultural background or hearing capacity. If we castigate society as a whole for the way deaf people are portrayed, e.g. in films like "Children of a Lesser God," implying that this treatment is primarily related to the issue of deafness, as some of the reviewed deaf newspapers have done, we stretch the limits of causality. Being victims of distorted or atypical press coverage or sensationalism is not unique to any subset of people, and believing that one group is singled out for stereotyping toward its extremes overlooks larger realities which may be inherent in press coverage tendencies. i.e. The press and other media coverage dwell on the aberrant rather than the unobtrusive as part of notice-appeal. A happy person, deaf or hearing, leading a quiet, peaceful life draws no media attention, sells no papers, etc. It may be irrelevant to our present study to focus on the appeals of sensationalism.

Bemoaning the lack of films, books, talk show coverage, etc. produced by the larger society which show "normal" deaf people leading "normal" lives, while it is not likely to compel the point to be redressed by mainstream film-makers, authors, talk-show hosts, etc., might, however, encourage ambitious deaf people who care how they appear to others to produce alternative offerings to more accurately present the typical deaf person's life. Pointing out that the Deaf culture is not alone in being misrepresented or is being inadequately represented to the larger society does not imply that inaccurate portrayal of people in public media is to be condoned or excused. So, even though Deaf people are not the only victims of sensationalism and stereotyping by public media, these articles' comments calling attention to and objecting to these behaviors, may ultimately be useful in getting inaccurate representation discontinued.

In the areas of alcoholism and substance abuse, also, additional material has been written since the previous survey of this work was completed. A few of these writings have been selected to summarize the bulk of writings in this area. The format of these writings is largely profile interview with self-report disclosure.

Numerous newspaper feature articles offer additional testimony that deaf people are becoming aware the traps that addiction pose and are freeing themselves from these.[25] Implications of the Americans with Disabilities Act regarding the employment of people who are substance abusers are spelled out in such diverse publications as Woman's World and Ability Magazine.[26] The Americans with Disabilities Rehabilitation Act of 1973 is the primary federal law prohibiting discriminatory treatment against handicapped individuals, both in the workplace and in all public places. Emboldened by this law, increasing numbers of deaf people have felt empowered to work through advocacy for accessible substance abuse and alcoholism treatment facilities and programs.[27] Conferences and networking efforts, such as these writers participated in, help workers in substance abuse areas to keep current on

---

[25] e.g. "Ex-First Ladies Push Mental Health Aid" L.A. Times. March 8, 1994. p. A12.

[26] Annette Fogline. Woman's World, March 22, 1994. p. 41, & ADA - Drug and Alcohol Abuse, in ABILITY Magazine of Health, Disability & Human Potential. n.d. pp. 55-59.

[27] Jeffrey T. Rosen, Esq. "Legal Rights of Drug Addicts and Alcoholics in the Workplace" Substance Abuse and Recovery: Empowerment of Deaf Persons. wash. D.C., Gallaudet Univ. June, 1990. pp. 136-143. and John P. Layh, Ph.D., Margaret J. Rhodes, M.S., and Bonnie L. Smith, B.A. "Regional Consortiums: A Strategy for increasing Deaf Helpers and Strengthening Support Networks" in Ibid. pp. 159-176.

research and to pool ideas for improving treatment programs.

As a further deterrent to the tragedy of alcoholism, Dr. Andrew Avins of UC San Francisco reported that problem drinkers, all heterosexuals, in five public school treatment centers in San Francisco, had a much higher rate of HIV infection than did other participants.[28] An alarming fact about Dr. Avins' results is that the HIV prevalence among heterosexual people in San Francisco is only a fraction of one percent of HIV incidence. This finding has alarming implications for gay/lesbian people in that geographical region.

As substance abuse treatment centers, prevention programs, educational endeavors aimed at avoiding substance abuse and other efforts continue to accumulate statistical documentation of such things as vulnerability to HIV infection among problem drinkers and percentage of recidivism in treatment centers, their insights form bases for future treatment efforts. As clinical experience in the substance abuse field also accumulates, workers in the field will have broader parameters and guidelines within which to base their clinical judgments.

People such as John de Miranda encourage people to look at the factors common to alcoholism, addiction and disability. He notes, "The unhealthy patterns that develop when individuals and families adjust to addiction and disability are quite similar."[29] He further notes eight similarities between the areas of disability and substance abuse movements. These are: 1) both owe their existence

---

[28] "Alcoholics have higher rate of HIV infection, study says" <u>Press Telegram.</u> Feb. 16, 1994. p. A4.

[29] John de Miranda, Ed.M. "The Common Ground: Alcoholism, Addiction and Disability;" <u>Addiction & Recovery,</u> August, 1990. p. 43.

to efforts of grass-roots advocates, rather than being empowered from the top down; 2) both movements try to create new services for their constituents; 3) both areas use the insights of self-help; 4) both movements offer competing medical and sociological models for interpretation and treatment; 5) in both areas, the reciprocal relationship between an individual and his/her environment are stressed; 6) both fields have both negative and moralistic histories; 7) both conditions may be perceived through the existential viewpoint of paradox: i.e. if recovery is to succeed, the individual must first accept the condition's reality and power; and 8) both conditions share elements of spiritual regeneration, surrender and rebirth.[30]

Such studies, and others previously noted, which endeavor to keep meticulous records and accumulative data, are valuable for tailoring future remedial attempts to documented needs of participants. Miranda and other workers in the field continually face inequities of the system, the frustrating confines of inadequate budget and facilities, and even such relatively minor, but still important, factors as the seemingly incompatible desire of most all people to be viewed by others both as similar to each other and as discrete and unique from one another, yet they persevere toward optimum treatment programs.

As the problems of substance abuse among deaf people have come to the light of public scrutiny, certain needs and guidelines for treatment have emerged. These have been covered in previous chapters, but workers may now be disseminating available data more widely, with the help of conferences and writings such as those reviewed.

There still remain a number of glaring needs for the treatment of substance abuse among the deaf, most

---

[30] Ibid. pp. 44-45.

obviously and compellingly being the need for clear, precise communication. ASL, the language of choice of most deaf people within the Deaf culture, but not necessarily that of other people with hearing impairment, needs to be available on a widespread basis in facilities which attempt to offer help to deaf people, while hard-of-hearing and late-deafened people still require communication options appropriate to their situations. This thought is not new, but it still has not been given adequate consideration. Deaf patrons still indicate they feel the lack of a common language coming between them and adequate treatment for substance abuse. Communication is such a basic essential of life, from everyday exchanges to complicated or formal messages, e.g. a doctor's prescription, that it seems to this writer that meeting the communication needs of deaf people among hearing people remains a primary goal.

This researcher recommends that universities/colleges having more than a minimum number of deaf students might offer certification programs for deaf students in the areas of alcohol and drug abuse counseling, since there exists a shortage of deaf counselors to meet needs of chemically dependent deaf people. Additionally, deaf students, from all majors at the college, might be given incentives to act as tutors for signing classes for hearing students. Such certification programs could be sub-sets of general education programs, special education coursework, communication studies or could be offered under the auspices of psychology departments. In addition to the obvious topic-related subjects to be covered in such programs would be an emphasis on developing optimum communication skills for interacting with deaf people.

As research, surveys of existing literature, public opinion polls, and other writings on the fields of deafness, disability in general, addiction, alcoholism specifically, multiple and cross addictions, etc. continue to emerge, it is hoped that the points which need to be addressed will receive adequate attention, and that feedback obtained will be used to reshape maladaptive behaviors and inadequate responses to these problems. The scourge of addiction or the underlying propensity to abuse substances is a disability which can ultimately be overcome, this research has suggested throughout, so that deaf people have a greater probability of living well-adjusted lives.

EPILOGUE BIBLIOGRAPHY

ADA Communication Accommodation Project, with the National Center for Law and Deafness; via the U.S. Dept. of Justice. Gallaudet University; Wash. D.C. n.d.

"ADA - Drug and Alcohol Abuse" n.a.; Ability: Health-Disability-Human Potential, n.p.; n.d. pp. 56-59.

Alcoholics have higher rate of HIV infection, study says" n.a., Press Telegraph, Feb., 16, 1994. p. A4.

Barge, Bruce N. & Carlson, John G. The Executive's Guide to Controlling Health Care & Disability Costs: Strategy-Based Solutions. John Wiley & Sons, Inc. Publisher. N.Y.; 1993.

Bliss, Al and Cramer, Christine. Indicence of Alcohol Use by People with Disabilities: A Wisconsin Survey of Persons with a Disability. The Department of Health & Social Services, Division of Community Services; Bureau of Community Programs & the Office for Persons with Physical Disabilities. Madison, WI. August, 1989.

Bowe, Frank "Doing Our Part: SSI, Medicaid, and People with Disabilities" In the Mainstream. May-June 1993. pp 1-4.

Brauer, Barbara A., Ph.D. "Implications for the Deaf Community of President Clinton's Health Care Reform Plan" The NAD Broadcaster. Jan., 1994. p. 10.

Brennan, Bruce, "Deb & Sarah Tell it Boldly" The Community Ear. Vol. 7 #8; May 1994. pp. 4B, 8B.

Delgado, Gilbert L., Editor. The Hispanic Deaf: Issues & Challenges for Bilingual Special Education. Gallaudet College Press. Wash., D.C. n.d.

DeMiranda, John, Ed.M. "The Common Ground: Alcoholism, Addiction and Disability" Addiction & Recovery, August 1990. pp. 42-46.

"Did You Know;" NCADD South Bay Newsletter, Torrance, CA Vol. 7; #2; 1992. p. 4.

Dixon, Jennifer, "Report: Disability pay feeds addiction" Daily Breeze. Feb. 6, '94. p. A6.

"Drug Dealer Gets Gov't Handout - Because It's Not a Full-Time Job" Star Magazine. L.A. Times, March 28, 1994.

Eaton, William J. "Senate OKS Ban on Benefits to Drug Addicts, Alcoholics;" Los Angeles Times. March 3, 1994. p. A4.

"Ex-First Ladies Puch Mental Health Aid" L.A. Times. March 8, 1994, p. A12.

Foglino, Annette. "Fired for Telling the Truth;" Woman's World; March 22, 1994.

Garretson, Mervin D. Deafness 1993-2013; a NAD monograph; vol. 43; 1993.

Higgins, Paul C., Ph.D. & Nash, Jeffrey E., Ph.D., Editors. Understanding Deafness Socially. Charles C. Thomas, Publisher. Springfield, IL. n.d.

Luetke-Stahlman, B., Ph.D. "Recruiting Black Teacher-Trainees into Programs for the Hearing Impaired," American Annals of the Deaf. Oct., 1993. pp. 851-853.

Makipaa, Ann "Focus on the Human Rights Dimension of Deafness" WFD News., Vol. #2, July 1993. pp. 13-14.

Makipaa, ann, "Medical Profession Needs a New Approach to Deafness," WFD News. Vol. #2, July 1993. pp. 15-17.

Meddis, Sam Vincent. "Nation's Drug Scene Again Degenerating" USA Today, n.d.

Pickens, Roy W., Ph.D. Children of Alcoholics. Hazelden Press, Center City, MN. 1984.

Randell, Joan, Forget, Daniel, and Miller, Jean Somers, "The Americans with Disabilities Act: Implications in Working with Substance Abusers," Journal of Job Placement. Vol. 9 (3) 1993. pp. 27-31.

Shapiro, Joseph P. Shapiro. No Pity: People with Disabilities Forging a New Civil Rights Movement. Times Books of Random House; N.Y., N.Y., 1993.

Substance Abuse and Recovery: Empowerment of Deaf Persons. Conference Proceedings Wash., D.C.; Gallaudet University, June 5-9, 1990.

Sussman, Allen E., Ph.D. "Characteristics of a Well-Adjusted Deaf Person or The Art of Being a Deaf Person," Deaf Life Plus. July 1991. pp. 13-17.

A~Z FINGERSPELLING

FIRST NEW DESIGNS F I N G E R S ADDRESS LABELS

YOU CAN PUT YOUR PERSONALIZED ADDRESS LABELS ON IDENTIFICATION, BOOKS, ENVELOPES, POSTCARDS, ORDER FORMS, GIFTS, ETC.

WHITE LABELS & BLACK FINGERSPELLINGS / LOGOS Labels are not actual size. The size is 1" X 2 5/8"	CIRCLE **O N E** FINGER INITIAL OR LOGO FOR YOUR PERSONALIZED ADDRESS LABELS	QUANTITY ADDRESS LABELS YOUR OR GIFT LABELS

PEEL & SELF-STICK
30 SPACES PER LINE
FINGER INITIAL / LOGO

NEW

(SAMPLE)
F I N G E R S MART
7012 ANSBROUGH DRIVE
CITRUS HEIGHTS, CA 95621

 YOUR NAME
ADDRESS
CITY, STATE ZIP

ARIAL Check here ☐

 Your Name
Address
City, State Zip

Univers Check here ☐

 YOUR NAME
ADDRESS
CITY, STATE ZIP

TIMES Check here ☐

 ☐ Please send me more information about Mugs, Caps, Key Tags, T-Shirts.

All Match Same As
Fingerspellings
and Logos.

  A B C D E
F G H I J
K L M N O
P Q R S T
U V W X Y
Z ☺

$2.49 **60 LABELS**
$1.00 Postage & Handling
$3.49 TOTAL ☐

$3.99 **120 LABELS**
$1.50 Postage & Handling
$5.49 TOTAL ☐

$7.99 **240 LABELS**
$2.00 Postage & Handling
$9.99 TOTAL ☐

ID # _____

PLEASE PRINT CLEARLY ♦ LINE TO APPEAR ON YOUR LABELS

L
O
G
O

_____
N A M E

_____
A D D R E S S

_____
CITY, STATE ZIP

MAKE CHECK OR MONEY ORDER PAYABLE TO:

 F I N G E R S MART
E-mail: fingersmart@juno.com